GREAT IDEAS IN THE LAW

THE
IDEA OF LIBERTY

First Amendment Freedoms

By

ISIDORE STARR, J.S.D., Ph.D.
Professor Emeritus of Education
Queens College, City University of New York

ST. PAUL, MINN.
WEST PUBLISHING CO.

COPYRIGHT © 1978
By
WEST PUBLISHING CO.

1st Reprint September, 1980

Library of Congress Cataloging in Publication Data

Starr, Isidore.
    The idea of liberty.
    (Great ideas in the law)
    Includes index.
    1. United States. Constitution. 1st amendment. 2. Religious liberty—United States. 3. Liberty of speech—United States. 4. Assembly, Right of—United States. I. Title. II. Series.
KF4770.S8   342'.73'085   78–1655
ISBN 0–8299–1017–4

FOREWORD

Writing about the idea of liberty presents many problems. It is not an easy subject to study because it is abstract. It deals with relationships between individuals and the State as they impinge on beliefs, thoughts, expression, and action. As the individual condemns the State for injustices, the State is placed in the dilemma of protecting that individual's liberty and, at the same time, protecting the community against dangers to the public welfare.

The problems of liberty also spill over into confrontations between or among individuals or groups. Hate-mongering, slurs and epithets have brought speakers and audiences or marchers and onlookers to the verge of riots. Which side can legitimately lay claim to liberty? How should the State use its power in such cases?

Writers on liberty have the option of writing technical tomes for scholars or simplified exercises for students. We have attempted to walk the line between the two. Our plan has been to present scholarly materials and yet, at the same time, to use a format which will be interesting to the general reader.

In treating the six principles of the idea of liberty in six sections, we have tried, wherever possible, to present historical background materials and landmark Supreme Court rulings. A special feature of this volume is the section entitled: *Issues to be Analyzed*. Here we present statements of facts from important cases and we ask you to play the role of judge. That should be an interesting exercise because here you have the opportunity to use the case study method:

1. What are the relevant facts?
2. What are the arguments of the opposing sides—the adversaries?
3. What are the issues?
4. What is your decision?
5. What is your opinion—the reasons for your decision?

Now, and only now, are you ready to compare your ruling with that of the Court. You will find the court opinions presented in a section following the case studies.

Do not be disappointed if your opinion differs from that of the Court! After all, yours may have great merit in its own right. Under liberty, you are always free to disagree with and criticize even the opinions of the Supreme Court of the United States.

Isidore Starr

TABLE OF CONTENTS

SECTION I

AN ESTABLISHMENT OF RELIGION—SEPARATION OF CHURCH AND STATE

SECTION II

FREEDOM OF RELIGION

SECTION III

FREEDOM OF SPEECH

SECTION IV

FREEDOM OF THE PRESS

SECTION V

THE RIGHT PEACEABLY TO ASSEMBLE

SECTION VI

THE RIGHT TO PETITION THE GOVERNMENT FOR REDRESS OF GRIEVANCES

To The Memory
of
My Parents
Who Came To This Country
Seeking Liberty

✝

THE IDEA OF LIBERTY

First Amendment Freedoms

LOUIS DEMBITZ BRANDEIS (1856–1941)

Nominated by President Woodrow Wilson, he served as an Associate Justice on the Supreme Court from 1916 to 1939. He became one of our great justices and his opinions have become part of the literature of great Supreme Court rulings.

THE IDEA OF LIBERTY

"Those who won our independence believed that the final end of the state was to make men free to develop their faculties; and that in its government the deliberative forces should prevail over the arbitrary. They valued liberty both as an end and as a means. They believed liberty to be the secret of happiness and courage to be the secret of liberty. They believed that freedom to think as you will and to speak as you think are means indispensable to the discovery and spread of political truth; that without free speech and assembly discussion would be futile; that with them, discussion affords ordinarily adequate protection against the dissemination of noxious doctrine; that the greatest menace to freedom is an inert people; that public discussion is a political duty; and that this should be a fundamental principle of the American government. . . . Those who won our independence by revolution were not cowards. They did not fear political change. They did not exalt order at the cost of liberty."

Justice Louis D. Brandeis
Whitney v. California, 274 U.S.
357 at 375, 47 S.Ct. 641 at 648,
71 L.Ed. 1095 at 1105 (1927)

*

INTRODUCTION

The idea of liberty winds its way through American history and literature. It is proclaimed on the Liberty Bell; it is designated an inalienable right in the Declaration of Independence; it is pronounced a blessing in the Preamble to the Constitution; it is protected in the Fifth and Fourteenth Amendments against arbitrary acts by government; it is recited as part of the Pledge of Allegiance; and it is symbolized by the Statue of Liberty.

What does the idea of liberty mean? Perhaps the best operational definition—the way the idea of liberty functions in our society —is found in the provisions of the First Amendment:

Congress shall make no law respecting an establishment of religion or prohibiting the free exercise thereof; or abridging the freedom of speech, or of the press; or the right of the people peaceably to assemble, and to petition the government for a redress of grievances

Why is the First Amendment first in the Bill of Rights? Have you ever thought about this question? After all, the Bill of Rights could have started with the right to a fair trial or the right to bear arms. As a matter of fact, when a Bill of Rights was being considered by the First Congress of The United States, the First Amendment was not first. When the Bill of Rights was finally ratified in 1791, however, the First Amendment led all the rest. Was it an accident, style, or intent?

Perhaps the First Amendment heads the constellation known as the Bill of Rights because it is basic to all the other rights. Those who drafted the first ten amendments knew at first hand the importance of freedom of thought, belief, inquiry, expression, assembly and petition as a means of guaranteeing the other rights against the capricious or malicious whims of rulers. The First Amendment remains the best operating definition of liberty and as such, it describes the meaning of the phrase—the dignity and integrity of the individual. It is understandably the first of what President James Madison referred to as the "Great Rights". Remove the First Amendment from the United States Constitution and you strike out the very means of testing the other rights and of protesting abuses of government.

We turn now to an examination of the provisions of the First Amendment as they relate to the idea of liberty.

5

In exploring the meaning of the ideas of liberty, we shall examine each of the phrases of the First Amendment. In doing so, we shall look at each phrase through the great cases which the Supreme Court has decided. In this way, we shall try to bring to life the meaning of separation of church and state, religious freedom, freedom of speech, freedom of press, the right to assemble peaceably, and the right to petition for redress of grievances.

INTERPRETING THE
FIRST AMENDMENT FREEDOMS

As one reads the material which follows, it will soon become evident that there is no one single interpretation of the idea of liberty. As judges look at the value conflicts in each case, they look to the past for guidance. The precedents do not speak with one voice. Judges come to their cases with philosophies about society and the individual and they tend to express their system of ideas within the language of the law. The tendency of the courts is to follow precedents as a means of sustaining continuity in decision-making so that the law will convey a sense of predictability. In other words, if we are to be held accountable for the consequences of what we say and do, we must be able to predict in some fashion how the judges will decide similar facts and circumstances.

The idea of liberty, which goes to the very heart of the nature of government and the dignity and integrity of the governed, does not lend itself to easy generalizations. In interpreting the provisions of the First Amendment, judges tend to differ on the meaning of phrases, such as freedom of speech, freedom of the press, freedom of religion, the right to assemble, the right to petition, and separation of church and state. And in addition as Mr. Dooley has reminded us, "the Supreme Court follows the election returns." The Court is sensitive to public opinion.

What follows is a brief summary of some of the interpretations which have emerged from the thinking of those who have grappled with this issue.

THE ABSOLUTE POSITION

It is my belief that there *are* "absolutes" in our Bill of Rights, and that they were put there on purpose by men who knew what words meant, and meant their prohibitions to be absolutes.

Justice Hugo L. Black in *The Great Rights* edited by Edmund Cahn

HUGO L. BLACK
1886–1971

Associate Justice
1937–1971

THE PREFERRED POSITION

The case confronts us again with the duty our system places on the Court to say where the individual's freedom ends, and the state's power begins. Choice on that border, now as always delicate, is perhaps more so where the usual presumption supporting legislation is balanced by the preferred place given in our scheme to the great, the indispensable democratic freedoms secured by the First Amendment.

Justice Wiley Rutledge in *Thomas v. Collins* (1944)

WILEY B. RUTLEDGE
1894–1949

Associate Justice
1943–1949

THE CLEAR AND PRESENT DANGER RULE

The question in every case is whether the words used are used in such circumstances and are of such a nature as to create a clear and present danger that they will bring about the substantive evils that Congress has a right to prevent. It is a question of proximity and degree.

Justice Oliver Wendell Holmes, Jr.,
Schenk v. United States (1919)

OLIVER WENDELL HOLMES
1841–1935

Associate Justice
1902–1932

THE BALANCING DOCTRINE

FELIX FRANKFURTER
1882–1965

Associate Justice
1939–1962

The demands of free speech in a democratic society as well as the interest in national security are better served by candid and informed weighing of the competing interests, within the confines of judicial process, than by announcing dogmas too inflexible for the . . . problems to be solved. . . .

Justice Felix Frankfurter in *Dennis v. United States* (1951)

There are other rules which have been formulated to settle the perennial problem of individual's rights and society's needs: the Bad Tendency Test and the Gravity-of-the-Evil Test. Suffice it to say, that the ones that have been presented above are sufficient as guides through the thicket of problems which follow. Try to apply each of these guidelines to the cases and try to determine which one can best serve the idea of liberty.

The existence of these rules or guidelines should, in no way, discourage you from devising principles of your own. As you study the cases, give your imagination free rein and create principles which help to resolve the problems presented. Keep in mind that we are dealing with the idea of liberty—its meaning today and its implications for the future.

SECTION I

AN ESTABLISHMENT OF RELIGION—
SEPARATION OF CHURCH AND STATE

AMENDMENT I

"Congress shall make no law respecting an establishment of religion. . . ."

AMENDMENT XIV

". . . nor shall any state deprive any person of life, liberty, or property without due process of law . . ."

"I contemplate with sovereign reverence that act of the whole American people which declared that their legislature should 'make no law respecting an establishment of religion or prohibiting the free exercise thereof,' thus building a wall of separation between church and state."

Thomas Jefferson

"When they have opened a gap in the hedge or wall of separation between the garden of the church and the wilderness of the world, God hath ever broke down the wall itself, removed the candlestick, and made His garden a wilderness, as at this day."

Roger Williams

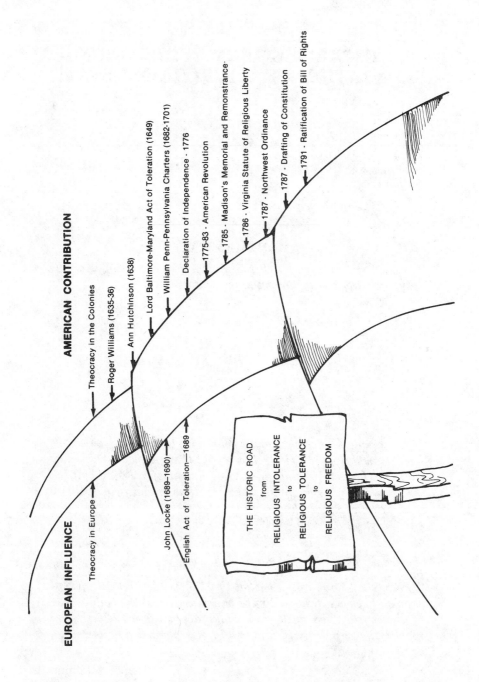

EUROPEAN INFLUENCE

AMERICAN CONTRIBUTION

Theocracy in Europe

Theocracy in the Colonies

Roger Williams (1635-36)

Ann Hutchinson (1638)

John Locke (1689-1690)

English Act of Toleration—1689

Lord Baltimore-Maryland Act of Toleration (1649)

William Penn-Pennsylvania Charters (1682-1701)

Declaration of Independence - 1776

1775-83 - American Revolution

1785 - Madison's Memorial and Remonstrance

1786 - Virginia Statute of Religious Liberty

1787 - Northwest Ordinance

1787 - Drafting of Constitution

1791 - Ratification of Bill of Rights

THE HISTORIC ROAD
from
RELIGIOUS INTOLERANCE
to
RELIGIOUS TOLERANCE
to
RELIGIOUS FREEDOM

CHAPTER 1

THE ROAD FROM RELIGIOUS INTOLERANCE
TO RELIGIOUS FREEDOM

Why do the first ten words of the First Amendment read as they do? Why do they deal with religion?

One obvious answer is that the Founding Fathers were deeply concerned about church and state, as well as about religious liberty, and as we shall see, they had good cause to be.

Their concern with religion can be understood if we look at Article VI of the Constitution. This is the last article in the Constitution that deals with substantive matters. Article VII deals with the procedure of ratification. The last sentence in Article VI reads:

. . . no religious test shall *ever* be required as a qualification to any office or public trust under the United States. (emphasis supplied)

This sentence cannot be amended at any time. Amendment I prohibits any law respecting an establishment of religion.

Since the original Constitution ends with a restriction on religion and the opening sentence of the First Amendment continues on the theme of religion, it is reasonable to say that the Founding Fathers were determined to clarify the role of religion in American life.

Why were they so involved with this important subject? They knew their history and they wanted this nation to avoid the excesses of the past by insisting that God and Caesar go their separate ways.

Perhaps the best way to understand their state of mind is to take a journey on the road of history.

Let us begin our journey with England in the seventeenth century. The government was a theocracy in which state and church were united. In a theocratic state a sin is a crime and a crime is a sin. Those who did not belong to the Anglican Church—the official or established church of England—were discriminated against in many ways and those who opposed it were punished. When the Puritans left their homeland for the New World, they came seeking religious freedom for themselves.

When the Puritans set up their Bible Commonwealth in Massachusetts Bay, they established a theocratic government in which church and state were united. Dissenters were not tolerated and were persecuted. Two famous cases show us how the once-persecuted Puritans treated nonconformists.

Roger Williams, it has been said, was sent to earth before his time. In 1636 he was banished from Massachusetts Bay colony because he "broached and divulged divers new and dangerous opinions." What were these "dangerous opinions"? Williams favored separating church and state because he said that there should be a wall of separation between "the Garden of the Church and the wilderness of the world." In addition, he advocated democracy and equality. Government rests on the consent of the people, he wrote, and, in addition, he preached equality for all, including the Indians.

The seventeenth century was not ready for Roger Williams and the Puritans expelled him. He carried his radical views of democracy, equality, and religious freedom to Providence, which became a haven for dissenters.

Anne Hutchinson suffered a similar fate but with a tragic ending. She held meetings at her home in Boston. What made these meetings unusual were that they were "for women only." The men who ruled the colony were suspicious and they had reason to be. Anne was preaching a doctrine that placed an individual's direct intuition of God's love as superior to obedience to the laws of theocratic Massachusetts Bay. In 1638 she was tried for heretical and seditious teachings. Forced to incriminate herself, she was excommunicated and banished. She took her fourteen children and fled to New York, where she and many of her children were killed in an Indian raid.

Roger Williams and Anne Hutchinson stood out like giants in a world of religious intolerance. Their ideas on religious freedom—so basic to the idea of liberty—could not be exiled or banished. The idea had been planted and it was not forgotten.

A quick survey of the landmarks on the *Historic Road* shows a steady movement from religious intolerance to religious freedom. Lord Baltimore established a colony for Catholics and, fearful that the Protestants might eventually become a majority, he espoused the Maryland Act of Toleration of 1649, which granted religious tolerance to all who believed in Christ. William Penn went one step further by granting religious tolerance to all who believed in God.

The spirit of religious tolerance was gradually making its way into history. The writings of John Locke influenced the English Toleration Act of 1689, granting religious toleration to all Protestants. The Maryland Act of Toleration, as we have seen granted toleration to all Christians. William Penn, in his colony, granted religious tolerance to all who believed in God. This action extended toleration for Jews. But religious freedom for all—the right to believe or not to believe—had not yet achieved respectability. It took a number of giant steps forward to achieve the separation of church and state. The Declaration of Independence proclaimed the inalienable rights of life, liberty, and the pursuit of happiness. It was a declaration, not a law.

In 1784 the Virginia Legislature passed a bill that levied a tax for the support of Christian Churches. Each taxpayer was given the option of choosing the church to which the tax was to be paid. If no choice was indicated, the tax went for education.

James Madison's analysis and attack on this Assessment Bill has become a classic. His famous Memorial and Remonstrance Against Religious Assessments has been referred to in numerous Supreme Court opinions. Since Madison was the leading architect of the Religion Clauses of the First Amendment, the arguments in the Memorial and Remonstrance are worth reading even at this time.

> 1. . . . we hold it for a fundamental and undeniable truth, "that Religion or the duty which we owe to our Creator and the Manner of discharging it, can be directed only by reason and conviction, not by force or violence." The Religion then of every man must be left to the conviction and conscience of every man; and it is the right' of every man to exercise it as these may dictate. This right is in its nature an unalienable right. . . .

> 3. Because, it is proper to take alarm at the first experiment on our liberties. We hold this prudent jealousy to be the first duty of citizens, and one of [the] noblest characteristics of the late Revolution. . . . Who does not see that the same authority which can establish Christianity, in exclusion of all other Religions, may establish with the same ease any particular sect of Christians, in exclusion of all other sects? That the same authority which can force a citizen to contribute three pence only of his property for the support of any one establishment, may force him to conform to any other establishment in all cases whatsoever?

> 4. Because, the bill violates that equality which ought to be the basis of every law, ... If "all men are by nature equally free and independent," all men are to be considered . . . as retaining an "*equal* title to the free exercise of Religion according to the dictates of conscience."

In 1786 the Virginia Statute of Religious Liberty, drafted by Thomas Jefferson, incorporated and expanded the meaning of the ideas proclaimed by Madison. In this famous law, Jefferson declared:

> *Be it enacted by the General Assembly* that no man shall be compelled to frequent or support any religious worship, place, or ministry whatsoever, nor shall be enforced, restrained, molested, or burdened in his

body or goods, nor shall otherwise suffer on account of his religious opinions or belief; but that all men shall be free to profess, and by argument to maintain, their opinion in matters of religion, and that the same shall in no wise diminish, enlarge, or affect their civil capacities.

One year later the Northwest Ordinance of 1787, in its first Article, stated that: "No person demeaning [behaving] himself in a peaceable and orderly manner, shall ever be molested on account of his mode of worship or religious sentiments in the said territory." In the same year the newly drafted Constitution prohibited religious tests for public office. Finally, it was the Bill of Rights that converted the dream of Roger Williams into the First Amendment of the Bill of Rights. The policy of disestablishment, or separation of church and state, was not achieved in reality until 1833. It was in that year that Massachusetts finally separated church and state, the last of the original colonies to do so.

What were the historic forces and conditions which moved the thoughts of men and women away from religious intolerance toward religious freedom? Can you offer any explanations for this change in thoughts and feelings?

Leo Pfeffer, one of the most respected lawyers and scholars in the field of religious liberty, offers us some interesting ideas on this question in his revised edition of *Church, State, and Freedom*. In chart form, this is his answer to these questions.

CHART

Practical	Ideological
1. **Religious pluralism resulting from the multiplicity of sects.** As ethnic groups continued to migrate to the new world, they found themselves living close to others with the same problems. Voltaire put it best when he said: "If there were one religion in England, its despotism would be terrible. If there were two, they would destroy each other; but there are thirty, and therefore they live in peace and harmony."	1. **The Influence of Roger Williams, Anne Hutchinson, Lord Baltimore and William Penn.** Their ideas and contentions moved colonial America away from the policy of established religions and religious intolerance toward religious tolerance and, ultimately, toward separation of church and state and religious freedom.
2. **Trade and Commerce led to secularization.** Businessmen were not necessarily interested in the religion of their customers.	2. **Writings of John Locke and the English Act of Toleration (1689).** John Locke's *Letter Concerning Toleration* and the English Act of Toleration gave support to the movement away from intolerance and persecution.
3. **Limited affiliation with churches.** Only a small number or percentage of colonists either belonged to or attended church because of the hardships of frontier life and the difficulties of earning a living.	3. **The social contract theory** developed by John Locke stated that civil government is a contract among the people and that religion is not within the scope of powers of the governors.
4. **The American Revolution and Alliances with Catholic France.** Protestant America fighting Protestant England found the assistance of Catholic France and Catholic Spain invaluable. This cooperation tended to soften religious animosities.	4. **Influence of Deism.** Many of the leaders at the time of the Declaration of Independence were Deists, who believed in an impersonal God, "Nature's God" and were not members of formal religious groups.
	5. **Evangelical Revivalism of the Mid-Eighteenth Century.** This movement, by concentrating on religion as a personal affair, contributed to the thought that church and state had to be separated.

Chart material based on Leo Pfeffer, *Church, State, and Freedom*, Revised Edition, Boston, Beacon Press, 1967, pp. 93–104.

Having taken this very brief journey into the past, we are now ready to look at the first ten words of the First Amendment—the culmination of the movement to achieve complete religious freedom. What did the men who drafted this amendment mean when they said that "Congress shall make *no law* respecting an establishment of religion"?

This has become known as the Establishment Clause and its interpretation has been greatly influenced by President Jefferson's now famous letter of January 1, 1802, to the Danbury Baptist Association. It was here that he wrote:

> Believing with you that religion is a matter which lies solely between man and his God, that he owes account to none other for his faith or his worship, that the legislative forces of government reach actions only, and not opinions, I contemplate with sovereign reverence that the act of the whole American people which declared that their legislature should "make no law respecting an establishment of religion, or prohibiting the free exercise thereof," thus building a wall of separation between church and state.   .   .   .

Jefferson's phrase—a wall of separation between church and state—was probably borrowed from Roger Williams. In his writings Williams favored a wall of separation between the garden that is the church and the wilderness that is the world. While Williams wanted to protect the *church from the state*, it was Jefferson's interpretation that the First Amendment was intended to protect the *state from the church*.

CHAPTER 2

STATE AND FEDERAL FINANCIAL
AID TO PAROCHIAL SCHOOLS

We have traced the events that led to the writing of the prohibition against an establishment of religion into the First Amendment. The test of a principle is its application. The following cases show how judges have interpreted the meaning of this clause.

CASES

CASE 1

THE NEW JERSEY PAROCHIAL SCHOOL BUSING CASE

Everson v. Board of Education of Ewing Township
330 U.S. 1, 67 S.Ct. 504, 91 L.Ed. 711 (1947)

Ewing Township in New Jersey did not have any high schools. When the children in that community graduated from elementary school, they went to high schools outside the community. The parents of these children paid for the public bus transportation of their children to three public high schools and four Catholic parochial schools outside the district. Under state law, the school board had the authority to pay for this bus transportation and they did so by reimbursing the parents for this expenditure.

Those who protested the use of public funds to pay for the transportation of Catholic children to parochial schools argued as follows:

1. A state cannot tax A to reimburse B for the cost of transporting his children to church schools. This violates that part of the Fourteenth Amendment which prohibits a state from taking a person's property without due process of law. When the state does this, it satisfies the personal wishes of parents rather than the state's interest in the general education of the children.

2. When the state uses tax money to transport children to parochial schools, it is aiding religion. Such action violates the Establishment of Religion Clause of the First Amendment which applies to the states under the Fourteenth Amendment's Due Process Clause. By declaring that "no state shall deprive any person of life, liberty, or property without due process of law," the Fourteenth Amendment incorporates the First Amendment's prohibition against an establishment of religion.

The nine Justices apparently had a hard time with this issue. When the case was finally decided, it was a 5 to 4 landmark ruling with some very puzzling features. Speaking for the majority of five, Justice Black began with a long history of events leading to the Establishment Clause of the First Amendment. He then stated the case for the wall-of-separation rule in these oft-quoted words:

> The "establishment of religion" clause of the First Amendment means at least this: Neither a state nor the Federal Government can set up a church. Neither can pass laws which aid one religion, aid all religions, or prefer one religion over another. Neither can force nor influence a person to go to or to remain away from church against his will or force him to profess a belief or disbelief in any religion. No person can be punished for entertaining or professing religious beliefs or disbeliefs, for church attendance or non-attendance. No tax in any amount, large or small, can be levied to support any religious activities or institutions, whatever they may be called, or whatever form they may adopt to teach or practice religion. Neither a state nor the Federal Government can, openly or secretly, participate in the affairs of any religious organizations or groups and vice versa. In the words of Jefferson, the clause against establishment of religion by law was intended to erect "a wall of separation between Church and State."

Up to this point, it seems as though Justice Black and the majority are going to declare unconstitutional the New Jersey practice of paying out of public funds the busing of students to parochial schools. But as we read, suddenly, an interesting line of argument develops.

1. In answering the first objection that the New Jersey law taxes some people to help others achieve their private wishes, the majority argues that the use of tax funds to assist parochial school children in reaching their schools furthers a public program mandated by the state.

2. Does the New Jersey law violate the First and Fourteenth Amendments' mandate that neither the Congress nor the states may make laws respecting an establishment of religion? The Court answers this important question as follows:

> . . . we cannot say that the First Amendment prohibits New Jersey from spending tax-raised funds to pay the bus fares of parochial school pupils as a part of a general program under which it pays the fares of pupils attending public and other schools. It is undoubtedly true that children are helped to get to church schools. There is

even a possibility that some of the children might not be sent to the church schools if the parents were compelled to pay their children's bus fares out of their own pockets when transportation to a public school would have been paid for by the State. . . . Similarly, parents might be reluctant to permit their children to attend schools which the state had cut off from such general government services as ordinary police and fire protection, connections for sewage disposal, public highways and sidewalks. Of course, cutting off church schools from these services, so separate and so indisputably marked off from the religious function, would make it far more difficult for the schools to operate. But such is obviously not the purpose of the First Amendment. That Amendment requires the state to be a neutral in its relations with groups of religious believers and non-believers; it does not require the state to be their adversary. State power is no more to be used so as to handicap religions, than it is to favor them.

This Court has said that parents may, in the discharge of their duty under state compulsory education laws, send their children to a religious rather than a public school if the school meets the secular educational requirements which the state has power to impose. . . . It appears that these parochial schools meet New Jersey's requirements. The State contributes no money to the schools. It does not support them. Its legislation, as applied, does no more than provide a general program to help parents get their children, regardless of their religion, safely and expeditiously to and from accredited schools.

The First Amendment has erected a wall between church and state. That wall must be kept high and impregnable. We could not approve the slightest breach. New Jersey has not breached it here.

Four Justices dissented. Justice Jackson, with whom Justice Frankfurter agreed, begins his opinion by saying that, at first, he was inclined to agree with the majority. However, after a careful reading of the reasoning, he was convinced that Justice Black's opinion could not be supported. He remarked:

In fact, the undertones of the opinion, advocating complete and uncompromising separation of Church from State, seem utterly discordant with its conclusion yielding support to their commingling in educational matters.

He concludes with the warning that

. . . the Court today is unconsciously giving the clock's hands a backward turn.

Between his opening and closing remarks, Justice Jackson reasons that Catholic education is a vital part of the Catholic religion. To support the one is to aid the other and such action violates the

First and Fourteenth Amendments. In addition, the New Jersey law is discriminatory in its application to those who do not attend public or Roman Catholic parochial schools. Those who attend non-Catholic parochial schools or private schools are not aided. The legal point is that it is the character of the school which determines state aid, not the needs of the children.

Justice Jackson answers Justice Black's argument that the transportation service here is similar to police and fire protection of Catholic schools.

> It seems to me that the basic fallacy in the Court's reasoning, which accounts for its failure to apply the principles it avows, is in ignoring the essentially religious test by which beneficiaries of this expenditure are selected. A policeman protects a Catholic, of course—but not because he is a Catholic; it is because he is a man and a member of our society. The fireman protects the Church school—but not because it is a Church school; it is because it is property, part of the assets of our society. Neither the fireman nor the policeman has to ask before he renders aid "Is this man or building identified with the Catholic Church." But before these school authorities draw a check to reimburse for a student's fare they must ask just that question, and if the school is a Catholic one they may render aid because it is such, while if it is of any other faith or is run for profit, the help must be withheld.

Justice Rutledge's historically impressive dissenting opinion was concurred in by Justices Jackson, Frankfurter, and Burton. Tracing the origins of the religious clauses to the influence of Jefferson and Madison, Justice Rutledge concluded that the First Amendment prohibited:

> state support, financial or other, of religion in any guise, form or degree. It outlaws all use of public funds for religious purposes. . . . For Madison, as also for Jefferson, religious freedom was the crux of the struggle for freedom in general.

Rutledge raises the question: "Does New Jersey's action furnish support for religion by use of the taxing power?" He answers it in this way:

> Here parents pay money to send their children to parochial schools and funds raised by taxation are used to reimburse them. This not only helps the children to get to school and the parents to send them. It aids them in a substantial way to get the very thing which they are sent to the particular school to secure, namely, religious training and teaching. . . .

New Jersey's action therefore exactly fits the type of exaction and the kind of evil at which Madison and Jefferson struck. Under the test they framed it cannot be said that the cost of transportation is no part of the cost of education or of the religious instruction given. . . . It is precisely because the instruction is religious and relates to a particular faith, whether one or another, that parents send their children to religious schools. . . . And the very purpose of the state's contribution is to defray the cost of conveying the pupil to the place where he will receive not simply secular, but also and primarily religious, teaching and guidance. . . .

Public money devoted to payment of religious costs, educational or other, brings the quest for more. It brings too the struggle of sect against sect for the larger share or for any. Here one by numbers alone will benefit most, there another. That is precisely the history of societies which have had an established religion. . . .

In this passage Rutledge pinpoints two important ideas. Religion is a private matter to be sustained and supported by private means. Once the state enters this private domain, "the kingdom of the individual man and his God," it opens a Pandora's Box of competition among religious sects for state favors. It is for this reason, he says, that "we have staked the very existence of our country on the faith that complete separation between the state and religion is the best for the state and best for religion."

Let us suppose, however, that the New Jersey law paid for the transportation of children attending all public and all religious schools. Would this take care of the discrimination argument? After all, such a law would show no preferences. This, too, would be unconstitutional, argued Rutledge, because the childless taxpayer and the non-believer would be paying for transporting children to religious institutions and the believers of one religious sect would be assessed to support the religious instruction of another sect.

We have discussed the New Jersey Bus case at length because it poses clearly the division in judicial thinking about church-state financial aid issues. Rutledge and his colleagues see the wall of separation as impregnable so far as money is concerned. Any use of tax money is a breach, regardless of the sum. Permit one break, no matter how minor, and the hole will grow so large that the wall will collapse.

Black and his colleagues agree that the wall of separation must be respected but they see the issue in this case as assistance to the child, not to religion. This Child Benefit Theory, supported in some states, opens the door to financial aid in a variety of ways.

With the passage of time, Rutledge's reasoning influenced some of the Justices who had disagreed with him at the time. Notably, Black and Douglas, in later opinions, reflected the position of Rutledge and they even gave him credit for being more perceptive about this issue than they were in 1947.

CASE 2

THE NEW YORK STATE TEXTBOOK CASE

Board of Education of Central School District No. 1 v. Allen
392 U.S. 236, 88 S.Ct. 1923, 20 L.Ed.2d 1060 (1968)

Is there a difference between a school bus and a school textbook? In the *Everson* case, students were transported by bus to their parochial schools. The bus stopped at the schoolhouse door. Could the *Everson* decision be used to support the supplying of textbooks to parochial schools at public expense? Let us see.

New York State enacted a law requiring school districts to purchase and loan textbooks free of charge to students enrolled in grades 7 to 12 in public and parochial schools. Such textbooks had to be approved by local boards of education.

The trial court declared the law unconstitutional under the First and Fourteenth Amendments, the Appellate Division reversed, and the highest court in New York State by a 4 to 3 vote upheld the law. The case was then carried to the Supreme Court.

> Assume you are the attorney for the Board of Education of Central District No. 1 which opposes this law. What points would you present? Then, place yourself as counsel for Allen, the Commissioner of Education of New York State, and try to answer the reasons you have just presented. Which side seems to have the more powerful argument?

Based on the *Everson* case, the Justices have a choice. They can base their ruling either on the Child Benefit Theory or on the Neutrality Doctrine—that on matters of religion the state must be neutral. As is to be expected in subjects that touch the sensitive chords of religion, the Justices differed 6–3.

Justice White's opinion for the majority recognizes that the line between state neutrality toward religion and state support of religion is not easy to locate. He agrees that the constitutional standard is separation of church and state, but how does one apply a sweeping constitutional rule to the issue of the needs of children and the laws of the state? He resolves it by invoking the Child Benefit Theory:

> The law merely makes available to all the children the benefits of a general program to lend school books free of charge . . . ownership remains, at least technically, in the State. Thus no funds or books are furnished to parochial schools, and the financial benefit is to parents and children, not to schools.

In this case, he goes on to say, only secular books can be loaned to the schools and there is no evidence in the record that religious literature has or will be distributed. Nor does he see any merit in the argument that in a parochial school secular and religious training are so intertwined that even secular textbooks can become instruments in religious instruction. No evidence was offered, he points out, to show that this has taken place.

Justice Black's dissenting opinion is of special significance because the majority quoted with approval his opinion in the *Everson* case. That opinion, he argues, has been misinterpreted by Justice White and, therefore, misapplied. What the *Everson* case really stated is that the state can pay out of its taxes the transportation fare *of all* the school children, police protection for *all* the school children, police and fire protection for *all* buildings, and lunches for *all* school children. What differentiates the New Jersey Busing Case from the New York State Textbook Case is that the former directed itself *to all the children*, while the latter makes it possible to use state funds *to help a religious school*. Looking into the future, Justice Black predicts accurately, as we shall see, the consequences of upholding the New York State law.

> This New York law, it may be said by some, makes but a small inroad and does not amount to complete state establishment of religion. But that is no excuse for upholding it. It requires no prophet to foresee that on the argument used to support this law others could be upheld providing for state or federal government funds to buy property on which to erect religious school buildings or to erect the buildings themselves, to pay the salaries of the religious school teachers, and finally to have the sectarian religious groups cease to rely on voluntary contributions of members of their sects while waiting for the Government to pick up all the bills for the religious schools. . . .

Justice Douglas, who had agreed with Justice Black's majority opinion in the *Everson* case, now found himself once again on the side of Justice Black, but as a dissenter. Like Justice Black, he states bluntly that the facts of life are such that "the parochial school will ask for the books that it wants,"—and that these books will be those —"that best promote its sectarian creed". The school board will then be faced with a dilemma. If it accepts such books, "the struggle to keep church and state separate has been lost." If it resists, "the battle line between church and state will have been drawn and the contest will be on to keep the school board independent or to put it under church domination and control." Strong words!

He then proceeds to distinguish between "the bus" and "the book."

> Whatever may be said of *Everson*, there is nothing ideological about a bus. There is nothing ideological about a school lunch, or a public nurse, or a scholarship. The constitutionality of such public aid to students in parochial schools turns on considerations not present in this textbook case. The textbook goes to the very heart of education in a parochial school. It is the chief, although not solitary, instrumentality for propagating a particular religious creed or faith. How can we possibly approve such state aid to a religion? A parochial school textbook may contain many, many more seeds of creed and dogma than a prayer.

Justice Fortas' dissenting opinion accentuates the unique nature of the New York law.

> This statute calls for furnishing special, separate, and particular books, specially, separately, and particularly chosen by religious sects or their representatives for use in their sectarian schools. This is the infirmity, in my opinion. This is the feature that makes it impossible, in my view, to reach any conclusion other than that this statute is an unconstitutional use of public funds to support an establishment of religion.

Having seen the appeal to the historic wall of separation, we are now confronted with two rules of interpretation: the Child Benefit Theory and the Neutrality Doctrine.

ISSUES TO BE ANALYZED

Up to this point, we have examined the historical background and two landmark rulings relating to separation of church and state. The following five cases (Cases 3–7) present issues which reached the Supreme Court. Try your skill in deciding these cases and then compare your opinions with those of the Supreme Court. The Supreme Court decisions are presented on pp. 31–39, but we suggest that you refrain from "peeping" at them before you have arrived at your own ruling. You may check each case separately or wait until you have tried to solve all five cases.

CASE 3

PENNSYLVANIA AND RHODE ISLAND CASES— SUPPLEMENTING TEACHERS' SALARIES

Since parochial schools, like public schools, have been in financial difficulty, states have sought to assist them in a variety of ways. Rhode Island passed a law providing state financial assistance in supplementing the salaries of teachers of secular subjects in non-public elementary schools. *The money was to be paid directly to the teacher* and could not be in excess of 15% of the current salary. The law required that the teachers eligible for this financial assistance must use only teaching materials which are used in the public schools. In addition, they must agree in writing not to teach a course in religion so long as they receive the salary supplement.

It should be noted that 25% of the children were attending non-public elementary schools and that 95% of this number were students in Catholic parochial schools. About 250 teachers, all of them employed by Catholic parochial schools, applied for the benefits.

The Pennsylvania law also sought to assist non-public schools for their expenditures for teachers' salaries, textbooks and instructional materials. The state reimbursed the non-public schools for their expenditures. The conditions for payment were that the courses taught must be secular and similar to those presented in the public school curriculum. Textbooks and instructional materials must be approved by the State Superintendent of Public Instruction. No reimbursement was permitted for any course that contains "any subject matter expressing religious teaching, or the morals or forms of worship of any sect."

Under this law, the state entered into contracts with 1181 non-public elementary and secondary schools, which enrolled more than 20% of the total number of students in the state. More than 96% of these students attended parochial schools, and most of these were Roman Catholic.

> What differences do you see between the Rhode Island and Pennsylvania laws? How would you decide these cases?

CASE 4

FEDERAL AID TO CHURCH–RELATED COLLEGES AND UNIVERSITIES

In 1963 Congress passed the Higher Education Facilities Act which provides for federal grants to colleges and universities for the construction of buildings. The law prohibited the use of funds for any building used for sectarian instruction, religious worship, or department or divinity school. The United States retained a twenty-year interest in any building constructed with federal funds. Any violation of this prohibition required the return of such funds to the government. The U. S. Office of Education was required to conduct on-site inspections.

Four church-related colleges and universities in Connecticut received federal grants for two library buildings, a music, drama, and arts building, science building, and a language laboratory. Tilton and others sued Richardson, Secretary of the Department of Health, Education and Welfare, arguing that such grants were unconstitutional.

> What do you think? Do you see any differences between public aid to parochial schools and public assistance to colleges?

CASE 5

MAINTENANCE AND REPAIR GRANTS, TUITION REIMBURSEMENT, AND TAX BENEFITS

In 1972 New York State passed a number of laws which were challenged immediately.

1. The first law provided for direct state grants to non-public elementary and secondary schools in low-income urban areas. These grants were to be used for the maintenance and repair of school buildings and equipment "to ensure the health, welfare and safety of enrolled pupils."

2. Another law granted partial reimbursement to low-income parents who paid tuition for their children in non-public elementary and secondary schools. Parents eligible for this payment had to have an annual taxable income of less than $5,000. The reimbursement was limited to $50 for each elementary school student and $100 for each high school student.

3. A third law provided for tax relief for parents of non-public school children who failed to qualify for tuition reimbursement. These deductions from state income tax ranged from $1,000 for each dependent of parents with adjusted gross income of less than $9,000 to $400 per dependent for incomes of $15,000, to no exemptions for those with $25,000 or more.

Those who favored this law argued as follows:

1. Maintenance and repair of schools are necessary for a healthy and safe school environment. This benefits the child, the neighborhood, the city and the state.

2. The tuition reimbursement plan and the tax relief program make it possible for parents and their children to select alternative educational systems. In a pluralistic society, freedom of choice or diversity is important. If the non-public schools closed down because of a financial crisis, public school enrollments would increase greatly, and so would the cost of public education, endangering the quality of education for all students. Almost 20% of the state's students (700,000–800,000) attend non-public schools. About 85% are church affiliated.

3. This assistance is secular, neutral, non-ideological and, therefore constitutional. In the *Everson* and *Allen* cases, grants were made by the state to aid children and they were upheld.

Do you agree or disagree? If you disagree, how do you answer these arguments? You can decide, of course, that one provision is constitutional, while the others are not.

CASE 6

AUXILIARY SERVICES, INSTRUCTIONAL MATERIALS, AND TEXTBOOK LOANS TO PAROCHIAL SCHOOLS

To assist its non-public school children, the state of Pennsylvania enacted two laws. One provided auxiliary services (counseling, testing, psychological services, speech and hearing therapy, and services for exceptional, remedial, and disadvantaged students) and the loan of textbooks acceptable for use in the public schools. The auxiliary services were to be performed by public school personnel in the parochial schools. The second law provided for loans directly to the non-public schools of instructional materials (magazines, maps, photographs, charts, recordings and films) and instructional equipment (projectors, recorders, and laboratory paraphernalia).

> Consider yourself to be a Justice on our High Court. How would you rule on these laws? Would you apply the Child Benefit Theory or can you develop a theory of your own supporting your position?

CASE 7

OHIO SEEKS TO AID PAROCHIAL SCHOOLS IN SIX WAYS

In 1976 the Ohio Legislature appropriated funds for the assistance of parochial schools in the following ways:

1. The loan of secular textbooks or book substitutes used as textbooks.

2. Supply of standardized tests and scoring services—tests would be prepared by outside consultants, would deal with secular subjects, and non-public school personnel would not be involved in the scoring.

3. Furnishing diagnostic services: such as speech, hearing and psychological specialists hired by the local school board.

4. Furnishing therapeutic, guidance, and remedial services to assist those with speech and hearing problems, the deaf, blind, handicapped, crippled, emotionally disturbed. Only employees of local school boards would be used, and such services would be available only in public schools, public centers, and in mobile units located off non-public premises.

5. Purchase and loan of instructional materials and equipment to parochial school students or their parents upon request. Such equipment would include projectors, tape recorders, record players, maps and globes, science kits, weather forecasting equipment, etc.

6. Field Trip transportation is to be provided on the same basis as that provided to public school students.

Examine each of these six provisions and decide which is constitutional and which is unconstitutional. In arriving at your conclusion, try to use previous rulings as precedents. For example, the *Allen* case (the New York Textbook Case) and the *Meek* case (the Pennsylvania case dealing with auxiliary services, instructional materials, and textbook loans) should be consulted.

DECISIONS

The following decisions are the Supreme Court's rulings in Cases 3–7. Did your reasoning correspond with that of the majority or the dissenters? Were you able to come up with some principles that the Court has not as yet considered? Can you foresee future problems in this area?

CASE 3

Lemon v. Kurtzman

Early v. DiCenco

Robinson v. DiCenco

403 U.S. 602, 91 S.Ct. 2105, 29 L.Ed.2d 745 (1971)

Chief Justice Burger wrote the opinion of the Court declaring both laws unconstitutional under the religion clauses of the First and Fourteenth Amendments. In his reasoning he brings together three rules to be applied to Establishment of Religion cases:

1. **Purpose:** The statute must have a secular (non-religious) purpose.

2. **Effect:** The principle or primary effect of the law must be one that neither advances nor inhibits religion.

3. **Entanglement:** The statute must not foster an excessive government entanglement with religion.

In applying these rules, Chief Justice Burger concluded that the purpose of these laws was secular not religious. The legislative intent was to improve the quality of education. It was not necessary to discuss the effect of these laws because their cumulative effect amounted to *excessive entanglement* and, therefore, they were unconstitutional.

In the Rhode Island case, it was noted that most of the teachers were nuns and that most of the lay teachers were Catholics. The Chief Justice notes that:

> With the best of intentions such a teacher would find it hard to make a total separation between secular teaching and religious doctrine. What would appear to some to be essential to good citizenship might well for others border on or constitute instruction in religion.

> To make sure that the subsidized teachers do not inculcate religion, the state will have to undertake continuing surveillance which is bound to lead to excessive entanglement between church and state. Such a development is "pregnant with dangers of excessive government direction of church schools and hence of churches."

> As in the Rhode Island case, the Pennsylvania law is unconstitutional because it creates excessive entanglement between church and state. The state will have to develop a system of continuous inspection to make sure that the teachers being paid by the state refrain from any religious indoctrination. The religious schools will have to keep financial records subject to audit by the state. All of these conditions create "an intimate and continuing relationship between church and state" which the First and Fourteenth Amendments prohibit.

> Two other considerations contribute to the unconstitutionality of the Pennsylvania law. It involves a cash subsidy—direct financial aid to parochial schools. Even more significant is that, when the issue of financial aid becomes part of the political process, "the potential divisiveness of such conflict is a threat to the normal political process . . . ." It conflicts with our whole history and tradition to permit questions of the Religion Clauses to assume such importance in our legislatures and in our elections that they could divert attention from the myriad issues and problems that confront every level of government.

Justice Harlan did not participate in the Rhode Island case.

Justice Douglas wrote a concurring opinion in which Justice Black concurred. He invokes Madison's *Memorial* and *Remonstrance* and he reminds the Court of Black's famous quote in *Everson*: "No tax in any amount, large or small, can be levied to support any religious activities or institutions."

Justice Brennan's separate opinion concludes also that the laws in question are unconstitutional because they provide for a direct subsidy from public funds for activities essential to sectarian schools. He is troubled by the conditions which these grants impose on parochial schools. He sees state inspectors prowling the halls of schools and auditing classroom instruction. This may have a chilling effect on teachers and administrators in those schools and may lead to self-censorship.

Justice White dissented on several grounds. Parochial schools, he pointed out accomplish a dual purpose. They educate children both in secular subjects and in the tenets of a particular sect. This dual function can be and has been kept separate. State or federal funds for secular education in a parochial institution, therefore, do not violate the Establishment Clause. Actually, they assist the state in carrying out the compulsory education law. The fact that religion may benefit *indirectly* from such assistance does not breach the wall of separation.

Since there was no evidence that there was a co-mingling in the schools of the secular and the religious, the statutes should have been upheld.

BYRON R. WHITE
1917–
Associate Justice
1962–

CASE 4

Tilton v. Richardson

403 U.S. 672, 91 S.Ct. 2091, 29 L.Ed.2d 790 (1971)

Chief Justice Burger announced the judgment of the Court in an opinion supported by Justices Harlan, Stewart, and Blackmun. Justice White wrote a separate concurring opinion. The four Justices, a minority of the Court, concluded that the purpose of the law was secular not religious. However, the twenty-year limit of governmental interest makes it possible for the colleges to use the buildings for sectarian purposes after the twenty years. Therefore, concludes the Chief Justice, the twenty-year limit enhances religion and it is unconstitutional. But the rest of the law is constitutional. There is no evidence to support the argument of excessive governmental interference with religion.

Colleges and universities are not elementary and secondary schools, and college students are not as impressionable as younger students. In the words of the Court, there is less likelihood that religion will permeate the area of secular education in the university with its tradition of academic freedom. This reduces the need for government surveillance. Nor does the law interfere with religious freedom because there is no evidence of this fact.

Justice White agreed with the majority opinion, arguing that the secular and the sectarian can be and have been kept separate in church related colleges and universities. Certainly clerics in parochial schools, as well as church-related colleges are as trustworthy in obeying the law as are their counterparts in elementary and secondary public schools. They can be trusted to keep religious instruction out of sectarian education. He concludes by saying that, if the Court can approve federal support for church-related colleges, he sees no reason why states like Rhode Island and Pennsylvania could not be permitted to assist financially their parochial schools.

Justice Douglas wrote a dissent concurred in by Justices Black, and Marshall. The point is repeated here, as before, that religious and secular teaching in parochial institutions are "so enmeshed . . . that only the strictest supervision and surveillance would insure compliance" with the prohibition against sectarian use for twenty years. In addition, since a parochial school operates on one budget, the money saved through federal grants can be used for religious purposes. How can the government know, asks Douglas, what will be taught in the buildings constructed with federal grants without constant supervision? Wouldn't this be excessive entanglement?

Once again, in his closing remarks, he invokes the warning of Madison:

> It is almost unbelievable that we have made the radical departure from Madison's Remonstrance . . . The million-dollar grants sustained today put Madison's miserable "three pence" to shame. But he even thought, as I do, that even a small amount coming out of the pocket of taxpayers and going into the coffers of a church was not in keeping with our constitutional ideal.

Justice Brennan sides with the dissenters on the ground that a federal construction grant to sectarian colleges and universities is unconstitutional because giving "tax monies directly to a sectarian institution necessarily aid the proselytizing function of the institution."

CASE 5

Committee for Public Education and Religious Liberty v. Nyquist, Commissioner of Education of New York State

413 U.S. 756, 93 S.Ct. 2955, 37 L.Ed.2d 948 (1973)

Justice Powell delivered the opinion of the Court, finding all three provisions an unconstitutional infringement of the Establishment Clause. He begins his opinion with a reference to Madison's *Memorial and Remonstrance Against Religious Assessments* and then imposes the three-part test of constitutionality: a secular legislative *purpose*, an *effect* that neither inhibits nor advances religion, and no excessive *entanglement*.

The maintenance and repair provisions, he finds, are unconstitutional because they enhance religion. If a classroom is renovated with public funds, what guarantee is there that it will not be used for religious purpose? Since it is impossible to restrict maintenance and repair for secular education in this religious institution, the law must of necessity subsidize religious education.

Tuition reimbursement also fails the *Effect* test because the financial aid to parents in reality provides financial support for nonpublic, sectarian institutions. It is true that the tuition reimbursement is given to the parents only after they paid the school, but that makes no difference because the grant is an incentive to send children to parochial schools.

Although the system of income tax benefits goes to the parents and not to the sectarian institutions, there is really no way of telling how this money will be used. It could be used to advance religion and is, therefore, unconstitutional.

This case, points out Justice Powell, differs from the *Allen* and *Everson* cases. The latter applied to both public and non-public schools, while this case deals only with non-public schools.

The majority opinion closes on a theme which must be uppermost in the minds of the Justices. Although the theme is not based on a constitutional principle, it is rooted along the road from religious intolerance to religious freedom. Competition among different groups for public monies has inherent dangers for a community. Justice Powell puts it very well, when he says:

> But we know from long experience with both Federal and State Governments that aid programs of any kind tend to become entrenched, to escalate in cost, and to generate their own aggressive constituencies. And the larger the class of recipients, the greater the pressure for accelerated increases. . . . In this situation, where the underlying issue is the deeply emotional one of Church-State relationships, the potential for seriously divisive political consequences needs no elaboration. . . .

Justice Rehnquist, Chief Justice Burger, and Justice White concurred in the maintenance and repair decision of the majority, but dissented from the ruling which held that the tax benefits for low-income families were unconstitutional. Justice Rehnquist, writing the opinion, asks: "If the tax exemption of church property is constitutional, why isn't a tax benefit to the parents constitutional, too? The tuition reimbursement and tax benefit plans should be upheld because the aid is to students and their parents and not to the schools."

He goes on to say:

> The reimbursement and tax benefit plans today struck down, . . . are consistent with the principle of neutrality. New York has recognized that parents who are sending their children to nonpublic schools are rendering the State a service by decreasing the costs of public education and by physically relieving an already overburdened public school system. Such parents are nonetheless compelled to support public school services unused by them and to pay for their own children's education. Rather than offering "an incentive to parents to send their children to sectarian schools," . . . as the majority suggests, New York is effectuating the secular purpose of the equalization of the costs of educating New York children that are borne by parents who send their children to nonpublic schools. As in *Everson* and *Allen*, the impact, if any, on religious education from the aid granted is significantly diminished by the fact that the benefits go to the parents rather than to the institutions.

CASE 6

Meek v. Pittinger

421 U.S. 349, 95 S.Ct. 1753, 44 L.Ed.2d 217 (1975)

The Justices had some real problems with this case. They finally found themselves in several clusters or groups without being able to agree completely on the reasoning behind the decision.

Justice Stewart announced the judgment of the Court and delivered the opinion of the Court holding all parts of these laws unconstitutional, except the textbook loan provision. He reasoned that the direct loan of instructional materials and equipment amounts to a direct and substantial advancement of religious activity. Also, the auxiliary services are provided at predominantly church-related schools and violate the Establishment Clause as it applies to the states under the Fourteenth Amendment. On the other hand, the textbook loan section of the law is constitutional because it is similar to the precedent established in the *Allen* case. Where the financial benefit is to the parents and children, it is not to the schools.

Justice Stewart emphasizes that 75% of the non-public schools qualifying for this financial assistance are church-related. It would require constant surveillance and, therefore, excessive entanglement by the government in religious institutions to make sure that the public funds were limited to secular education. Justices Blackmun and Powell agreed with Stewart on all points.

Justices Brennan, Douglas and Marshall concurred with most of the points in the Stewart opinion, but dissented from his decision on textbook loans. Justice Brennan was deeply concerned about political divisions along political lines. He argued that the need for massive annual appropriations for textbooks would create a divisive conflict over the issue of aid to religion and would violate the very goal which the Establishment Clause was designed to achieve.

Brennan and his colleagues hammer away at the Child Benefit Theory, arguing that it no longer applies because transactions concerning textbooks really take place between church (religious schools) and state (State Education Department or Boards of Education). The textbooks are loans to the schools, not to the children.

Chief Justice Burger concurred with the Court majority on the textbook provision, but dissented on the auxiliary services. The Court's opinion, he holds, discriminates against the poor. The rich can afford private schools and auxiliary services. The poor who exercise their right to religious freedom and send their children to parochial schools will find that those who are handicapped will now be denied the special assistance offered by the state.

Justices Rehnquist and White concurred in the textbook ruling and dissented in all other respects. They maintained that the auxiliary services and the instructional equipment and materials were secular, neutral and non-ideological. Public school personnel, who will furnish the auxiliary services in the parochial schools, will be able to walk the secular line without invading the religious sphere.

The result of these differences among the Justices led to the following conclusion: the textbook provision was constitutional; the others were not.

CASE 7

Wolman v. Walter

97 S.Ct. 2593, 433 U.S. 229, 53 L.Ed.2d 714 (1977)

Once again the Court was badly divided over the various provisions of the legislation. Justice Blackmun's opinion for the Court won the support of only Justices Stewart, Powell, and the Chief Justice.

1. The textbook loan provision was upheld on the basis of the *Allen* and *Meek* precedents.

2. The testing and scoring provisions were upheld on the ground that there was no excessive entanglement with religion.

3. The diagnostic services were upheld on two grounds: child benefit theory and no excessive entanglement with religion. The Court differentiated the *Meek* case from this case by pointing out that the Pennsylvania law required excessive surveillance, while such action was not necessary under the Ohio law.

4. The therapeutic services were constitutional because they were given on neutral sites.

5. The instructional materials and equipment provisions were unconstitutional because this was an indirect way of assisting the parochial schools. Lending the materials and equipment to parents and students was in reality a way of giving them to the schools. The materials were to be stored in the schools. According to the Court: "If a grant in cash is impermissible, a grant in kind is impermissible."

6. Field trip transportation was unconstitutional because it represented direct aid to parochial schools. In addition, this provision would require constant surveillance by school authorities to make sure that the trip was secular in nature.

Justice Brennan felt that all the provisions were unconstitutional, while the Chief Justice and Justices White and Rehnquist felt that all the provisions were constitutional. Justice Marshall was willing to support only some of the diagnostic and therapeutic services as necessary to protect "children's health and well-being." Justice Powell felt that field trips were permissible because only the bus and the driver are supplied by the state. Justice Stevens thought that the textbook and testing and scoring provisions were unconstitutional. In other words, the Court in 1977 continued to have problems applying the establishment clause to the attempts by states to aid parochial schools.

SUMMARY

Those who support state and federal aid to elementary and secondary schools, as well as to colleges and universities, present impressive arguments. Large numbers of students attend these institutions. If they should shut down because of lack of funds, the public schools, and even the public colleges and universities would be flooded by students who would be clamoring to be admitted. Elementary and secondary school enrollments would swell. By supporting parochial schools the state benefits itself, the students and their parents.

In addition, the position is taken that parents of parochial school students pay taxes for public schools and they pay tuition to parochial schools. This, they contend, is a form of double taxation.

By aiding parochial schools, the state keeps open the doors to alternative forms of education. In this way it recognizes the needs of a pluralistic society.

As for the constitutional argument of separation of church and state, the state can aid the secular part of the parochial school curriculum without intruding on the religious domain.

Opponents of state and federal aid to parochial schools base their position on the historic road from religious intolerance to religious freedom. We have come a long way, they argue, in separating church from state and any one exception can become a turning of the road back toward establishment. They refer to Madison and Jefferson and their crusade for a wall of separation.

They see no double taxation. Parochial school parents have the right to give their children a religious education. There are many ways to do it. One way is to send their children to public school in the morning and to religious schools in the afternoon or on Sundays.

It is impossible, they emphasize, to separate religious instruction and secular education in the parochial schools. State aid can easily and even unconsciously pass through the "wall of separation" within the school and be used for religious purposes. This is unconstitutional and must not be tolerated.

The Supreme Court cases relating to the Establishment Clause of the First Amendment have produced the following interpretations:

1. The Madison-Jefferson-Rutledge Position of a wall of separation which tolerates no exceptions. One breach in the wall weakens it and invites another.

2. The Child Benefit Theory.

3. The Neutrality Doctrine.

   (a) Purpose—Legislative purpose must be secular.

   (b) Effect—Primary effect must be neither to enhance or hinder religion.

   (c) Entanglement—No excessive entanglement between the state and religion.

4. Political Divisiveness Test. Aid to parochial schools engenders annual jockeying for funds with the possibility of serious political consequences for the community. Such legislation must be examined with great care.

SUMMARY OF WALL OF SEPARATION CASES
PUBLIC FINANCIAL ASSISTANCE TO PAROCHIAL SCHOOLS

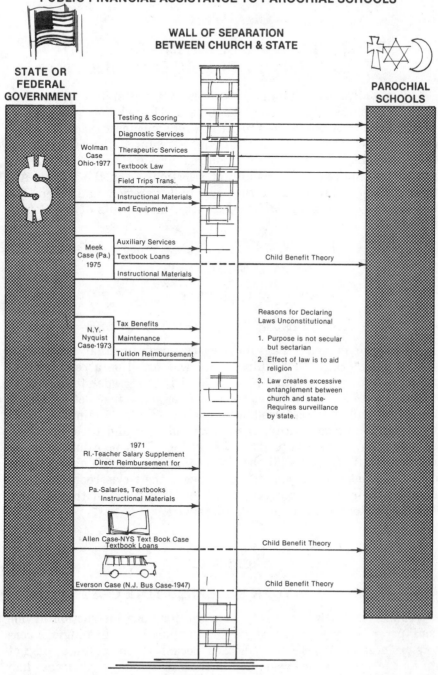

WALL OF SEPARATION
BETWEEN CHURCH & STATE

STATE OR
FEDERAL
GOVERNMENT

PAROCHIAL
SCHOOLS

Testing & Scoring

Diagnostic Services

Wolman
Case
Ohio-1977

Therapeutic Services

Textbook Law

Field Trips Trans.

Instructional Materials
and Equipment

Meek
Case (Pa.)
1975

Auxiliary Services

Textbook Loans — Child Benefit Theory

Instructional Materials

N.Y.-
Nyquist
Case-1973

Tax Benefits

Maintenance

Tuition Reimbursement

Reasons for Declaring
Laws Unconstitutional

1. Purpose is not secular
   but sectarian

2. Effect of law is to aid
   religion

3. Law creates excessive
   entanglement between
   church and state-
   Requires surveillance
   by state.

1971
RI.-Teacher Salary Supplement
Direct Reimbursement for

Pa.-Salaries, Textbooks
Instructional Materials

Allen Case-NYS Text Book Case
Textbook Loans — Child Benefit Theory

Everson Case (N.J. Bus Case-1947) — Child Benefit Theory

CHAPTER 3

RELEASED TIME, BIBLE READING, AND PRAYERS IN PUBLIC SCHOOLS

The wall of separation between church and state cuts across a number of areas. Some states have used released time programs to permit public school students to receive religious instruction for about one hour per week. Other states have required the recitation of daily prayers. Generally, the required prayers have been accompanied by required daily reading of selections from the Bible. Are these practices breaches in the wall of separation and, therefore, in violation of the First and Fourteenth Amendments of the Constitution?

CASES

CASE 8

THE ILLINOIS RELEASED TIME CASE

The accompanying diagram poses two problems that came before the Supreme Court. The Illinois case was based on a released time policy in the town of Champaign. Students in grades four to nine, whose parents consented, were given religious instruction within the school building for periods ranging from 30 to 45 minutes. Religious teachers came within the school building and used the classrooms. They were not paid by the school. This plan had been developed jointly by the Catholic, Protestant and Jewish faiths. Students who did not participate had to leave their classrooms and had to spend their time in secular studies in other parts of the building. The regular teachers kept attendance reports.

CASE 9

THE NEW YORK RELEASED TIME CASE

Under the New York City plan the religious instruction of one hour per week was given outside the public schools in religious centers. Those who were not released because their parents did not consent to this practice remained in their classrooms. Churches had to make weekly attendance reports to the schools. No teacher or administrator could comment on attendance or non-attendance.

RELEASED TIME CASES

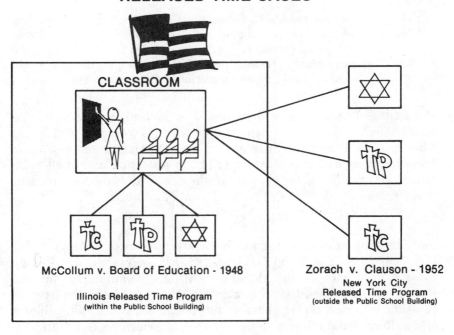

McCollum v. Board of Education - 1948

Illinois Released Time Program
(within the Public School Building)

Zorach v. Clauson - 1952
New York City
Released Time Program
(outside the Public School Building)

What differences can you see between the two plans? In taking
your position as to the constitutionality of each of these practices,
how would you reason your way through the arguments posed by
each side?

DECISIONS IN CASES 8 AND 9

The Supreme Court had very little trouble with the first case, *McCollum v. Board of Education*, 333 U.S. 203, 68 S.Ct. 461, 92 L.Ed. 649 (1948). In an 8 to 1 decision, the Court declared the practice unconstitutional. Justice Black, speaking for the majority, concluded:

> Here not only are the state's tax-supported public school buildings used for the dissemination of religious doctrines. The State also affords sectarian groups an invaluable aid in that it helps to provide pupils for their religious classes through use of the state's compulsory public school machinery. This is not separation of Church and State . . .

Justice Reed, the sole dissenter, saw nothing wrong with "released time" in this case. Religious instructors were not paid by the schools. What was taking place in the Champaign schools was a friendly accommodation between religious education and public education—a practice growing out of the ideal of religious freedom. It had nothing to do with the establishment of a Church.

The New York case was another matter. *Zorach v. Clauson*, 343 U.S. 306, 72 S.Ct. 679, 96 L.Ed. 954 (1952). Here the Justices divided 6 to 3, with Justice Douglas, writing the opinion for the majority. He concluded that the main difference here was the practice of using religious centers outside the public schools. The influence of the Reed dissent seems to be reflected in Douglas's concluding remarks:

> In the *McCollum* case the classrooms were used for religious instruction and the force of the public schools was used to promote that instruction. Here, as we have said, the public schools do no more than accommodate their schedules to a program of outside religious instruction. We follow the *McCollum* case. But we cannot expand it to cover the present released time program unless separation of church and state means that public institutions can make no adjustments of their schedules to accommodate the religious needs of the people. We cannot read into the Bill of Rights such a philosophy of hostility to religion.

Justice Douglas elaborates this time in an especially stirring passage which is often referred to in subsequent opinions.

> We are a religious people whose institutions presuppose a Supreme Being. We guarantee the freedom to worship as one chooses. We make room for as wide a variety of beliefs and creeds as the spiritual needs of man deem necessary. We sponsor an attitude on the part of government that shows no partiality to any one group and that lets

each flourish according to the zeal of its adherents and the appeal of its dogma. When the state encourages religious instruction or co-operates with religious authorities by adjusting the schedule of public events to sectarian needs, it follows the best of our traditions. For it then respects the religious nature of our people and accommodates the public service to their spiritual needs. To hold that it may not would be to find in the Constitution a requirement that the government show a callous indifference to religious groups. That would be preferring those who believe in no religion over those who do believe. . . . we find no constitutional requirement which makes it necessary for government to be hostile to religion and to throw its weight against efforts to widen the effective scope of religious influence . . . it can close its doors or suspend its operations as to those who want to repair to their religious sanctuary for worship or instruction. No more than that is undertaken here. . . .

Justices Jackson, Frankfurter, and Black dissented sharply and with an eloquence that matched the rhetoric of Justice Douglas. Justice Black, who wrote the *McCollum* opinion, said that he saw no difference between the two cases. Each represented a combination of Church and State and he warned: "Government should not be allowed under cover of the soft euphemism of 'co-operation,' to steal into the sacred area of religious choice."

The three dissenters focused on the nature of coercion—using the state compulsory education law and the public school educators paid by the state "to help religious sects get pupils." Justice Jackson's response to Justice's Douglas passage on religion was sharp and critical. In quotable phrases, he reminded the majority:

. . . my evangelistic brethren confuse an objection to compulsion with an objection to religion. It is possible to hold a faith with enough confidence to believe that what should be rendered to God does not need to be decided and collected by Caesar.

The day that this country ceases to be free for irreligion it will cease to be free for religion—except for the sect that can win political power . . . We start down a rough road when we begin to mix compulsory public education with compulsory Godliness. . . .

Justice Frankfurter drew a distinction between "dismissed time" and "released time." In dismissed time students are excused from school to go their separate ways. This is constitutionally acceptable. On the other hand, "released time" involves pressure on parents and students to engage in religious education and that violates the wall of separation.

CASE 10

REQUIRED PRAYERS AND SECTARIAN BIBLE READING

Engel v. Vitale

370 U.S. 421, 82 S.Ct. 1261, 8 L.Ed.2d 601 (1962)

In 1951 the Board of Regents of the State of New York, a group of men and women who supervise the educational system, composed a short prayer:

> Almighty God, we acknowledge our dependence upon Thee, and we beg thy blessings upon us, our parents, our teachers, and our country.

This was done at a time when we were engaged in the Korean War and in the Cold War with the Soviet Union—a time when the fear of communism and subversion troubled the nation. In order to prepare students to develop the moral and spiritual stamina to defend the American way of life, various programs were suggested. The Regents' prayer was a recommendation, but the school system of New Hyde Park in New York made it a daily requirement. It was no surprise to anyone that this practice was challenged in the High Court.

In a 6 to 1 ruling (Justices Frankfurter and White did not take part), the Supreme Court struck down the compulsory prayer. The essence of the majority opinion written by Justice Black was that it was not the business of the Board of Regents—public officials—to write prayers for public school children. The prayer was religious in nature and, therefore, unconstitutional.

Justice Douglas' concurring opinion is sweeping in its condemnation of tax exemptions for religious institutions, the "In God We Trust" slogan, "Under God" in the pledge of allegiance and other practices. He proclaims that he was wrong in the *Everson* case and that the ruling there should be overruled. Once again he refers to Rutledge's dissent in that case as one of the best essays on the philosophy of the First Amendment.

Justice Stewart dissented on the ground that prayers of this type permit students to share in the spiritual heritage of this nation. The prayer, he pointed out, was voluntary and non-denominational.

Although this case dealt only with the Regents prayer and the ruling was limited to the point that government officials could not constitutionally write prayers for public school students and require them to recite it, the ruling was attacked by many as atheistic and pro-communist. This sensitive issue apparently struck a tender chord in a large segment of the American public. This reaction influenced the Court's strategy in announcing a more sweeping decision the following year.

CASE 11

Abington Township v. Schempp

Murray v. Curlett

374 U.S. 203, 83 S.Ct. 1560, 10 L.Ed.2d 844 (1963)

The *Schempp* case dealt with a Pennsylvania law requiring the reading of at least ten verses from the Holy Bible without comment at the opening of each public school day. This was followed by the recitation of the Lord's Prayer. Students could be excused from this exercise upon written request from the parents.

The Schempps were Unitarians and they objected to this procedure on the ground that the Bible reading and prayers in the public schools violated the Establishment Clause of the First Amendment as applied to the states. In response to the question as to why he didn't request that his children be excused, Mr. Schempp replied that to do so might have labeled his son and daughter as "odd-balls," un-American, atheists, and undesirable non-conformists.

The case of *Murray v. Curlett* was different in that the Murrays were professed atheists who objected to the Maryland law requiring the opening exercises in the public schools to consist of reading without comment of a chapter in the Bible and/or the use of the Lord's Prayer. The Murrays based their case on religious freedom and separation of church and state.

The Bureau of the Census lists many religious organizations in this country. In the early 1960's, at the time of this case, there were at least 83 separate religious bodies, each with a membership of 50,000. More than 64% of the American people belonged to churches, while less than 3% indicated that they did not belong to any religion.

Are these statistics relevant in deciding these cases?

Five opinions resulted from these two cases. Justice Clark delivered the opinion of the Court, which outlawed required sectarian prayers and devotional Bible reading in public schools under the First and Fourteenth Amendments. This conclusion was based on the following conditions: the exercises were required as part of the curriculum; students recited the exercises in unison; they were held in public school buildings; and they were supervised by teachers paid by the state. This violated the wall of separation rule because it enhanced religion.

Doesn't this decision of the Court have the effect of permitting a "religion of secularism" to be established in the schools? Justice Clark replies as follows:

It is insisted that unless these religious exercises are permitted a "religion of secularism" is established in the schools. We agree of course that the State may not establish a "religion of secularism" in the sense of affirmatively opposing or showing hostility to religion, thus "preferring those who believe in no religion over those who do believe." . . .

TOM C. CLARK
1899–1977
Associate Justice
1949–1967

We do not agree, however, that this decision in any sense has that effect. In addition, it might well be said that one's education is not complete without a study of comparative religion or the history of religion and its relationship to the advancement of civilization. It certainly may be said that the Bible is worthy of study for its literary and historic qualities. Nothing we have said here indicates that such study of the Bible or of religion, when presented objectively as part of a secular program of education, may not be effected consistently with the First Amendment. But the exercises here do not fall into those categories. They are religious exercises, required by the States in violation of the command of the First Amendment that the Government maintain strict neutrality, neither aiding nor opposing religion.

Justice Douglas' concurring opinion focused on the use of state funds to finance religious exercises. Justice Brennan's long concurring opinion points to the options available to parents: a secular public school or a private or sectarian school. When a parent sends the child to a public school, he is entitled to certain expectations.

The public schools are supported entirely, in most communities, by public funds—funds exacted not only from parents, nor alone from those who hold particular religious views, nor indeed from those who subscribe to any creed at all. It is implicit in the history and character of American public education that the public schools serve a uniquely *public* function: the training of American citizens in an atmosphere free of parochial, divisive, or separatist influences of any sort—an atmosphere in which children may assimilate a heritage common to all American groups and religions. . . . This is a heritage neither theistic nor atheistic, but simply civic and patriotic. . . .

He goes on to say that the procedure set up by the state to excuse students from the Bible reading and prayers does not convert an unconstitutional law into a constitutional one. What the excusal procedure does is to create a dilemma for the student. If he or she remains, they participate in exercises which are unacceptable; if he or she does not, they may be stigmatized as atheists or non-conformists. The power of the peer-group is most persuasive.

Justice Brennan agrees with Justice Clark's views on the relationship of religion to the teaching of history, literature and philosophy.

The holding of the Court today plainly does not foreclose teaching *about* the Holy Scriptures or about the differences between religious sects in classes in literature or history. Indeed, whether or not the Bible is involved, it would be impossible to teach meaningfully many subjects in the social sciences or the humanities without some mention of religion. To what extent, and at what points in the curriculum, religious materials should be cited are matters which the courts ought to entrust very largely to the experienced officials who superintend our Nation's public schools. They are experts in such matters, and we are not.

WILLIAM J. BRENNAN

1906–

Associate Justice

1956–

Justice Goldberg wrote a concurring opinion, in which Justice Harlan joined. His brief statement points out that, when the power and prestige of the school authorities support Bible reading and prayers, young impressionable children required to attend school are strongly influenced. This is not accommodation; it is a violation of the First Amendment.

Once again, Justice Stewart dissented. He found the record deficient in evidence as to whether variations in the exercises were permitted. In addition, he took the position that "if religious exercises are held to be an impermissible activity in schools, religion is placed at an artificial and state-created disadvantage." To refuse the religious exercises is to favor a religion of secularism; to permit them is to take a position of neutrality on the church-state issue. In concluding his views, Justice Stewart raises a point, perhaps unintentionally, that contains some serious problems for educators.

POTTER STEWART

1915–

Associate Justice

1958–

What our Constitution indispensably protects is the freedom of each of us, be he Jew or Agnostic, Christian or Atheist, Buddhist or Freethinker, to believe or disbelieve, to worship or not worship, to pray or keep silent, according to his own conscience, uncoerced and unrestrained by government. It is conceivable that these school boards, or even all school boards, might eventually find it impossible to administer a system of religious exercises during school hours in such a way as to meet this constitutional standard—in such a way as completely to free from any kind of official coercion those who do not affirmatively want to participate. But I think we must not assume that school boards so lack the qualities of inventiveness and good will as to make impossible the achievement of that goal.

I would remand both cases for further hearing.

We might well ask: Were five opinions necessary? Could it be that the widespread attacks on the prayer ruling of the previous year had sensitized the Justices to the need to explain to the public that they were expounding a Constitution, not their personal views? It may very well be that Justice Brennan, a Catholic, and Justice Goldberg, a Jew, joined their Protestant Brothers in trying to convey to the American community the difference between constitutional policy and private judgments.

"What Do They Expect Us To Do —— Listen To The Kids Pray At <u>Home</u>?"

—from *Straight Herblock* (Simon & Shuster, 1964)

SECTION II
FREEDOM OF RELIGION

AMENDMENT I

Congress shall make no law respecting an establishment of religion or prohibiting the free exercise thereof.
. . .

AMENDMENT XIV

. . . *nor shall any state deprive any person of life, liberty or property without due process of law.*

"If there is any fixed star in our constitutional constellation, it is that no official, high or petty, can prescribe what shall be orthodox in politics, nationalism, religion, or other matters of opinion or force citizens to confess by word or act their faith therein. If there are any circumstances which permit an exception, they do not now occur to us."

> Justice Robert A. Jackson
> *West Virginia State Board of Education v. Barnette,*
> 319 U.S. 624, 63 S.Ct. 1178, 87 L.Ed. 1628 (1943)

INTRODUCTION

There is an obvious connection between the two religion clauses. One sets up a wall of separation between church and state by disestablishing religion. The other gives us the right to believe and not to believe—the right to join a church or the right to be an agnostic or an atheist.

As we have seen in the cases involving church-state relations, it is very easy to quote the First Amendment but very difficult to apply its eighteenth century ideals to twentieth century realities. As we probe the issues of freedom of religion, we inevitably find ourselves holding the scales of justice and weighing the merits of each side.

To understand the familiar phrase, freedom of religion, we shall have to take a journey through the landscape of constitutional law with stops at the Mormon polygamy issue, flag salutes, parochial schools, religious test oaths, blue laws, Sabbatarians, vaccinations, X-rays, blood transfusions, peyote, snake cults, conscientious objectors, and creation-evolution controversy. We shall meet Jehovah's Witnesses and Amish and we shall observe their contributions to the clarification of religious fredom and freedom of conscience issues.

The constitutional argument in these cases is based on the First and Fourteenth Amendments. Since the Due Process Clause of the Fourteenth Amendment absorbs the Religion Clauses of the First Amendment according to Supreme Court rulings, the constitutional principle as now applied holds that neither Congress nor the states can pass any law prohibiting the free exercise of religion.

There is a particularily moving quality about most of these cases. We are dealing here not only with matters of the mind but with affairs of the heart and the spirit. It is this very matter which makes these issues so compelling and so difficult.

CHAPTER 4

THE MORMON POLYGAMY CASE

CASE 12

Reynolds v. United States

98 U.S. 145, 25 L.Ed. 244 (1878)

George Reynolds, a Mormon living in the Utah Territory, was charged with violating a law passed by Congress and applicable to all territories of the United States.

> Every person having a husband or wife living, who marries another, whether married or single, in a Territory, or other place over which the United States have exclusive jurisdiction, is guilty of bigamy, and shall be punished by a fine of not more than $500, and by imprisonment for a term of not more than five years.

The Mormon religion at the time supported plural marriages and polygamy was even regarded as a religious obligation. Reynolds argued that the First Amendment states clearly that Congress shall make *no* law prohibiting the free exercise of religion. Since the Constitution is the supreme law of the land, the anti-polygamy statute of Congress is unconstitutional because it prohibits Mormons from practicing the tenets of their religion.

How do you feel about so sensitive an issue? Would you have supported Reynolds or the Congress?

Chief Justice Waite wrote the unanimous opinion for the Court. He poses the issue as follows: Can religious beliefs justify an act made criminal by the law of the land? He begins his answer by saying that religious freedom is "guaranteed everywhere throughout the United States, so far as congressional interference is concerned." The issue here is whether this law is a constitutional exercise of the powers of Congress. Freedom of religion, says the Chief Justice, means freedom to hold an opinion or belief, it does not apply to those actions "in violation of social duties or subversive of good order."

MORRISON R. WAITE
1816–1888
Chief Justice
1874–1888

Does polygamy fall within that area which is "of good order"?

The Chief Justice answered:

. . . we think it may safely be said there never has been a time
in any State of the Union when polygamy has not been an offence
against society, cognizable by the civil courts and punishable with
more or less severity. In the face of all this evidence, it is impossible
to believe that the constitutional guaranty of religious freedom was
intended to prohibit legislation in respect to this most important feature of social life. Marriage, while from its very nature a sacred
obligation, is nevertheless, in most civilized nations, a civil contract,
and usually regulated by law. . . .

Can Congress outlaw polygamy even though it is a tenet in a
religious faith?

The Court replied:

Laws are made for the government of actions, and while they cannot
interfere with mere religious belief and opinions, they may with
practices. Suppose one believed that human sacrifices were a necessary part of religious worship, would it be seriously contended that

the civil government under which he lived could not interfere to prevent a sacrifice? Or if a wife religiously believed it was her duty to burn herself upon the funeral pyre of her dead husband, would it be beyond the power of the civil government to prevent her carrying her belief into practice?

So here, as a law of the organization of society under the exclusive dominion of the United States, it is provided that plural marriages shall not be allowed. Can a man excuse his practices to the contrary because of his religious belief? To permit this would be to make the professed doctrines of religious belief superior to the law of the land, and in effect to permit every citizen to become a law unto himself. Government could exist only in name under such circumstances.

We have quoted at length from this opinion because it has set an important precedent—a principle established in 1878 which continues to influence decisions relating to free exercise of religion issues.

The *Reynolds* case did not end the Mormon polygamy issue in our courts. In 1890 two other cases were decided. One involved a statute passed by the territorial legislature of Idaho requiring that anyone who voted in the general election must take an oath that he was not a member of any church which required or encouraged bigamy or polygamy as a religious duty. The other case dealt with another law passed by Congress which forfeited all of the property of the Mormon Church except for that portion which was used exclusively for religious worship.

The Supreme Court upheld both laws and, as a result, in that year the Mormon Church announced that plural marriages were no longer a tenet of that faith. The properties were thereupon returned.

Some Mormons, however, continued to disregard this Church ruling and have persisted in the practice of polygamy. In 1946 the Supreme Court was confronted with the issue of a number of Mormons who crossed state lines with their plural wives. They were convicted under the Mann Act, making it a crime to transport women across state lines for immoral purposes and the Supreme Court upheld the government's action.

CHAPTER 5

THE FLAG SALUTE CASES

CASES

CASE 13

Minersville School District v. Gobitis

310 U.S. 586, 60 S.Ct. 1010, 84 L.Ed. 1375 (1940)

Like the Mormons, the sect known as Jehovah's Witnesses had its day before the Supreme Court. As a matter of fact, the cases initiated by Jehovah's Witnesses have done more than any other religious group to probe the nature, scope, and limits of the principle of religious freedom. It has been estimated that between 1938 and 1943 they began twenty major cases before the Supreme Court, winning fourteen of them.

Among the most famous of these issues are The Flag Salute Cases. The first case was argued before the Supreme Court on April 25, 1940 and decided with unusual speed on June 3, 1940. Justice Frankfurter, delivering the opinion of the Court, stated the facts as follows:

> Lillian Gobitis, aged twelve, and her brother William, aged ten, were expelled from the public schools of Minersville, Pennsylvania, for refusing to salute the national flag as part of a daily school exercise. The local Board of Education required both teachers and pupils to participate in this ceremony. The ceremony is a familiar one. The right hand is placed on the breast and the following pledge recited in unison: "I pledge allegiance to my flag, and to the Republic for which it stands; one nation indivisible, with liberty and justice for all." While the words are spoken, teachers and pupils extend their right hands in salute to the flag. The Gobitis family are affiliated with "Jehovah's Witnesses," for whom the Bible as the Word of God is the supreme authority. The children had been brought up conscientiously to believe that such a gesture of respect for the flag was forbidden by command of scripture.

Since the Pennsylvania law required school attendance, the parents had to place their children in private schools. Because this financial expense was a hardship on the family, the father and the children brought this action against the school authorities, requesting that they be excused from the flag salute requirement.

How does one reconcile the individual's liberty of conscience, protected by the First and Fourteenth Amendments, with the state's authority to require school children to engage in such compulsory patriotic exercises as the flag salute? In this conflict of two important and desirable values, which one deserves priority?

Justice Frankfurter's answer is interesting. Religious liberty is an individual, precious right, he said, but each citizen also has political responsibilities to the community which protects this and other rights. A state can require ceremonies for all children in the promotion of national unity because "national unity is the basis for national security."

In defending the required flag salute as a means designed to achieve the goal of national cohesion, Justice Frankfurter speaks with eloquence:

FELIX FRANKFURTER
1882-1965
Associate Justice
1939-1962

The ultimate foundation of a free society is the binding tie of cohesive sentiment. Such a sentiment is fostered by all those agencies of the mind and spirit which may serve to gather up the traditions of a people, transmit them from generation to generation, and thereby create that continuity of a treasured common life which constitutes a civilization. "We live by symbols." The flag is the symbol of our national unity, transcending all internal differences, however large, within the framework of the Constitution. This Court has had occasion to say that ". . . the flag is the symbol of the nation's power,—the emblem of freedom in its truest, best sense. . . . it signifies government resting on the consent of the governed; liberty regulated by law; the protection of the weak against the strong; security against the exercise of arbitrary power; and absolute safety for free institutions against foreign aggression."

In developing a spirit of patriotism among school children the legislature has the authority, under Amendment X of the Constitution, to select any appropriate means to achieve its goals.

Justice Frankfurter then refers to the subject of school discipline. To require the flag salute of all children and then to permit dissenters to be excused on the basis of conscience would weaken the exercise by raising doubts in the minds of those who conformed.

In concluding, he takes the position that this type of issue belongs in the forum of public opinion and should be fought out in the halls of the legislature rather than the judicial arena.

Justice Stone dissented on several grounds. These children, he declared, were not lawbreakers in the usual sense of the word. What they were asked to do was contrary to their religious beliefs. In addition, the flag salute is not the only way of teaching patriotism. There are alternative procedures, such as the teaching of history, government, and civil liberty.

Finally, Justice Stone turns to Justice Frankfurter's observation that the legislature is the place to seek redress, rather than the judiciary. We are dealing here, he notes, with a small minority which is subject to the majority in the legislature. There is little reason to believe that the religious convictions of this unpopular minority will be tolerated or respected in a legislature which seeks conformity of belief and opinion in the interests of school discipline. It is issues of this nature which call for judicial scrutiny and protection of the liberty of religious and racial minorities. "A possible adjustment of school discipline," he concludes, "is necessary to protect the higher priorities set forth in the Bill of Rights."

CASE 14

West Virginia State Board of Education v. Barnette et al.

319 U.S. 624, 63 S.Ct. 1178, 87 L.Ed. 1628

In 1943 the United States was involved in World War II and patriotism and loyalty were issues of great moment. With millions of Americans in the Armed Forces, the Pledge of Allegiance and the National Anthem were recited frequently and with fervor. It was during this period of crisis that the Supreme Court agreed to review another Flag Salute case.

The facts, according to the Court's opinion, were as follows:

The Board of Education [of West Virginia] on January 9, 1942, adopted a resolution containing recitals taken largely from the Court's *Gobitis* opinion and ordering that the salute to the flag become "a regular part of the program of activities in the public schools," that all teachers and pupils "shall be required to participate in the salute honoring the Nation represented by the Flag; provided, however, that refusal to salute the Flag be regarded as an Act of insubordination, and shall be dealt with accordingly."

The resolution originally required the "commonly accepted salute to the Flag" which it defined. Objections to the salute as "being too much like Hitler's" were raised by the Parent and Teachers Association, the Boy and Girl Scouts, the Red Cross, and the Federation of Women's Clubs. Some modification appears to have been made in deference to these objections, but no concession was made to Jehovah's Witnesses. What is now required is the "stiff-arm" salute, the saluter to keep the right hand raised with palm turned up while the following is repeated: "I pledge allegiance to the Flag of the United States of America and to the Republic for which it stands; one Nation, indivisible, with liberty and justice for all."

Failure to conform is "insubordination" dealt with by expulsion. Readmission is denied by statute until compliance. Meanwhile the expelled child is "unlawfully absent" and may be proceeded against as a delinquent. His parents or guardians are liable to prosecution, and if convicted are subject to fine not exceeding $50 and jail term not exceeding thirty days.

In West Virginia a group of children belonging to Jehovah's Witnesses and their parents refused to obey the flag salute law on the ground that their religious beliefs forbade them to bow down or to serve "graven images." For them, the flag was such an "image" and they contended that God's law is superior to any governmental law. Instead, the children and their parents offered to make the following pledge:

"I have pledged my unqualified allegiance and devotion to Jehovah, the Almighty God, and to His Kingdom, for which Jesus commands all Christians to pray.

"I respect the flag of the United States and acknowledge it as a symbol of freedom and justice to all.

"I pledge allegiance and obedience to all the laws of the United States that are consistent with God's law, as set forth in the Bible."

The state refused to accept this as a suitable substitute. The children were expelled. State officials threatened to send them to reformatories maintained for juvenile delinquents. Their parents were prosecuted and threatened with prosecutions for causing delinquency.

This case poses some interesting issues. Should the *Gobitis* case serve as a precedent? Are there any facts that distinguish the two cases? Would you, as a judge, support or overrule the *Gobitis* precedent? Would the fact that a World War is being waged influence your decision? Is the Constitution a document for all seasons or should it be interpreted differently in wartime and in peacetime?

These issues were not easy ones to handle, as we can see by the Court's 6 to 3 decision. Between 1940 and 1943 two new Justices had joined the Court. Justice Jackson wrote the Court's opinion and Justice Rutledge joined him. By this time, Justice Stone, who had dissented in *Gobitis*, was now Chief Justice and he joined Jackson. Who were the other three who made up the majority of six? They were Justices Murphy, Black and Douglas, who had sided with the majority in 1940 and who decided to change their views in 1943. Justice Frankfurter, who had written the majority opinion in *Gobitis* was now a dissenter, as were Justices Reed and Roberts.

What led the Court to change its mind between 1940 and 1943 was, in part, the change in the composition of the Court. Two other developments were influential. The *Gobitis* ruling was attacked in many newspaper editorials, law reviews, and magazines. During the period between these two cases, members of Jehovah's Witnesses were mobbed, beaten, and harassed because of their views toward the flag salute.

Justice Jackson's opinion for the majority is studded with memorable quotations. The issue is one of the state's power to control access to the schools by requiring a flag salute against the individual's right of self-determination that touch individual opinion and personal attitude.

Recognizing the desirability of national unity, loyalty, and patriotism, Justice Jackson warns that there are many ways of achieving this end.

Ultimate futility of such attempts to compel coherence is the lesson of every such effort from the Roman drive to stamp out Christianity as a disturber of its pagan unity, the Inquisition, as a means to religious and dynastic unity, the Siberian exiles as a means to Russian unity, down to the fast failing efforts of our present totalitarian enemies. Those who begin coercive elimination of dissent soon find themselves exterminating dissenters. Compulsory unification of opinion achieves only the unanimity of the graveyard.

ROBERT H. JACKSON
1892–1954
Associate Justice
1941–1954

It seems trite but necessary to say that the First Amendment to our Constitution was designed to avoid these ends by avoiding these beginnings. There is no mysticism in the American concept of the State or of the nature or origin of its authority. We set up government by consent of the governed, and the Bill of Rights denies those in power any legal opportunity to coerce that consent. Authority here is to be controlled by public opinion, not public opinion by authority.
.   .   .

To believe that patriotism will not flourish if patriotic ceremonies are voluntary and spontaneous instead of a compulsory routine is to make an unflattering estimate of the appeal of our institutions to free minds. We can have intellectual individualism and the rich cultural diversities that we owe to exceptional minds only at the price of occasional eccentricity and abnormal attitudes. When they are so harmless to others or to the State as those we deal with here, the price is not too great. But freedom to differ is not limited to things that do not matter much. That would be a mere shadow of freedom. The test of its substance is the right to differ as to things that touch the heart of the existing order.

His concluding words have become one of the most quoted passages in constitutional law.

If there is any fixed star in our constitutional constellation, it is that no official, high or petty, can prescribe what shall be orthodox in politics, nationalism, religion, or other matters of opinion or force citizens to confess by word or act their faith therein. If there are any circumstances which permit an exception, they do not now occur to us.

We think the action of the local authorities in compelling the flag salute and pledge transcends constitutional limitations on their power and invades the sphere of intellect and spirit which it is the purpose of the First Amendment to our Constitution to reserve from all official control.

Justices Black and Douglas explained their switch to the majority view in a concurring opinion. They had voted with the majority in the *Gobitis* ruling because they were reluctant to have the Constitution used as a "rigid bar" against state regulation of conduct in the school. Now, they say, they were wrong because a "patriotic formula" can become a test oath and this is unconstitutional.

Justice Murphy concurred in the majority ruling.

Justice Frankfurter was understandably annoyed by the Court's refusal to follow the precedent of the *Gobitis* case and, in his long dissenting opinion, he points out that a line must be drawn between the feelings of a judge as a person and the function of a judge as an interpreter of the Constitution. The one must not be permitted to dominate the other. He states his position with vigor and conviction:

One who belongs to the most vilified and persecuted minority in history is not likely to be insensible to the freedoms guaranteed by our Constitution. Were my purely personal attitude relevant I should wholeheartedly associate myself with the general libertarian views in the Court's opinion, representing as they do the thought and action of

FELIX FRANKFURTER
1882–1965
Associate Justice
1939–1962

a lifetime. But as judges we are neither Jew nor Gentile, neither Catholic nor agnostic. We owe equal attachment to the Constitution and are equally bound by our judicial obligations whether we derive our citizenship from the earliest or the latest immigrants to these shores. As a member of this Court I am not justified in writing my private notions of policy into the Constitution, no matter how deeply I may cherish them or how mischievous I may deem their disregard. The duty of a judge who must decide which of two claims before the Court shall prevail, that of a State to enact and enforce laws within its general competence or that of an individual to refuse obedience because of the demands of his conscience, is not that of the ordinary person. It can never be emphasized too much that one's own opinion about the wisdom or evil of a law should be excluded altogether when one is doing one's duty on the bench. The only opinion of our own even looking in that direction that is material is our opinion whether legislators could in reason have enacted such a law.

He goes on to make a point which became a pivot in his judicial philosophy. In dealing with the interpretation of laws, judges must exercise self-restraint. The judiciary is one of three branches of government. If people dislike laws enacted by the legislature, the resort should be to the legislature to change the law. In this case, Jehovah's Witnesses and their supporters should have tried to persuade West Virginia to excuse them from the required flag-salute.

Furthermore, minorities can disrupt civil society and there is nothing in the Constitution which subordinates "the general civil authority of the state to sectarian scruples." In this case we have an act of the state legislature promoting good citizenship and national allegiance. It may not be wise, but it is an exercise of constitutional power.

If parents do not like the compulsory flag salute, they have the option of sending their children to non-public schools. After all, he points out, there are 250 distinctive established religious denominations in the United States. Of these, 120 are in Pennsylvania and 65 are in West Virginia. Think of the consequences of trying to adjust education to the religious scruples of each of these sects! In addition, those who do not belong to sects, may also object to laws on the claims of conscience. To avoid these consequences, educational programs designed to foster patriotism should be left to the state legislature and the public opinion which will either support it or initiate change. The courts ought to stand aloof from this type of controversy.

A TEACHER REFUSES TO SALUTE THE FLAG

CASE 15

Russo v. Central School District No. 1

469 F.2d 623 (2nd Cir. 1972)

Almost thirty years after the Flag Salute Cases, another case found its way into the courts. This time, however, the facts involved a teacher. The school regulation required teachers to participate with their students in the daily flag salute ceremonies. Susan Russo refused to join in the flag salute because she believed that the phrase "liberty and justice for all" did not "reflect the quality of life in America today." To mouth these words of the pledge were to her hypocritical. While the pledge was read over the school's loud-speaker system, Ms. Russo remained at attention. The class did recite the pledge, which was led by another teacher who was assigned to the class for this exercise. There was no disruption. Although Ms. Russo had not recited the pledge from the beginning of the semester in September, the Board of Education took no action until the following April. She was subsequently dismissed from her job and she appealed to the courts.

In November, 1972, the United States Court of Appeals of the Second Circuit decided in favor of Ms. Russo. The Court concluded that she was obviously sincere in her belief that the words of the pledge were neither accurate nor efficacious. Since "the First Amendment ranks among the most important of our constitutional rights, we must recognize that the previous right of free speech requires protection even when the speech is personally obnoxious."

Although the judges speak of freedom of speech, another issue which hovers over this case is that of freedom of conscience—an issue which has a spiritual quality about it and which was present in the Jehovah's Witnesses cases.

CHAPTER 6

THE RIGHT TO ESTABLISH PAROCHIAL SCHOOLS

CASES

CASE 16

Pierce v. Society of Sisters
and
Pierce v. Hill Military Academy

268 U.S. 510, 45 S.Ct. 571, 69 L.Ed. 1070 (1925)

In 1922 Oregon passed a Compulsory Education Act which required all normal children between the ages of 8 and 16 years with certain exceptions to attend public school. Failure to do so was a misdemeanor for each day the law was violated and was punishable by fines from $5 to $100 or imprisonment from 2 to 30 days, or both. The law grew out of the post-World War I feeling of nationalism and it reflected the influence of the Ku Klux Klan in Oregon.

The law was challenged by the Society of Sisters, a Catholic religious order, and by the Hill Military Academy. The former owned and operated elementary and secondary parochial schools, as well as junior colleges. The latter was a military training school for boys between the ages of 5 and 21.

> If you were the attorneys for the state, what would be the basis for your arguments? If you represented the religious order or the military school, how would you respond to the points raised by the state?

The issue comes down to the fundamental question: Does the state have the power to compel all children to attend the public schools?

The state, arguing from Amendment X, takes the position that it has the responsibility for teaching citizenship by designing the proper curriculum and selecting teachers of "good moral character and patriotic disposition." It is the responsibility of the state to make sure that "nothing be taught which is manifestly inimical to the public welfare."

The Society of Sisters and the Hill Military Academy base their case on the right to property and the right to liberty under the Fourteenth Amendment. The state law deprives them of their property without due process of law. In addition, there is nothing in the Constitution which gives the government a monopoly over the right to educate children.

Justice McReynolds, who spoke for a unanimous Court, stated:

. . . we think it entirely plain that the Act of 1922 unreasonably interferes with the liberty of parents and guardians to direct the upbringing and education of children under their control. As often heretofore pointed out, rights guaranteed by the Constitution may not be abridged by legislation which has no reasonable relation to some purpose within the competency of the state. The fundamental theory of liberty upon which all governments in this Union repose excludes any general power of the state to standardize its children by forcing them to accept instruction from public teachers only. The child is not the mere creature of the state; those who nurture him and direct his destiny have the right, coupled with the high duty, to recognize and prepare him for additional obligations.

Appellees are corporations, and therefore, it is said, they cannot claim for themselves the liberty which the Fourteenth Amendment guarantees. Accepted in the proper sense, this is true. . . . But they have business and property for which they claim protection. These are threatened with destruction through the unwarranted compulsion which appellants are exercising over present and prospective patrons of their schools. And this court has gone very far to protect against loss threatened by such action.

This case has become the precedent for supporting private and parochial schools.

THE AMISH REFUSE TO SEND THEIR CHILDREN TO PUBLIC SECONDARY SCHOOLS

CASE 17

THE AMISH SECONDARY SCHOOL CASE

State of Wisconsin v. Jonas Yoder et al.

406 U.S. 205, 92 S.Ct. 1526, 32 L.Ed.2d 15 (1972)

Can members of a religious sect refuse to send their children to the public secondary school because the teachings at the school are in conflict with the tenets of the religion?

Jonas Yoder and Wallace Miller are members of the Old Order Amish religion and Adin Yutzy is a member of the Conservative Amish Mennonite Church. They live in Green County, Wisconsin and their children graduated from the eighth grade in elementary school. They refuse to send their children, Frieda Yoder and Barbara Miller, age 15, and Vernon Yutzy, age 14 to public or private high school. The Wisconsin compulsory education law requires attendance at public or private schools until the age of 16. Penalties for violating the law range from fines of $5 to $50, and imprisonment for not more than three months or both. The parents were each fined $5.

Before the case went to trial, the attorney for the Amish suggested a compromise settlement to the State Superintendent of Public Instruction. He proposed that the Amish establish their own vocational training center. Using the Pennsylvania plan as a model, it was suggested that the children would attend the center for three hours a week, where they would be taught English, social studies, math and health by an Amish teacher. During the rest of the week, the children would perform farm and household duties under the supervision of their parents. In addition, they would keep a journal of their daily activities. The Superintendent refused to accept this plan on the ground that this type of education would not be "substantially equivalent" to that given in the schools of that community.

The arguments presented on behalf of the Amish are based on the Religion Clauses of the First Amendment, as applied to the states by the Fourteenth Amendment. First, an appeal is made to history. The Amish religion traces its roots to the sixteenth century Anabaptists, who sought a return to the simple life of the early Christian era. A basic tenet of their faith is that religion pervades all of life and that salvation requires living in a church community apart from worldly influence.

The second argument poses a conflict of values. The Amish do not object to public elementary school education because they regard basic training in the "three R's" as useful in Bible reading, in civic education and in dealing with daily affairs in a non-Amish world. Their objection to the public secondary schools is stated in the following terms in the Court's opinion:

> . . . The high school tends to emphasize intellectual and scientific accomplishments, self-distinction, competitiveness, worldly success, and social life with other students. Amish society emphasizes informal learning-through-doing; a life of "goodness," rather than a life of intellect; wisdom, rather than technical knowledge, community welfare, rather than competition; and separation from, rather than integration with, contemporary worldly society.

According to one expert, if the Amish children are required to attend public high schools, the conflict between the worldly values of a secular society and the non-worldly values of a religious society would do psychological harm to the Amish children. Torn between the requirements of the school and the demands of their religion, the children might leave their church and this would mean the end of the Amish Community.

A second expert testified that the Amish way of raising their children by "learning through doing" farm and vocational work is superior to the ordinary high school education. Not only do these children become self-sufficient members of society, they have an excellent record as law-abiding citizens.

These arguments, presented on behalf of the Amish, are difficult to answer. This is especially so when one considers the Court's opinion in *Pierce v. Society of Sisters*, permitting the establishment of parochial schools. Using that case as a precedent, the argument could be advanced that freedom of religion sanctions exceptions to compulsory public school attendance.

However, how far can one go with this argument? Since there are several hundred religious sects, would you approve many exceptions to compulsory education? After all, the public schools, unlike the private and parochial schools, bring together children from the neighborhood or the community. The public schools seek to develop a commonality of interests in the pursuit of the goals of American life. It is here that all creeds, colors, and religious groups meet on an equal footing and learn to live together. At least this is one of the foundation stones upon which the public schools are built. To ask for exceptions from this requirement, one must present a value which has greater priority than universal public education. Can freedom of religion make this claim?

Chief Justice Burger delivered the opinion of the Court, with which Justice Douglas dissented only in part. The Chief Justice begins his opinion with the observation that we are dealing here with a 300-year old religion. For this religious group to sustain its claim that religious freedom has priority over the claim of compulsory public education, it must prove that its religious faith and its mode of life are inseparable. The record of the trial shows that the Amish way of life is church-oriented, while the life around them is secular and charged with pressures to conform. To force them to comply with the compulsory education law means that they either leave the state and search for a more tolerant environment or risk the loss of their children to a secular society.

In the first place, says Chief Justice Burger, it should be remembered that religious sects, like the Amish, have played an important role in history.

> We must not forget that in the Middle Ages important values of the civilization of the Western World were preserved by members of religious orders who isolated themselves from all worldly influences against great obstacles. There can be no assumption that today's majority is "right" and the Amish and others like them are "wrong." A way of life that is odd or even erratic but interferes with no rights or interests of others is not to be condemned because it is different.

We agree, replies the State of Wisconsin, but let us suppose that some of the Amish children decide to leave their religious sanctuaries and venture out into the world at large. Wouldn't they be ill-equipped for life in a secular society?

There is no merit in this type of argument, answered Chief Justice Burger, because the Amish offer their children an "ideal" vocational education during the adolescent years. Skills in farming and manual labor are developed, as are qualities of reliability, self-reliance, and dedication to work. The Amish instill in their children the social and political responsibilities of citizenship. The record in this case disclosed that the Amish in Green County had never been known to commit crimes, to receive public assistance, and to be unemployed. One or two years of high school would not necessarily match this type of education.

The Court had to answer two other interesting lines of argument. The first was based on the state's police power to protect the lives, health, morals, safety, and welfare of all the people. Under this power, argued the State of Wisconsin, the state stands in *parens patriae* to the children. That is, according to the Latin phrase, the government stands in the place of the parents when it becomes necessary to take care of minors and others who cannot take care of themselves. The Court responded that there is nothing in the record to show that the health, or safety, or welfare of the children have been endangered by the actions of the parents.

The second point deals with the charge of Justice Douglas, in his dissenting opinion, that this case disregards the wishes of the children. Only one of the three children testified that she agreed with her parents. The other two children were not called so that we do not know their thoughts and feelings on the issue. To this, Chief Justice Burger replied that the children are not the parties in this case. Furthermore, the State of Wisconsin never raised this point.

The opinion concluded with a summary of the findings and with this instruction to the State:

> Nothing we hold is intended to undermine the general applicability of the State's compulsory school-attendance statutes or to limit the power of the State to promulgate reasonable standards that, while not impairing the free exercise of religion, provide for continuing agricultural vocational education under parental and church guidance by the Old Order Amish or others similarly situated. The States have had a long history of amicable and effective relationships with church-sponsored schools, and there is no basis for assuming that, in this related context, reasonable standards cannot be established concerning the content of the continuing vocational education of Amish children under parental guidance, provided always that state regulations are not inconsistent with what we have said in this opinion.

Justices Powell and Rehnquist took no part in the consideration of the case or the decision.

Justice Stewart wrote a concurring opinion, in which Justice Brennan joined. Justice White wrote a concurring opinion, in which Justices Brennan and Stewart joined.

Justice Douglas' opinion agrees with the judgment of the Court concerning Frieda Yoder, since she had testified as to her opinion. He dissents from their opinion concerning Vernon Yutzy or Barbara Miller, because they had not testified as to their views. His opinion is a moving statement on behalf of the rights of children.

> These children are "persons" within the meaning of the Bill of Rights. We have so held over and over again. . . . It is the future of the student, not the future of the parents, that is imperiled by today's decision. If a parent keeps his child out of school beyond the grade school, then the child will be forever barred from entry into the new and amazing world of diversity that we have today. The child may decide that that is the preferred course, or he may rebel. It is the student's judgment, not his parents', that is essential if we are to give full meaning to what we have said about the Bill of Rights and of the right of students to be masters of their own destiny. If he is harnessed to the Amish way of life by those in authority over him and if his education is truncated, his entire life may be stunted and deformed.

The child, therefore, should be given an opportunity to be heard before the State gives the exemption which we honor today.

Justice Douglas then directs his attention to other aspects of the Court's opinion. Chief Justice Burger had made reference to "the law and order" record of the Amish people. Irritated by this point, Justice Douglas responds:

> I think the emphasis of the Court on the "law and order" record of this Amish group of people is quite irrelevant. A religion is a religion irrespective of what the misdemeanor or felony records of its members might be. I am not at all sure how the Catholics, Episcopalians, the Baptists, Jehovah's Witnesses, the Unitarians, and my own Presbyterians would make out if subjected to such a test. It is, of course, true that if a group or society was organized to perpetuate crime and if that is its motive, we would have rather startling problems akin to those that were raised when some years back a particular sect was challenged here as operating on a fraudulent basis. . . . But no such factors are present here, and the Amish, whether with a high or low criminal record, certainly qualify by all historic standards as a religion within the meaning of the First Amendment.

In its opinion the Court had referred to the *Reynolds* case, often referred to as the Mormon Polygamy Case. In that case the judgment against the Mormons was based on a distinction between belief and action growing out of the principle of freedom of religion. Belief was permitted, but action regarded as anti-social by the state was prohibited. The Court's ruling in the Amish case seems to contradict the precedent of the *Reynolds* case. It is a good thing, too, remarks Justice Douglas, and hopefully, the *Reynolds* precedent will be overruled in time.

CHAPTER 7

RELIGIOUS TEST OATHS, BLUE LAWS, AND SABBATARIANS

Now that we have examined some of the landmark cases dealing with the Establishment and the Freedom of Religion Clauses of the First and Fourteenth Amendments, we should be ready to decide some other interesting and important issues which deal with religion and the state.

ISSUES TO BE ANALYZED

Cases 18–23 present a series of problems relating to freedom of religion. Place yourself in the position of a judge. Using historical background materials and the legal precedents that you have read up to this point, decide the following cases. Justify your position with reasons and principles.

CASES

CASE 18

THE MARYLAND RELIGIOUS TEST OATH CASE

The Constitution of the State of Maryland provided that no religious test could ever be required "as a qualification for any office of profit or trust in this State, other than a declaration of belief in the existence of God." Torcaso, who had been appointed a notary public, would not declare his belief in God and he was refused the commission. He then sued the state for his commission on the ground that his right to freedom of religion under the First and Fourteenth Amendments had been violated.

The State of Maryland argued that no one is compelled to hold public office. If a person doesn't like the conditions, he or she does not have to serve. In addition, there is no invasion of Torcaso's freedom of religion because the law does not require him to believe or to disbelieve.

How would you answer these arguments?

In answering Maryland, would you invoke Article VI of the United States Constitution: "No religious test shall ever be required as a qualification for any office or public trust under the United States."

How would you decide this case?

BLUE LAWS—SUNDAY CLOSING LAWS

Blue Laws, originally, were those that imposed religious restrictions—generally puritanical standards—on people's conduct. In recent years these laws have been associated with prohibitions on working and selling on Sundays.

What do these laws have to do with religion? Originally, they were designed to set up Sunday as the Lord's Day, as a day of religious observance, when people refrained from work and play and attended church. Derived from English law, the American colonists incorporated this legislation into their codes and the Sunday Closing Laws were enforced to a greater or lesser extent.

In 1961 the Supreme Court was confronted with four cases involving violations of these laws.

CASE 19

MARYLAND SUNDAY CLOSING LAW

Seven employees of a large department store were indicted for violating the Maryland Sunday Closing Law and were fined $5 and costs.

The Maryland law was attacked on a number of grounds. An important objection to the law was that it was designed to help the Christian religion and the argument ran as follows: Sunday is the Sabbath Day of the predominant Christian sects and the purpose of the stoppage is to encourage church attendance. In addition, the purpose of the law is to induce people with no religion or the uncommitted to join the predominant Christian sects. Furthermore, the Sunday closing contributes to the atmosphere of tranquillity and aids the conduct of the church services. All in all, these laws contribute to an establishment of religion and, therefore, violate the First and Fourteenth Amendments.

CASE 20

SUNDAY CLOSING LAWS AND THE ORTHODOX
JEWISH RELIGION

The Massachusetts Sunday Closing Laws prohibited the opening of shops and doing business on Sunday. There were many exceptions to the law. The Crown Kosher Super Market, owned by Orthodox Jews, kept their business open on Sunday. No other supermarket remained open on Sunday. Since the Jewish sabbath is on Saturday, Orthodox Jews do not shop on that day. For this reason, it was argued that the Crown Kosher Super Market should have the right to be open on Sunday. About one-third of its weekly business was conducted on Sunday. To prohibit them from doing so was to deny them the equal protection of the laws, their freedom of religion, and, in addition, contributed to the establishment of religion.

---

1. What differences do you see between Case 19 and 20?
2. How would you decide this issue?

CASE 21

SUNDAY CLOSING LAWS AND THE PROSECUTION OF EMPLOYEES

A Pennsylvania law made unlawful Sunday retail sales of certain commodities. The plaintiff, Two Guys from Harrison-Allentown, a large discount department store, kept their place open on Sunday. The County District Attorney prosecuted a number of its employees under the law. The Department Store sought an injunction against the prosecutor on the ground that the Sunday Closing Law violated the First and Fourteenth Amendments.

---

1. What differences do you see among Cases 19, 20, and 21?
2. Will these differences influence your decision?
3. In each of these cases there is a claim that one group is being discriminated against by the state. What do you think?

CASE 22

SUNDAY CLOSING LAWS AND ORTHODOX JEWS

The Pennsylvania law mentioned in Case 20 applies here. It prohibits Sunday retail sales of certain commodities, including clothing and home furnishings. The plaintiffs are Philadelphia merchants of the Orthodox Jewish faith. Their religion requires them to close their place of business and to abstain from all work from nightfall each Friday until nightfall each Saturday. They maintained that they kept their business open on Sunday in order to compensate for their closing on Saturday. If forced to close on Sunday, they will be closed on two days and will lose so much business that they might be forced to close. In this way, they are put at a serious economic disadvantage with their competitors. To remain in business and to conform to the law, they might have to give up one of the basic tenets of their religion and remain open on Saturday. This is religious discrimination and violates the First and Fourteenth Amendments.

> Can you formulate a legal principle that will apply to the cases considered up to this point?

SABBATARIANS

Sabbatarians are those who regard Saturday as their day of religious observance and rest. In addition to the Orthodox Jews, Sabbatarians include a variety of Christian sects, among which are the Seventh Day Adventists. What happens when Sabbatarians are asked to work on Saturday? Let us suppose that they refuse to do so? Can they be fired? Can they receive unemployment insurance?

CASE 23

SEVENTH-DAY ADVENTIST IS DENIED
UNEMPLOYMENT INSURANCE

Adell H. Sherbert was a member of the Seventh-Day Adventist Church. A basic tenet of her religion is prohibition against any work on Saturday. At first her employer permitted her to work a five-day week. When the work week was changed to six days, including Saturday, she refused to do so and was discharged. She tried to get a job at other textile mills in the area, but could not do so because none of them would employ her on a five-day week. She filed a claim for unemployment insurance, but it was refused because she had refused to accept "available suitable work" as required by the South Carolina law. She argued that this action was a restriction on her freedom of religion.

> 1. In what way is her case different from those of the Orthodox Jews?
> 2. Would you grant her unemployment insurance?
> Justify your decision.

DECISIONS

The following decisions for Cases 18–23 can now be compared with your reasoning. Were you able to anticipate the court's analysis?

RELIGIOUS TEST OATH

CASE 18

Torcaso v. Watkins

367 U.S. 488, 81 S.Ct. 1680, 6 L.Ed.2d 982 (1961)

The Court decided in favor of Torcaso in a unanimous ruling. Justices Frankfurter and Harlan concurred in the result without an opinion.

The Maryland Constitution requiring a belief in God as a condition for holding public office violated the Freedom of Religion Clause of the First and Fourteenth Amendments. The Court decided that the Maryland Constitution set up a religious test which was designed to, and does, bar every person who refuses to declare a belief in God from holding a public office in Maryland. Justice Black's opinion declares:

> The power and authority of the State of Maryland thus is put on the side of one particular sort of believers—those who are willing to say they believe in "the existence of God." . . .

Article VI in the Constitution applies only to federal office holders. Amendment XIV, incorporating the First Amendment Freedoms, applies this prohibition to this case. Justice Black concludes that:

> neither a State nor the Federal Government can constitutionally force a person "to profess a belief or disbelief in any religion." Neither can constitutionally pass laws nor impose requirements which aid all religions as against non-believers, and neither can aid those religions based on a belief in the existence of God as against those religions founded on different beliefs. (For example, Buddhism, Taoism, Ethical Culture, and Secular Humanism)

BLUE LAWS—SUNDAY CLOSING LAWS

CASE 19

McGowan v. Maryland

366 U.S. 420, 81 S.Ct. 1101, 6 L.Ed.2d 393 (1961)

Chief Justice Warren wrote the opinion for the Court, with Justice Douglas as the only dissenter. He concluded that, although the Sunday Closing Laws were religious in their origin, they were now secular in character. They were designed to improve "the health, safety, recreation and general well-being of our citizens."

In order to accentuate this point, the Chief Justice continues:

> . . . it is common knowledge that the first day of the week has come to have special significance as a rest day in this country. People of all religions and people with no religion regard Sunday as a time for family activity, for visiting friends and relatives, for late-sleeping, for passive and active entertainments, for dining out and the like. . . . The cause is irrelevant; the fact exists.

EARL WARREN
1891–1974
Chief Justice
1953–1969

CASE 20

Gallagher, Chief of Police of City of Springfield, Mass. v.
Crown Kosher Super Market of Mass.

366 U.S. 617, 81 S.Ct. 1122, 6 L.Ed.2d 536 (1961)

Chief Justice Warren delivered the judgment of the Court in which Justices Black, Clark, and Whittaker concurred. The first thing to note here is that only four judges agreed on the Court's opinion. Since two other Justices—Frankfurter and Harlan—concurred in a separate opinion, it is obvious that the Court's opinion represents a minority of the Justices, although a majority of six agreed on the decision. Finally, in this case we find three dissenters—Justices Brennan, Stewart and Douglas.

The Court's opinion upheld the Massachusetts law on the ground that it did not deny the Jewish merchant the equal protection of the laws required by the Fourteenth Amendment. Nor did this law establish a religion by requiring the closing of most businesses on Sunday. The point is made again that these laws, originally religious in nature, are now secular in character. *McGowan v. Maryland* is given as the precedent.

As for the argument that this law discriminated against Jews by interfering with their religious freedom, the Court saw no need to decide this issue at this time.

Justices Brennan and Stewart dissented on this very point that the Massachusetts law prohibited the free exercise of religion.

CASE 21

Two Guys from Harrison–Allentown v. McGinley, District
Attorney of County of Lehigh, Pa.

366 U.S. 582, 81 S.Ct. 1135, 6 L.Ed.2d 551 (1961)

Chief Justice Warren delivered the opinion of the Court. Justices Frankfurter and Harlan concurred and Justice Douglas dissented. Quoting their reasoning in *McGowan v. Maryland*, the Chief Justice ruled that "neither statute's purpose nor its effect is religious."

CASE 22

Braunfeld v. Brown, Commissioner of Police of Philadelphia, Pa.

366 U.S. 599, 81 S.Ct. 1144, 6 L.Ed.2d 563 (1961)

Chief Justice Warren, once again, spoke for a minority of the Court when he announced the judgment of the Court. Agreeing with his reasoning were Justices Black, Clark and Whittaker. The other Justices either concurred or dissented on various grounds.

The Court's opinion upheld the Pennsylvania law on three grounds: There was no denial of equal protection of the laws; There was no establishment of religion; and, there was no interference with freedom of religion. Using the three previous cases as precedents, the Court's opinion concluded that the Sunday Closing Law was secular in its purpose.

In this case the Court's opinion focuses on the freedom of religion issue and concludes that the Pennsylvania law does not outlaw any religious practices. It merely inconveniences some, but not all members of the Orthodox Jewish faith. The fact that the merchant in this case has to make a financial sacrifice in order to observe his religious beliefs is no reason for declaring the state law unconstitutional.

Justice Frankfurter wrote a long concurring opinion which contains a detailed and scholarly history of Sunday Closing laws.

Three Justices dissented in the cases involving Orthodox Jewish merchants on the ground that the Sunday Closing laws discriminated against their free exercise of religion. Justice Stewart put it succinctly:

> Pennsylvania has passed a law which compels an Orthodox Jew to choose between his religious faith and his economic survival. This is a cruel choice. It is a choice which I think no state can constitutionally demand. For me this is not something that can be swept under the rug and forgotten in the interest of enforced Sunday togetherness.

Justice Brennan's dissent asks why Pennsylvania could not have exempted Orthodox Jews from the law. He points out that a majority—21—of the 34 states which have Sunday laws have made exemptions of this kind. Freedom of conscience, he concludes, is too delicate a matter to be forced in the pattern of having everyone rest on the same day. This may be administratively convenient for the state, but it violates the freedom of religion protected by the First and Fourteenth Amendments.

Justice Douglas dissented in all four cases. He posed the issue as follows:

> The question is not whether one day out of seven can be imposed by a state as a day of rest. The question is not whether Sunday can by force of custom and habit be retained as a day of rest. The question is whether a state can impose criminal sanctions on those who, unlike the Christian majority that makes up our society, worship on a different day or do not share the religious scruples of the majority.

He then answers this question in a rather unique way.

> The issue of these cases would therefore be in better focus if we imagined that a state legislature, controlled by Orthodox Jews and Seventh Day Adventists, passed a law making it a crime to keep a shop open on Saturdays. Would a Baptist, Catholic, Methodist, or Presbyterian be compelled to obey that law or go to jail or pay a fine? Or suppose Moslems grew in political strength here and got a law through a state legislature making it a crime to keep a shop open on Fridays? Would the rest of us have to submit under the fear of criminal sanctions?

> But it is a strange Bill of Rights that makes it possible for the dominant religious group to bring the minority to heel because the minority, in the doing of acts which intrinsically are wholesome and not antisocial, does not defer to the majority's religious beliefs. . . .

> There is an "establishment" of religion in the constitutional sense if any practice of any religious group has the sanction of law behind it. There is an interference with the "free exercise" of religion if what in conscience one can do or omit doing is required because of the religious scruples of the community. Hence I would declare each of those laws unconstitutional as applied to the complaining parties, whether or not they are members of a sect which observes as their Sabbath day a day other than Sunday.

> When, however, the State uses its coercive powers—here the criminal law—to compel minorities to observe a second Sabbath, not their own, the State undertakes to aid and "prefer one religion over another"—contrary to the command of the Constitution. . . .

A SEQUEL TO THE SUNDAY CLOSING RULINGS

There was an interesting reaction to these decisions. The legislatures of Maryland, Massachusetts and Pennsylvania amended their Sunday Closing Laws to exempt Sabbatarians. Where these laws still remain in the statute books, police and prosecutors have shown little inclination to carry them out. At present it seems that, in most states, they are dead-letter laws, since the business community seems more and more inclined to keep open their establishments on Sunday.

SABBATARIANS

CASE 23

Sherbert v. Verner

374 U.S. 398, 83 S.Ct. 1790, 10 L.Ed.2d 965 (1963)

In a 6 to 2 ruling the Court upheld Sherbert's claim. Justice Brennan delivered the opinion of the Court. To uphold the state in this case, he pointed out, forces Sherbert

> to choose between following the percepts of her religion and forfeiting benefits, on the one hand, and abandoning one of the percepts of her religion in order to accept work on the other hand.

This, he said, is similar to imposing a fine for Saturday worship and is an unconstitutional burden on freedom of religion.

The Court's opinion concludes:

> This holding but reaffirms a principle that we announced a decade and a half ago, namely that no State may "exclude individual Catholics, Lutherans, Mohammedans, Baptists, Jews, Methodists, Nonbelievers, Presbyterians, or the members of any other faith, *because of their faith, or lack of it,* from receiving the benefits of public welfare legislation."

Justices Douglas and Stewart wrote concurring opinions.

Justice Harlan wrote a dissenting opinion, in which Justice White joined. The legislature did not provide any exceptions when it stated that unemployment insurance would be paid only if the claimant was "available for work." The fact that Sherbert is not available for work for religious reasons is irrelevant. The state was not discriminating against her for religious reasons. She was denied benefits for personal reasons.

More important, says the dissent, is the fact that the Court's opinion is singling out a religious group and granting it a benefit. This amounts to an establishment of religion in violation of the First and Fourteenth Amendments.

CHAPTER 8

X–RAYS, BLOOD TRANSFUSIONS, PEYOTE, AND SNAKES

CASES

ISSUES TO BE ANALYZED

Cases 24–28 present additional issues which impinge on freedom of religion. Once again, you have an opportunity to act the role of judge.

X–RAYS

CASE 24

The State Board of Regents in Washington instituted a requirement that all students registering at the University of Washington must have chest X-rays for the detection of tuberculosis. A member of the Christian Science Church objected to this requirement on the ground that it conflicted with the tenets of her church, as well as with her own personal religious convictions.

Would you make an exception in her case?

BLOOD TRANSFUSIONS

CASE 25

A child was born with a serious medical condition. According to medical experts, the child needed a blood transfusion immediately. Without it, death was inevitable. The child's parents were members of the Jehovah's Witnesses sect and they objected on the ground that blood transfusions were prohibited by their religion.

The case was taken to family court and the judge was asked to make a decision.

You are the judge. Decide.

CASE 26

A member of Jehovah's Witnesses pregnant with a child refused a blood transfusion, despite the decision of medical experts that it was necessary to save her life, as well as that of her unborn child. This is obviously an emergency and the parties come before you and ask for a ruling.

> Before giving your decision, consider:
>   (a) arguments on behalf of the mother;
>   (b) arguments on behalf of the unborn child;
>   (c) arguments on behalf of the hospital.
> Now—decide the case.

SNAKE HANDLERS

CASE 27

A city in North Carolina passed an ordinance prohibiting the handling of poisonous reptiles "in such a manner as to endanger public health, welfare, and safety." A cult of snake handlers, basing their practice on religious grounds, refused to obey the law. They were convicted and their case was carried to the Supreme Court of North Carolina.

The defendants argued that they had not violated the ordinance because the snakes were handled voluntarily among members of the cult only. This practice, they contended, did not "endanger public health, welfare, and safety."

> What do you think of this argument? Will you uphold the religious freedom of this group to engage in what they regard as a religious experience?

PEYOTE

CASE 28

Indians who belonged to the American Native Church smoked peyote, a hallucinogen, as a religious sacrament. The California narcotics law prohibited the use of harmful drugs. Those Indians who smoked peyote were arrested and convicted of violating the law and they appealed.

> Do you think the use of drugs as part of a religious ceremony exempts the Indians from the state law? How would you balance the right of the state to protect its citizens with the right of Indians to exercise their religious freedom?

DECISIONS IN CASES 24–28

X–RAYS

CASE 24

State ex rel. Holcomb v. Armstrong

39 Wash.2d 860 (1952), 239 P.2d 545

In 1952 the Supreme Court of Washington upheld the regulation on the ground that tuberculosis was a serious disease among students and that the state had the power to use reasonable means to stop the spread of the disease among the student body. The State Board of Regents has the obligation of protection of the community under its supervision. This concern for society has a priority over an individual's right to religious freedom.

BLOOD TRANSFUSIONS

CASE 25

People ex rel. Wallace v. Labrenz

411 Ill. 618 (1952), 104 N.E.2d 769, certiorari denied

344 U.S. 824 (1952)

In this case the family court judge took the child out of the custody of the parents and appointed a legal guardian who, then, approved the transfusion. The child's life was saved, but the parents decided to make an issue out of the proceedings. They appealed their right to control the life of their child to the Supreme Court of Illinois and they lost. The court, in its ruling, quoted with approval a statement made by the U. S. Supreme Court (*Prince v. Mass.*, 321 U.S. 158, 64 S.Ct. 438, 88 L.Ed. 645 [1944]) :

The right to practice religion freely does not include liberty to expose the community or the child to communicable disease or the latter to ill health or death . . . Parents may be free to become martyrs themselves. But it does not follow they are free, in identical circumstances, to make martyrs of their children before they have reached the age of full and legal discretion when they can make that choice for themselves.

CASE 26

Raliegh Fitkin Hospital v. Anderson

42 N.J. 421, 201 A.2d 537, certiorari denied 377 U.S. 985 (1964)

In a New Jersey case decided in 1964 the court held that a mother could not sacrifice the life of an unborn child, even though she might be able to sacrifice her own life.

SNAKE HANDLING

CASE 27

State v. Massey

51 S.E.2d 179, 229 N.C. 734 (1949)

In 1949 the Supreme Court of North Carolina upheld the city ordinance as a valid exercise of police power—the power to protect the lives, health, morals, welfare, and safety of the people. This form of religious worship must give way to the greater value of public safety.

In Bunn v. North Carolina, 336 U.S. 942 (1949), the Supreme Court dismissed the appeal on the ground that it did not state a significant federal issue.

PEYOTE SMOKING

CASE 28

People v. Woody

394 P.2d 813 (1964), 61 C.2d 716

In 1964 the California Supreme Court upheld the right of the Indians to use peyote as part of their religious ceremony. The Court declared that, since there was no clear evidence that peyote was a dangerous drug, the Indians could not be prosecuted under the state's narcotics law.

CHAPTER 9

CONSCIENTIOUS OBJECTORS

In his dissenting opinion in *Braunfeld v. Brown*, one of the Sunday Closing Cases, Justice Douglas refers to a higher law in these words:

> The institutions of our society are founded on the belief that there is an authority higher than the authority of the state; that there is a moral law which the state is powerless to alter; that the individual possesses rights, conferred by the Creator, which government must respect. The Declaration of Independence stated the now familiar theme:

> "We hold these truths to be self-evident, that all men are created equal, that they are endowed by their Creator with certain inalienable rights, that among these are life, liberty, and the pursuit of happiness."

> And the body of the Constitution, as well as the Bill of Rights enshrined these principles.

Keeping this idea in mind—the idea of a higher law, a moral law—let us turn to an issue which involves a confrontation between this idea and the power of raising an army through the draft.

Under the Constitution, the Congress has the power to declare war, to raise an army, and to support a navy. Under this power Congress can draft men and women regardless of age. It has been the custom to limit the draft to men while, in recent years, women were permitted to volunteer for military service.

Now, let us suppose that we are at war and that the Congress has passed a law to draft men between certain ages for military service. Can a man refuse to fight because the tenets of his religion prohibit him from killing others? Suppose he does not belong to a recognized religious sect, but he objects to killing others because of his deeply held beliefs about humankind? Should these men be excused from the draft?

The conscientious objector is one who objects to the actions of the state whether it is directed to war or to discrimination. It has been said that the conscientious objector listens "to an inner voice" when all others in the nation march to "the drums of war" or to the lockstep of state-supported discrimination. In this conflict of values between the dictates of an individual's conscience and the commands of the state, a democratic people faces the dilemma of the individual's freedom of belief versus the states right to self-preservation.

Let us see how these principles are applied to actual cases.

The draft laws in this country have recognized the dilemma posed by conscientious objectors. The 1917 draft law exempted from military service those who belonged to well-recognized pacifist religious sects. The 1940 draft law exempted from military action those who by "religious training and belief" opposed killing in war. They were not exempt from the draft, but were assigned to non-combatant duties. If they refused induction, they could be and were imprisoned.

In 1948 Congress defined "religious training and belief" as "an individual's relation to a Supreme Being involving duties superior to those arising from any human relation, but [not including] essentially political, sociological, or philosophical views or a merely personal moral code." This was incorporated into the Universal Military Training and Service Act.

The war in Vietnam brought to court many cases of young men who claimed that they were conscientious objectors. How can a court differentiate between a real conscientious objector and one who is trying simply to evade the draft? This is, obviously, a difficult task.

CASE 29

In 1965 the Supreme Court handed down one of its most important decisions in this matter. The Justices considered three cases in each of which the young man claimed conscientious objection on grounds other than a belief in God. The first young man believed in goodness and virtue and moral and intellectual integrity. His draft board found him to be honest and sincere, but he was, nevertheless, drafted.

The second young man believed in "Godness" and claimed the military service would be a strain on his conscience. The third young man declared that it was against his moral code to take human life. He based his conscientious beliefs on democratic American culture and values derived from western religions and philosophical traditions. They, also, were drafted.

In a unanimous decision in *United States v. Seeger*, the Court upheld the positions advanced by the three young men. Justice Clark delivered the opinion of the Court. He posed the issue in this way:

> Our question, therefore, is the narrow one: Does the term "Supreme Being" mean the orthodox God, or the broader concept of a power or being, or a faith, "to which all else is subordinate or upon which all else is ultimately dependent"?

In answering, Justice Clark reminds us that there are more than 250 sects in this country with a variety and multiplicity of interpretations as to the meaning of God. There are Quakers, Mennonites, Hindus, and Buddhists, each of which has its own views of a supernatural diety.

Perhaps, reasoned Justice Clark, the way out of this complex issue rooted in conscience is to formulate a rule of law which can cover this diversity of viewpoints. The rule is stated in this way:

> The test might be stated in these words: A sincere and meaningful belief which occupies in the life of its possessor a place parallel to that filled by God.

On the basis of this rule, the three men qualify as conscientious objectors. Justice Clark noted that a purely "personal code" did not qualify anyone for exemption. It is to be noted, said Justice Clark, that this case does not deal with atheists.

TOM C. CLARK
1899–1977
Associate Justice
1949–1967

CASE 30

Welsh v. United States

398 U.S. 338, 90 S.Ct. 1792, 26 L.Ed.2d 308 (1970)

Welsh was convicted of refusing to submit to induction in the Armed Forces because he claimed he was a conscientious objector. He insisted that his opposition was not based on religious grounds and he even struck out the word "religious" in his conscientious objector application. Later, he wrote a letter to the Draft Board pointing out that his beliefs were "religious in the ethical sense of the word." Welsh's objection to war was based on his conception of world politics. He wrote his draft board that "the military complex wastes both human and material resources . . . that in our failure to recognize the political, social, and economic realities of the world, we *as a nation*, fail our responsibilities *as a nation*." He also contended that the taking of life is morally wrong. Killing, he declared is "immoral and totally repugnant."

The Government argued that this case was different from the *Seeger* case. Welsh's views, they contended, were "essentially political, sociological, or philosophical . . . or a merely personal moral code," and for this reason he was not entitled to exemption.

The High Court had problems with this issue and they split 5 to 3 with Justice Blackmun taking no part in the consideration or decision of the case. Justice Black announced the judgment of the Court and delivered an opinion in which Justices Douglas, Brennan, and Marshall joined. Justice Harlan concurred in the result and wrote a separate opinion. The three dissenters were Justices White, who wrote the opinion in which Chief Justice Burger and Justice Stewart concurred.

Justice Black reasoned as follows:

If an individual deeply and sincerely holds beliefs that are purely ethical or moral in source and content but that nevertheless impose upon him a duty of conscience to refrain from participating in any war at any time, those beliefs certainly occupy in the life of that individual "a place parallel to that filled by . . . God" in traditionally religious persons. Because his beliefs function as a religion in his life, such an individual is as much entitled to a "religious" conscientious objector exemption under § 6(j) as is someone who derives his conscientious opposition to war from traditional religious convictions. . . .

Welsh stated that he "believe[d] the taking of life—anyone's life—to be morally wrong." In his original conscientious objector application he wrote the following:

"I believe that human life is valuable in and of itself; in its living; therefore I will not injure or kill another human being. . . ." On the basis of these beliefs and the conclusion of the Court of Appeals that he held them "with the strength of more traditional religious convictions," . . ., we think Welsh was clearly entitled to a conscientious objector exemption.

The *Welsh* ruling obviously extended the *Seeger* principle to include deeply held beliefs that are rooted in morals and ethics as a qualification for conscientious objector status.

Justice Harlan concurs with the Court's decision but differs with its reasoning. By granting conscientious objector status only to those who believed in a Supreme Being, since that is the general meaning of "religion," Congress was discriminating between believers and non-believers. In this sense, according to Justice Harlan, the draft law violates the Religion Clauses of the First Amendment—an establishment of religion and the free exercise thereof. However, it is desirable to interpret this important law so as to find it constitutional. Hence, he is willing to accept the Court's decision.

Justice White's dissent is based on the necessity of enforcing the will of Congress, if it is not acting in an unconstitutional manner. He refuses to join the Court's interpretation of the Draft Law because it extends conscientious objector status to those whose views are rooted in a purely personal code based on philosophy, history and sociology rather than religious training and belief. Congress had no intention of exempting Welsh, and the Court ought to respect that intent.

CASE 31

THE SELECTIVE CONSCIENTIOUS OBJECTOR
Gillette v. United States
Negre v. Larsen

401 U.S. 437, 91 S.Ct. 828, 28 L.Ed.2d 168 (1971)

Gillette failed to report for induction into the Armed Forces. He defended his actions on the ground that he was a conscientious objector. He said that he was willing to fight in defense of the United States or in a war sponsored by the United Nations as a peace-keeping measure. He was, however, opposed to fighting in Vietnam because it was an unjust war. His views were based on a "humanist approach to religion" and a deeply held conviction concerning the purpose and obligations of human existence.

Negre, on the other hand, was inducted into the Army and completed his basic training. Upon receiving his orders to go to Vietnam, he applied for a discharge based on conscientious objection to that war.

Negre was a devout Catholic and believed that it was his duty as a faithful Catholic to discriminate between "just" and "unjust" wars. To participate in the Vietnam conflict, he claimed, would sear his conscience and force him to act against the principles that "I had been taught in my religious training."

The main issue here, simply stated is: Can a person claim conscientious objector status if he is opposed to a particular war, rather than to wars in general?

Justice Marshall delivered the Court's opinion, which held that the phrase in the Military Selective Service Act of 1967 providing for "conscientiously opposed to participation in war in any form" applied to all wars. In other words, a conscientious objector must be opposed to all wars; he cannot choose the wars in which he would refuse to fight.

Gillette and Negre had argued that limiting the conscientious objector interpretation of the draft law only to those who opposed all wars violated the Religion Clauses of the First Amendment. This is not so, answered the Court. The draft law does not discriminate among religious groups and, therefore, it does not contravene the prohibition against an establishment of religion. As a matter of fact, the law is neutral as to religious affiliation or religious belief. Although religious training or belief is required for exemption, no particular sectarian creed or religious organization is singled out for special treatment.

If there is no violation of the Establishment Clause, isn't there an interference with freedom of religion and conscience? The Court finds no interference with any religious ritual or practice. If there is an incidental burden to some, it is more than compensated for by the Government's interest in obtaining the necessary manpower for its Armed Forces.

Justice Black concurred with part of the Court's judgment.

Justice Douglas dissented. The majority of the Justices, he insists, miss the point. The issue is not that of service in the Armed Forces. The question is simply this:

> Can a conscientious objector, whether his objection be rooted in "religion" or in moral values, be required to kill?

This, he says, is a question the Court has never answered. If a person's conscience is opposed to killing, that conscience must be protected. To differentiate "conscience" based on "religion" from "conscience" based on philosophical grounds does harm to the First Amendment.

> I had assumed that the welfare of the single human soul was the ultimate test of the vitality of the First Amendment.

In this sense Gillette meets the criteria of a conscientious objector.

Negre's claim is different, according to Justice Douglas. Under Catholic doctrine there are just and unjust wars. The Fifth Commandment, "Thou Shalt Not Kill" is the guideline for an unjust war. A Catholic must determine the justice of a war on the basis of his own conscience. There is a rich Catholic literature on this subject to assist Catholics in their decisions. His application for discharge from the Army as a conscientious objector should have been granted.

CHAPTER 10

THE THEORY OF EVOLUTION AND THE THEORY OF CREATION

The theory of creation is based on the Biblical explanation of the divine origin of man and woman. The theory of evolution is based on the Darwinian explanation that men and women are descended from a lower order of animals. There are partisans on both sides, just as there are those who try to combine both theories into a unified explanation.

CASE 32

THE SCOPES TRIAL

In 1925 there took place in Tennessee the famous "monkey trial." It grew out of a law passed in that state which forbade public schools "to teach the theory that denies the story of the divine creation of man as taught in the Bible."

John T. Scopes, a biology teacher was tried for violating the law. The trial became world famous because of the participation of two of the most famous personalities of the time: William Jennings Bryan for the state and Clarence Darrow for the defense. Scopes was found guilty and the judge assessed a fine of $100. On appeal, the Tennessee Supreme Court upheld the law but reversed Scopes' conviction on the ground that the jury and not the judge should have assessed the fine. By this time Scopes was no longer in the employ of the state and the Court decided that in the interests of "peace and dignity of this state," this "bizarre case" should be ended. The Tennessee law was repealed in 1967.

The *Scopes* case never reached the Supreme Court, but forty-three years later a similar case confronted the Justices. In 1928 Arkansas enacted an anti-evolution statute prohibiting the teaching in public schools, colleges, and universities, of "the theory or doctrine that mankind ascended or descended from a lower order of animals". It also prohibited the selection and use of textbooks that expounded this theory. Violations were punishable by a fine not exceeding $500 and loss of job, upon conviction.

CASE 33

Epperson v. Arkansas

393 U.S. 97, 89 S.Ct. 226, 21 L.Ed.2d 228 (1968)

Susan Epperson was employed as a biology high school teacher in the Little Rock school system in the fall of 1964. In 1965, the school administration adopted and prescribed a biology textbook setting forth the theory of evolution.

She found herself in a quandry. She was supposed to use the new textbook. If she did so, however, and taught the chapter on evolution, she would commit a criminal offense. To resolve the problem for herself and others, she and a parent of students in the school started a lawsuit to have the court declare the Arkansas law void and to enjoin the school officials from dismissing her for violating the law.

> Assume you are the attorney for Susan Epperson. What arguments can you present on her behalf? How will you answer the argument that under the Constitution the state has the power to prescribe the curriculum for its public schools? What answer would you have for the argument that teaching the theory of evolution would cause children to disrespect the Bible?

ABE FORTAS
1910 –

Associate Justice
1965–1969

The Court was unanimous in its decision. Justice Fortas delivered the opinion of Court on behalf of Susan Epperson's position. Although there had never been a prosecution under the Arkansas law, the issue, said Justice Fortas, must be decided because of its importance. The Arkansas law is unconstitutional because it violates the Religion Clauses of the First Amendment, as incorporated into the Due Process Clause of the Fourteenth.

. . . the law must be stricken because of its conflict with the constitutional prohibition of state laws respecting an establishment of religion or prohibiting the free exercise thereof. The overriding fact is that Arkansas' law selects from the body of knowledge a particular segment which it proscribes for the sole reason that it is deemed to conflict with a particular religious doctrine; that is, with a particular interpretation of the Book of Genesis by a particular religious group.

Justice Fortas then proceeds to explain why it is necessary at times for the courts to intervene in educational matters, which are constitutionally under the jurisdiction of the states.

By and large, public education in our Nation is committed to the control of state and local authorities. Courts do not and cannot intervene in the resolution of conflicts which arise in the daily operation of school systems and which do not directly and sharply implicate basic constitutional values. On the other hand, "The vigilant protection of constitutional freedoms is nowhere more vital than in the community of American schools," . . . and "This Court will be alert against invasions of academic freedom. . . ." . . . As this Court said . . . the First Amendment "does not tolerate laws that cast a pall of orthodoxy over the classroom." . . . There is and can be no doubt that the First Amendment does not permit the State to require that teaching and learning must be tailored to the principles or prohibitions of any religious sect or dogma. . . .

Applying these principles to the facts in this case, Justice Fortas concludes:

In the present case, there can be no doubt that Arkansas has sought to prevent its teachers from discussing the theory of evolution because it is contrary to the belief of some that the Book of Genesis must be the exclusive source of doctrine as to the origin of man. No suggestion has been made that Arkansas' law may be justified by considerations of state policy other than the religious views of some of its citizens. It is clear that fundamentalist sectarian conviction was and is the law's reason for existence. Its antecedent, Tennessee's "monkey law," candidly stated its purpose: to make it unlawful "to teach any theory that denies the story of the Divine Creation of man, as taught in the Bible, and to teach instead, that man has descended from a lower order of animals." Perhaps the sensational publicity attendant upon the *Scopes* trial induced Arkansas to adopt less explicit language. It eliminated Tennessee's reference to "the story of the Divine Creation of man" as taught in the Bible, but there is no doubt that the motivation for the law was the same: to suppress the teaching of a theory which, it was thought, "denied" the divine creation of man.

Arkansas' law cannot be defended as an act of religious neutrality. Arkansas did not seek to excise from the curricula of its schools and universities all discussion of the origin of man. The law's effort was confined to an attempt to blot out a particular theory because of its supposed conflict with the biblical account, literally read. Plainly, the law is contrary to the mandate of the First, and in violation of the Fourteenth, Amendment to the Constitution.

Justice Black concurred in the decision, but not in the reasoning. In his opinion, the Arkansas law was so vague that reasonable people might differ as to its meaning. It is not clear whether the law forbids a teacher to mention the Darwinian Theory at all, or only to discuss it as long as he or she does not discuss its truth. To prosecute some-one on a vague statute is a denial of due process of law. The Court, he also declares, should have kept out of the establishment of religion issue because the Darwinian Theory, like the Genesis story, has been challenged by religionists and by scientists. In matters of this sort the Court ought to stay aloof.

Justice Harlan concurred on the ground that the law constituted an establishment of religion. He saw no need for the majority to go into the vagueness of the law or its interference with freedom of speech.

Justice Stewart's concurring opinion was based on freedom of communication protected by the First and Fourteenth Amendments. It is unconstitutional, in his opinion, "to make it a criminal offense for a public school teacher to so much as to mention the very existence of an entire system of respected human thought."

SECTION III
FREEDOM OF SPEECH

AMENDMENT I

Congress shall make no law . . . abridging freedom of speech . . .

AMENDMENT XIV

. . . nor shall any state deprive any person of . . . liberty . . . without due process of law . . .

President Woodrow Wilson on Freedom of Speech

I have always been among those who believed that the greatest freedom of speech was the greatest safety, because if a man is a fool, the best thing to do is to encourage him to advertise the fact by speaking. It cannot be so easily discovered if you allow him to remain silent and look wise, but if you let him speak, the secret is out and the world knows that he is a fool. So it is by the exposure of folly that it is defeated; not by the exclusion of folly, and in this free aid of free speech men get into that sort of communication with one another which constitutes the basis of all common achievement.

> Address at the Institute of France, Paris, May 10, 1919. Two selected Literary and Political Papers and Addresses of Woodrow Wilson (1926) 333.

It is the prized American privilege to speak one's mind, although not always with perfect good taste, on all public institutions.

> Justice Hugo Black
> *Bridges v. California,* 314 U.S. 252, 62 S.Ct. 190, 86 L.Ed. 192 (1941)

INTRODUCTION

Why should you or I or anyone else have the freedom to say what we think? After all, if I say what I really think about someone, it may injure his reputation. If you criticize the Government, you may lead people to lose faith in their representatives and in their leaders. Isn't it best to have people in authority set the limits regarding acceptable and non-acceptable speech?

This point of view has been expressed on many occasions by thoughtful men and women. In one of its important opinions, a majority of the Supreme Court Justices expressed this position in these words:

> It is a fundamental principle, long established, that the freedom of speech and of the press which is secured by the Constitution does not confer an absolute right to speak or publish, without responsibility, whatever one may choose, or an unrestricted and unbridled license that gives immunity for every possible use of language and prevents the punishment of those who abuse this freedom . . . .

> That a State in the exercise of its police power may punish those who abuse this freedom by utterances inimical to the public welfare, tending to corrupt morals, incite to crime, or disturb the public peace, is not open to question . . . .

> In short, this freedom does not deprive a State of the primary and essential right of self-preservation . . . .

> *Gitlow v. New York*
> 268 U.S. 652, 45 S.Ct. 625, 69 L.Ed. 1138 (1925)

On the other hand, the men who drafted the Bill of Rights declared that "Congress shall make no law . . . abridging freedom of speech." Why did they say "no law"? There does not seem to be any exception to this sweeping prohibition. What must have been in their minds?

They knew the story of Socrates, the Athenian teacher and philosopher, who was accused by his government of corrupting the youth and introducing new Gods. At his trial more than 2000 years ago, Socrates defended himself before his accusers in a memorable passage reported by Plato, one of his famous students.

> And now, Athenians, I am not going to argue for my own sake, as you may think, but for yours, that you may not sin against the God by condemning me, who am his gift to you. For if you kill me you will not easily find a successor to me, who, if I may use such a ludicrous figure of speech, am a sort of gadfly, given to the state by God; and the state is a great and noble steed who is tardy in his motions owing to his very size, and requires to be stirred into life. I am that gadfly which God has attached to the state, and all day long and in all places

am always fastening upon you, arousing and persuading and reproaching you. You will not easily find another like me, and therefore I would advise you to spare me.

Plato's Apology

This is the famous "Gadfly" argument. Let freedom of speech flourish. Let the Gadfly-critic bite the steed-society and the result may help people decide on the course to be taken. Societies tend to resist change and gadflies spread their ideas about change. When this is done freely, public opinion is best informed as to the options available to improve society.

Another defense of freedom of speech is based on the proposition that ideas come into our minds from a variety of sources. We are bombarded with ideas and the only way we can test their truth or falsity is by discussing them without fear of punishment. This line of reasoning was advanced by John Milton, the great seventeenth century English poet. In an essay entitled *Areopagitica,* he wrote:

> Where there is much desire to learn, there of necessity will be much arguing, much writing, many opinions; for opinion in good men is but knowledge in the making. . . .

> Give me the liberty to know, to utter, and to argue freely according to conscience, above all liberties. . . .

> And though all the winds of doctrine were let loose to play upon the earth, so Truth be in the field, we do injuriously, by licensing and prohibiting, to misdoubt her strength. Let her and Falsehood grapple; who ever knew Truth put to the worse, in a free and open encounter?
> . . . .

These are strong words. Perhaps the thoughts of Socrates and the ideas of Milton influenced the Founding Fathers to declare that Congress must pass *no law* abridging free speech.

This important principle has been tested many times before the Supreme Court. Unlike arithmetic problems where the correct answers are definite and verifiable, the answers to free speech issues vary with time, place, context and the judges who decide.

THE SMALL SOCIETY

AND IF ELECTED, I PROMISE TO...

HOO-BOY!

CLIK

ANOTHER POLITICIAN WHO HAS FREE SPEECH MIXED UP WITH CHEAP TALK—

Washington Star Syndicate, Inc.

BRICKMAN

CHAPTER 11

SPEAKERS, HECKLERS, AND DRAFT CARD AND FLAG BURNERS

He gets up on a soapbox on a street corner and begins his talk. An audience gathers around him. What he has to say is popular to some and disgusting to others. Some begin to heckle, while others heckle the hecklers. The audience is gradually changing into an unruly mob.

> What are the free speech issues here?

Now, suppose you are a police officer assigned to this area and you observe the episode.

> What should you do? Suppose you have a fellow officer, would that help you in any way?

In Great Britain there is Hyde Park where, each Sunday at Speaker's Corner, men and women mount their soapboxes or ladders and speak at length on their favorite subjects. British police are there, but generally few in numbers. This is the area where critics, crusaders, and dissenters voice their ideas amid few interruptions.

In this country there are some communities with their Hyde Parks, but in most areas a Speaker's Corner is missing. In most communities licenses are required for outdoor meetings, but the Supreme Court has not been sympathetic to those regulations which give administrators too much discretion in picking and choosing those to whom they would grant or deny permits. The regulations must be specific as to the time and place requirements. Nor may a permit be denied simply because the local authorities disagree with a speaker's views or fear trouble.

Before proceeding further, we should emphasize a familiar point. The First Amendment was designed to limit the powers of Congress only. In rulings by the Supreme Court, the First Amendment has been incorporated into the Fourteenth Amendment's Due Process Clause. Therefore, as we analyze the following cases, remember that they are to be decided on the measuring rod of the First and Fourteenth Amendments.

The following cases present a series of significant issues. Try to look at each issue from the position of the plaintiff, then from the position of the defendant, and then finally from the judge's bench. Think of the state's right to protect the lives, health, morals, welfare, and safety of its people. Then, consider the arguments in favor of freedom of speech.

> As they collide, to which would you give priority? Why?

THE UNPOPULAR SPEAKER AND THE HOSTILE AUDIENCE

> ## ISSUES TO BE ANALYZED
>
> Cases 34–39 present six freedom of speech problems. In deciding what should be done to resolve the conflict of values, think in terms of principles to be applied. The decisions appear on pp. 106–113, but try to restrain your curiosity.

CASE 34

THE CASE OF THE AMERICAN NAZI PARTY

George Lincoln Rockwell, the leader of the American Nazi Party, applied to the New York City Commissioner of Parks for a permit to speak on July 4, 1960 in Union Square, a popular meeting place for people advocating particular causes. The city official, fearing trouble because of Rockwell's anti-Semitic and anti-Black views, denied the request. Although the ordinance required that a denial of license be accompanied by an alternative time and place, it was not done so in this case. Rockwell asked the court to order the commissioner to issue the permit. The issue is obviously an important one: Should an American Nazi, hostile to the principles of democracy and preaching hate toward groups in the community, be permitted to spread his words in a public place where the audience would be hostile?

CASE 35

THE CASE OF THE "FIGHTING WORDS"

New Hampshire passed a law which declared: "No person shall address any offensive, derisive or annoying word to any other person who is lawfully in any street or other public place, nor call him by any offensive or derisive name."

Chaplinsky, a member of Jehovah's Witnesses, was distributing the literature of his sect on the streets of Rochester, New Hampshire on a busy Saturday afternoon. Some of the people complained to the City Marshall that the literature denounced religion as "a racket". The crowd became restless, a disturbance occurred, and the traffic officer started with Chaplinsky to the police station. On the way they met the City Marshall and Chaplinsky said to him:

You are a God damned racketeer. A damned Fascist and the whole government of Rochester are Fascists or agents of Fascists.

Chaplinsky was arrested for violating the law.

Is he guilty?

THE SMALL SOCIETY

THIS IS THE PART OF A DEMOCRACY I HATE —

Washington Star Syndicate, Inc.

BRICKMAN

CASE 36

THE SOAP BOX SPEAKER, THE UNRULY
BYSTANDERS, AND THE POLICE

On the evening of March 8, 1949, Irving Feiner, a Syracuse University student, was addressing an open-air meeting in Syracuse. The police received a telephone complaint concerning the meeting and two officers were sent to the scene. They found a crowd of about 75 to 80 people, Black and white, standing on the sidewalk and spreading out into the street. The purpose of the meeting was to urge listeners to attend a meeting to be held that night in the Syracuse Hotel.

According to the testimony, Feiner made the following remarks, although he denied making some of them:

Mayor Costello (of Syracuse) is a champagne-sipping bum.

The 15th ward is run by corrupt politicians, and there are horse rooms operating there.

President Truman is a bum.

Mayor O'Dwyer of New York is a bum.

The American Legion is a Nazi Gestapo.

The Negroes don't have equal rights; they should rise up in arms and fight for their rights.

The police were first concerned with pedestrian and vehicular traffic. The crowd was restless and there was some milling, pushing, and shoving. Some people approved of the speaker's remarks; others were hostile. Some of the onlookers commented to the police on their inability to handle the situation. At least one person threatened violence unless the police acted.

After Feiner had been speaking for about twenty minutes, a man in the crowd said to the policeman: "If you don't get that son of a bitch off, I will go over and get him off there myself." Thereupon, one of the police officers went up to Feiner and asked him to step down. Feiner refused and continued talking. The officer waited a minute and demanded a second time that he stop. Feiner refused and was thereupon arrested for violating the Disorderly Conduct Law. He was charged with "ignoring and refusing to heed and obey reasonable police orders . . . to regulate and control said crowd and to prevent a breach or breaches of the peace and to prevent injury to pedestrians attempting to use said walk . . . and prevent injury to the public generally."

Feiner was tried before a judge. If he had been tried before a jury and you had been on that jury, how would you have voted?

If you had been a police officer on the scene, would you have arrested the men in the crowd who threatened violence?

Do you think Feiner's remarks about the public officials were slanderous? Would it influence your judgment in deciding his guilt or innocence?

Feiner claimed that the police had violated his free speech rights under the First and Fourteenth Amendments.

Do you agree with him?

If a passerby on a street hears a speaker addressing a crowd and he dislikes what he hears, why shouldn't he or she simply walk away?

THE SMALL SOCIETY

Washington Star Syndicate, Inc.

CASE 37

BURNING A DRAFT CARD

On the morning of March 3, 1966 David Paul O'Brien and three friends burned their Selective Service certificates on the steps of the South Boston Courthouse. They did this to protest the Vietnam conflict. They were observed by a sizable crowd, including several FBI agents. After the burning, O'Brien and his companions were attacked by members of the crowd and they were taken by an FBI agent into the courthouse. He was arrested, read his rights, and charged with violating that section of the Universal Military Training and Service Act which made it a crime when anyone "knowingly destroys, knowingly mutilates" his draft card.

O'Brien said that he knew about the law and regarded it as an unconstitutional abridgement of his freedom of speech. In addition, he argued that the law served no legitimate legislative purpose.

> Do you agree with him? If not, what arguments would you raise in opposition to his position?

CASE 38

BURNING THE AMERICAN FLAG

On June 6, 1966, Street was listening to his radio, when a news report told of the shooting of James Meredith, a Southern civil rights leader, by a sniper. Angered, he took out a folded American flag, which he had displayed on National holidays, and walked to an intersection. There, in the presence of about thirty people, he burned the flag. A police officer observed him and heard him say: "We don't need no damn flag." When the officer asked him whether he had burned the flag, he replied: "Yes, that is my flag; I burned it. If they let that happen to Meredith, we don't need an American flag."

Street was tried under a New York law which makes it a misdemeanor "publicly [to] mutilate, deface, defile, or defy, trample upon, or cast contempt upon either by words or act [any flag of the United States]."

He was found guilty and given a suspended sentence. He appealed on the ground that his free speech rights under the First and Fourteenth Amendments had been violated.

> Do you agree with him? Why or why not? Is there an important difference between burning a draft card and burning an American flag? Would this difference influence your decision?

CASE 39

THREATENING THE PRESIDENT OF THE UNITED STATES

On August 27, 1966 a public rally was held on the Washington Monument grounds. Most of the participants were in their teens or early twenties. They broke up into small groups and Watts, who was eighteen years old, joined one of the groups. When someone suggested that young people should get more education before expressing their views, Watts replied:

> They always holler at us to get an education. And now I have already received my draft classification as I–A and I have got to report for my physical this Monday coming. I am not going. If they ever make me carry a rifle the first man I want to get in my sights is L. B. J. They are not going to make me kill my Black brothers.

An investigator for the Army Counter Intelligence Corps was present. Watts was arrested and charged with violating the federal law which made it a crime to threaten the life of the President, Vice President or other officer next in order of succession. He was found guilty and he appealed on several grounds. His attorney argued that the statement was made during a political debate; that the statement was made conditional upon an event which Watts vowed would never come; that Watts and the crowd laughed after the statement was made; that this was just a "very crude offensive method of stating political opposition to the President."

> Do you agree with Watts' attorney?
>
> If you were the prosecutor, how would you answer these points?

DECISIONS IN CASES 34 to 39

CASE 34

Rockwell v. Morris

**211 N.Y.S.2d 25, 12 A.D.2d 272 (1960), cert denied
368 U.S. 913, 82 S.Ct. 194, 7 L.Ed.2d 131 (1961)**

Although Rockwell lost in the lower court, the Appellate Division of New York upheld his right to a permit in a 4 to 1 vote. The case was appealed to the Supreme Court and in 1961 the Court refused to review the lower court ruling.

The Appellate Court's opinion, upholding Rockwell's position, stated:

> . . . A community need not wait to be subverted by street riots and stormtroopers; but, also, it cannot by its policemen or commissioners suppress a speaker, in prior restraint, on the basis of news reports, hysteria, or inference that what he did yesterday, he will do today. . . . if the speaker incites others to immediate unlawful action he may be punished—in a proper case, stopped when disorder actually impends . . . The evil to be prevented provokes evil means to that end. This is not good law or good morals. No doubt, too, suppression is easier than punishment. No doubt suppressing a minority is easier than keeping a misbehaving majority in line. But that is exactly the purpose of law, and of government under law.

CASE 35

Chaplinsky v. New Hampshire

315 U.S. 568, 62 S.Ct. 766, 86 L.Ed. 1031 (1942)

In a unanimous ruling, the Court upheld the conviction. Justice Murphy reasoned as follows:

> Allowing the broadest scope to the language and purpose of the Fourteenth Amendment, it is well understood that the right of free speech is not absolute at all times and under all circumstances. There are certain well-defined and narrowly limited classes of speech, the prevention and punishment of which have never been thought to raise any constitutional problem. *These include the lewd and the obscene, the profane, the libelous, and the insulting or "fighting" words—those which by very utterance inflict injury or tend to incite an immediate breach of the peace.* It has been well observed that such utterances are no essential part of the exposition of ideas, and are of such slight social value as a step to truth that any benefit derived from them is clearly outweighed by the social interest in order and morality. [Italics supplied]

The rule of law announced in this case is that if the words are of such a nature which, in the understanding of ordinary people will likely cause a fight, then they can be outlawed. The Free Speech Clause was not included in the Constitution to protect such words.

CASE 36

Feiner v. People of the State of New York

340 U.S. 315, 71 S.Ct. 303, 95 L.Ed. 295 (1951)

Feiner was found guilty and sentenced to 30 days in the County penitentiary. He appealed his case through the courts of New York State and lost. He then appealed to the Supreme Court.

Once again he lost by a 6 to 3 vote. Chief Justice Vinson delivered the majority opinion upholding the disorderly conduct conviction. He concluded, on the basis of the evidence, that Feiner encouraged the audience to become divided into hostile camps; he interfered with traffic; and he refused the request of the police to stop his speech. Feiner, he emphasized, was not arrested for the making or the content of his speech. He was arrested because of the audience reaction to his speech. He had created a clear and present danger of riot or disturbance.

The opinion concluded with these observations:

> We are well aware that the ordinary murmurings and objections of a hostile audience cannot be allowed to silence a speaker, and are also mindful of the possible danger of giving overzealous police officials complete discretion to break up otherwise lawful public meetings. "A State may not unduly suppress free communication of views, religious or other, under the guise of conserving desirable conditions." . . . But we are not faced here with such a situation. It is one thing to say that the police cannot be used as an instrument for the suppression of unpopular views, and another to say that, when as here the speaker passes the bounds of argument or persuasion and undertakes incitement to riot, they are powerless to prevent a breach of the peace. Nor in this case can we condemn the considered judgment of three New York courts approving the means which the police, faced with a crisis, used in the exercise of their power and duty to preserve peace and order. The findings of the state courts as to the existing situation and the imminence of greater disorder coupled with petitioner's deliberate defiance of the police officers convince us that we should not reverse this conviction in the name of free speech.

Three Justices dissented. Justice Black's response to the majority's reasoning is that Feiner had been sentenced because of his unpopular views. The trial judge, he pointed out, had fully accepted the testimony of the prosecution witnesses on all important points. In so important an issue, it is the responsibility of the Court to review the evidence in the record and to decide for itself whether a person's rights under the First and Fourteenth Amendments have been violated. He then goes on to say:

> I think this conviction makes a mockery of the free speech guarantees of the First and Fourteenth Amendments. The end result of the affirmance here is to approve a simple and readily available technique by which cities and states can with impunity subject all speeches, political or otherwise, on streets or elsewhere, to the supervision and censorship of the local police. I will have no part or parcel in this holding which I view as a long step toward totalitarian authority. . . .

Moreover, assuming that the "facts" did indicate a critical situation, I reject the implication of the Court's opinion that the police had no obligation to protect petitioner's constitutional right to talk. . . . Their duty was to protect petitioner's right to talk, even to the extent of arresting the man who threatened to interfere. Instead, they shirked that duty and acted only to suppress the right to speak.

In my judgment, today's holding means that as a practical matter, minority speakers can be silenced in any city. Hereafter, despite the First and Fourteenth Amendments, the policeman's club can take heavy toll of a current administration's public critics. Criticism of public officials will be too dangerous for all but the most courageous.

Justice Douglas's dissent, in which Justice Minton concurred, focuses on the role of police as censors in episodes involving unpopular speakers and hostile audiences.

A NOTE ON THE FEINER AND TERMINIELLO CASES

Would it have made any difference if Feiner had hired a hall?

Two years before the *Feiner* decision, the Court handed down a ruling in *Terminiello v. Chicago*, 337 U.S. 1, 69 S.Ct. 894, 93 L.Ed. 1131 (1949). In this case the meeting was held in a hall. The speaker, known for his racist and religious prejudices, attracted an audience of about 800 people, mostly sympathizers, while another 1000 milled about outside. There was disorder inside and outside the auditorium and the police had a difficult time with the crowd. Bricks and bottles were thrown. Terminiello hurled back such epithets as "slimy scum," "snakes," "bedbugs," while the people on the outside hurled their response: "Fascists! Hitlers!"

Terminiello managed to finish his speech and he and seventeen people in the outside group were arrested. He was charged with a breach of the peace. At his trial the judge instructed the jury that a breach of the peace includes speech which "stirs the public to anger, unites dispute, brings about a condition of unrest, or creates a disturbance." Terminiello was found guilty and he appealed.

In a 5 to 4 decision, Justice Douglas, writing for the majority, concluded that the judge's instruction to the jury was too broad and, therefore, the conviction had to be reversed. He defended the ruling on this ground:

> Accordingly, a function of free speech under our system of government is to invite dispute. It may indeed best serve its high purpose when it induces a condition of unrest, creates dissatisfaction with conditions as they are, or even stirs people to anger. Speech is often provocative and challenging. It may strike at prejudices and preconceptions and have profound unsettling effects as it presses for acceptance of an idea. That is why freedom of speech, though not absolute, is nevertheless protected against censorship or punishment, unless shown likely to produce a clear and present danger of a serious substantive evil that rises far above public inconvenience, annoyance or unrest.

In this passage Justice Douglas refers to the clear and present danger rule. He intimates that this should be the measuring rod which separates permissible from impermissible speech.

Four Justices dissented: Chief Justice Vinson and Burton, Frankfurter, and Jackson. The latter's long dissenting opinion has a number of significant passages which also seek to draw the line between speech protected by the First and Fourteenth Amendment and speech which is not immune from prosecution. He reasoned as follows:

> Rioting is a substantive evil, which I take it no one will deny that the State and the City have the right and the duty to prevent and punish. Where an offense is induced by speech, the Court has laid down and often reiterated a test of the power of the authorities to deal with the speaking as also an offense. "The question in every case is whether the words *used are used in such circumstances* and are of *such a nature* as to create a *clear and present danger* that they will bring about the substantive evils that Congress [or the State or City] has a right to prevent." [Emphasis supplied.] Mr. Justice Holmes in Schenck v. United States. . . . No one ventures to contend that the State on the basis of this test, for whatever it may be worth, was not justified in punishing Terminiello. In this case the evidence proves beyond dispute that danger of rioting and violence in response to the speech was clear, present and immediate. If this Court has not silently abandoned this long standing test and substituted for the purposes of this case an unexpressed but more stringent test, the action of the State would have to be sustained.

Only recently this Court held that a state could punish as a breach of the peace use of epithets such as "damned racketeer" and "damned fascists," addressed to only one person, an official, because likely to provoke the average person to retaliation. But these are mild in comparison to the epithets "slimy scum," "snakes," "bedbugs," and the like, which Terminiello hurled at an already inflamed mob of his adversaries.

CASE 37

United States v. O'Brien

391 U.S. 367, 88 S.Ct. 1673, 20 L.Ed.2d 672 (1968)

Chief Justice Warren wrote the opinion for the Court, with only Justice Douglas dissenting. The Court first considered O'Brien's argument that the law relating to draft card burning was an unconstitutional invasion of his right to "symbolic speech." This right, O'Brien had declared, is protected by the First Amendment.

The Chief Justice replied that Congress had the power to raise armies. In doing so, it can legitimately create a selective service or Draft Law and can require registrants to keep their draft cards in their possession at all times for purposes of identification and communication with Draft Boards. It can, therefore, punish those who intentionally destroy these cards.

Justice Douglas dissented on another ground. He said that the question in this case was really "whether conscription is permissible in the absence of a declaration of war." There had been no official declaration of war by Congress in the Vietnam conflict. Therefore, the country, he maintained, is entitled to a ruling on this issue and he suggested that the case be sent back for reargument.

CASE 38

Street v. New York

394 U.S. 576, 89 S.Ct. 1354, 22 L.Ed.2d 572 (1969)

The Court was badly split—a 5 to 4 decision. Writing for the majority, Justice Harlan overruled Street's conviction on the ground that he was "punished merely for speaking defiant or contemptuous words about the flag." The Fourteenth Amendment prohibits states from punishing those who advocate peaceful change in our institutions. The words used by Street were not "fighting words," nor did they shock anyone in the crowd. What Street did was to publicly express his opinion about the flag.

Justice Harlan concludes on this note:

> We add that disrespect for our flag is to be deplored, no less in these vexed times than in calmer periods of our history. . . . Nevertheless we are unable to sustain a conviction that may have rested on a form of expression, however distasteful, which the Constitution tolerates and protects. . . .

JOHN M. HARLAN
1899–1971

Associate Justice
1955–1971

It is on this very note that the dissenters parted company with the majority. Chief Justice Warren and Justices Black, Fortas, and White saw the issue as one involving action—the burning of the flag. Each felt that a state has the right to prohibit and punish those who desecrate the flag. Justice Fortas reasoned as follows:

> One may not justify burning a house, even if it is his own, on the ground, however sincere, that he does so as a protest. One may not justify breaking the windows of a government building on that basis. Protest does not exonerate lawlessness. And the prohibition against flag burning on the public thoroughfare, being valid, the misdemeanor is not excused merely because it is an act of flamboyant protest.

CASE 39

Watts v. United States

394 U.S. 705, 89 S.Ct. 1399, 22 L.Ed.2d 664 (1969)

The case was decided in a *per curiam* ruling—an unsigned opinion which expresses the decision of the Court. In this 5 to 4 decision, the Court overruled the conviction and sent it back to the District Court with instructions to enter a judgment of acquittal. The law protecting the life of a President is constitutional. Nevertheless, when a statute makes a form of pure speech a criminal offense, "it must be interpreted with the commands of the First Amendment clearly in mind." The government, under the law is required to prove a real "threat." This, said the Court, we cannot do, because the "language of the political arena . . . is often vituperative, abusive, and inexact." The Court agreed with Watts' point that his remarks were "a kind of crude offensive method of stating a political opposition to the President." The majority concluded that debates over public issues should be "uninhibited, robust, wide-open and it may very well include vehement, caustic, and sometimes unpleasantly sharp attacks on government and public officials."

Justice Douglas wrote a concurring opinion tracing the ancestry of laws designed to punish those who threaten rulers.

Justices Fortas and Harlan dissented on the ground that the constitutionality of the law in question should have been argued before the Court.

Justice White dissented without an opinion and Justice Stewart would have denied certiorari—an appeal to the Supreme Court.

THE SMALL SOCIETY

CHAPTER 12

FREEDOM OF SPEECH IN THE SCHOOLS

A public school is a special kind of institution. It is established and supported by the public to achieve a variety of goals that are generally designated as good citizenship, effective citizenship or civic education. The specific goals include a knowledge and understanding of a variety of subjects, a range of skills for analyzing problems, an attitude that is willing to look objectively at the options or alternative solutions to problems, and an appreciation of the American constitutional system of government referred to as a democratic republic and the American economic system designated as capitalism.

To achieve these ends the public schools are sometimes described as showcases or laboratories of democracy. Here the young are educated for their future responsibilities as citizens.

School systems, however, are also bureaucratic and hierarchial institutions. Principals and other administrators and teachers are required to carry out the mandates of the legislature and of departments and bureaus of education. There are times when the practices of the administrator run into conflict with the principles taught to students.

CASE 40

THE IOWA BLACK ARMBAND CASE

Tinker v. Des Moines Independent Community School District

393 U.S. 503, 89 S.Ct. 733, 21 D.Ed.2d 731 (1969)

In December, 1965 a group of adults and students decide to publicize their opposition to the Vietnam conflict by wearing black armbands during the holiday season and by fasting on December 16 and New Year's Eve. Several of the students present had engaged in similar activities in the past and they decided to participate in this program.

The principals of the Des Moines schools heard about it and on December 14, they adopted a policy that forbade the wearing of an armband to school. Students who refused to remove such armbands would be suspended until they complied.

On December 16, Mary Beth Tinker, a 13-year-old junior high school student, and Christopher Eckhardt, a 16-year-old high school student wore armbands to their schools. John Tinker, a 16-year-old high school student wore his armband the next day. All three knew about the regulation. They were suspended and were told not to come back unless they removed their armbands. They stayed away from school until after New Year's Day, when the planned period for wearing the armbands had expired.

The three students filed a complaint, through their parents, in the United States District Court, asking for an injunction ordering the school officials not to punish them. In addition, they sought nominal damages—a small or token sum of money (generally $1.00) to show that a legal injury had been suffered.

The District Court dismissed the complaint. The United States Court of Appeals was equally divided and the case was carried to the Supreme Court.

> If you were a school administrator, what arguments could you present?
>
> As a student who wore an armband, how would you present your position?
>
> What is the issue here?

Justice Fortas wrote the majority opinion in a case which has become famous in constitutional law. It is directed specifically at the relationship between the student's right to freedom of speech in the school and the administrator's obligation to maintain discipline.

He begins with the observation that the wearing of the armband was a symbolic act and therefore akin to "pure speech" as divorced from speech accompanied by disruptive conduct. Then comes one of the famous passages:

> First Amendment rights, applied in light of the special characteristics of the school environment, are available to teachers and students. It can hardly be argued that either students or teachers shed their constitutional rights to freedom of speech or expression at the schoolhouse gate. This has been the unmistakable holding of this Court for almost 50 years. . . .

This does not mean that the school authorities have no power at all.

> On the other hand, the Court has repeatedly emphasized the need for affirming the comprehensive authority of the States and of school officials, consistent with fundamental constitutional safeguards, to prescribe and control conduct in the schools. . . . Our problem lies in the area where students in the exercise of First Amendment rights collide with the rules of the school authorities. . . .
>
> The school officials banned and sought to punish petitioners for a silent, passive expression of opinion, unaccompanied by any disorder

or disturbance on the part of petitioners. There is here no evidence whatever of petitioners' interference, actual or nascent, with the schools' work or of collision with the rights of other students to be secure and to be let alone. Accordingly, this case does not concern speech or action that intrudes upon the work of the schools or the rights of other students. . . .

Outside the classrooms, a few students made hostile remarks to the children wearing armbands, but there were no threats or acts of violence on school premises. . . .

ABE FORTAS
1910 –

Associate Justice
1965–1969

In order for the State in the person of school officials to justify prohibition of a particular expression of opinion, it must be able to show that its action was caused by something more than a mere desire to avoid the discomfort and unpleasantness that always accompany an unpopular viewpoint. Certainly where there is no finding and no showing that engaging in the forbidden conduct would "materially and substantially interfere with the requirements of appropriate discipline in the operation of the school," the prohibition cannot be sustained. . . .

It is also relevant that the school authorities did not purport to prohibit the wearing of all symbols of political or controversial significance. The record shows that students in some of the schools wore buttons relating to national political campaigns, and some even wore the Iron Cross, traditionally a symbol of Nazism. The order prohibiting the wearing of armbands did not extend to these. Instead, a particular symbol—black armbands worn to exhibit opposition to this Nation's involvement in Vietnam—was singled out for prohibition. Clearly, the prohibition of expression of one particular opinion, at least without evidence that it is necessary to avoid material and substantial interference with schoolwork or discipline, is not constitutionally permissible.

In our system, state-operated schools may not be enclaves of totalitarianism. School officials do not possess absolute authority over their students. Students in school as well as out of school are "persons" under our Constitution. They are possessed of fundamental rights which the State must respect, just as they themselves must respect their obligations to the State. In our system, students may not be regarded as closed-circuit recipients of only that which the State chooses to communicate. They may not be confined to the expression of those sentiments that are officially approved. In the absence of a specific showing of constitutionally valid reasons to regulate their speech, students are entitled to freedom of expression of their views.
. . .

Justice Fortas then proceeds to set forth the rule of law which applies to the school-wide situation when a free speech issue arises.

Under our Constitution, free speech is not a right that is given only to be so circumscribed that it exists in principle but not in fact. Freedom of expression would not truly exist if the right could be exercised only in an area that a benevolent government has provided as a safe haven for crackpots. The Constitution says that Congress (and the States) may not abridge the right to free speech. This provision means what it says. We properly read it to permit reasonable regulation of speech-connected activities in carefully restricted circumstances. But we do not confine the permissible exercise of First Amendment rights to a telephone booth or the four corners of a pamphlet, or to supervised and ordained discussion in a school classroom. . . .

As we have discussed, the record does not demonstrate any facts which might reasonably have led school authorities to forecast substantial disruption of or material interference with school activities, and no disturbances or disorders on the school premises in fact occurred. These petitioners merely went about their ordained rounds in school. Their deviation consisted only in wearing on their sleeve a band of black cloth, not more than two inches wide. They wore it to exhibit their disapproval of the Vietnam hostilities and their advocacy of a truce, to make their views known, and, by their example, to influence others to adopt them. They neither interrupted school activities nor sought to intrude in the school affairs or the lives of others. They caused discussion outside of the classrooms, but no interference with work and no disorder. In the circumstances, our Constitution does not permit officials of the State to deny their form of expression.

Justice Stewart concurred but noted that he did not believe that the "First Amendment rights of students are co-extensive with those of adults."

Justice White concurred but indicated there is a distinction between communicating by words and communicating by acts "which sufficiently impinges on some valid state interest."

Justice Black's dissenting opinion contains some very surprising language. It amounts to a tirade against so-called permissive education.

HUGO L. BLACK
1886–1971

Associate Justice
1937–1971

He begins as follows:

The Court's holding in this case ushers in what I deem to be an entirely new era in which the power to control pupils by the elected "officials of state supported public schools . . ." in the United States is in ultimate effect transferred to the Supreme Court. The Court brought this particular case here on a petition for certiorari urging that the First and Fourteenth Amendments protect the right of school pupils to express their political views all the way "from kindergarten through high school." . . .

He then raises the question whether students have the constitutional right to use "symbolic" or "pure" speech at any time or at any place in the school. His answer is:

. . . the crucial remaining questions are whether students and teachers may use the schools at their whim as a platform for the exercise of free speech—"symbolic" or "pure"—and whether the courts will allocate to themselves the function of deciding how the pupils' school day will be spent. While I have always believed that under the First and Fourteenth Amendments neither the State nor the Federal Government has any authority to regulate or censor the content of speech, I have never believed that any person has a right to give speeches or engage in demonstrations where he pleases and when he pleases. This Court has already rejected such a notion. . . .

He continues on this theme at some length, disagreeing with Justice Fortas's conclusion that the Bill of Rights does not stop at the schoolhouse gate.

I deny, therefore, that it has been the "unmistakable holding of this Court for almost 50 years" that "students" and "teachers" take with them into the "schoolhouse gate" constitutional rights to "freedom of speech or expression." . . . The truth is that a teacher of kindergarten, grammar school, or high school pupils no more carries into a school with him a complete right to freedom of speech and expression than an anti-Catholic or anti-Semite carries with him a complete freedom of speech and religion into a Catholic church or Jewish synagogue. Nor does a person carry with him into the United States Senate or House, or into the Supreme Court, or any other court, a complete constitutional right to go into those places contrary to their rules and speak his mind on any subject he pleases. It is a myth to say that any person has a constitutional right to say what he pleases, where he pleases, and when he pleases. . . .

In my view, teachers in state-controlled public schools are hired to teach there . . . certainly a teacher is not paid to go into school and teach subjects the State does not hire him to teach as a part of its selected curriculum. Nor are public school students sent to the schools at public expense to broadcast political or any other views to educate and inform the public. The original idea of schools, which I do not believe is yet abandoned as worthless or out of date, was that children had not yet reached the point of experience and wisdom which enabled them to teach all of their elders. It may be that the Nation has outworn the old-fashioned slogan that "children are to be seen not heard," but one may, I hope, be permitted to harbor the thought that taxpayers send children to school on the premise that at their age they need to learn, not teach.

He also notes that there were some disturbances during the wearing of the armbands which distracted students. Since this had been anticipated by school officials, their regulation should have been upheld by the courts.

He concludes his opinion with a passionate appeal for the restoration of discipline in the schools—with the Court's blessing.

We cannot close our eyes to the fact that some of the country's greatest problems are crimes committed by the youth, too many of school age. School discipline, like parental discipline, is an integral and important part of training our children to be good citizens—to be better citizens. Here a very small number of students have crisply and summarily refused to obey a school order designed to give pupils who want to learn the opportunity to do so. One does not need to be a prophet or the son of a prophet to know that after the Court's holding today some students in Iowa schools and indeed in all schools will be ready, able, and willing to defy their teachers on practically all orders. . . . Turned loose with lawsuits for damages and injunctions against their teachers as they are here, it is nothing but wishful thinking to imagine that young, immature students will not soon believe it is their right to control the schools rather than the right of the States that collect the taxes to hire the teachers for the benefit of the pupils. This case, therefore, wholly without constitutional reasons in my judgment, subjects all the public schools in the country to the whims and caprices of their loudest-mouthed, but maybe not their brightest, students. I, for one, am not fully persuaded that school pupils are wise enough, even with this Court's expert help from Washington, to run the 23,390 public school systems in our 50 States. I wish, therefore, wholly to disclaim any purpose on my part to hold that the Federal Constitution compels the teachers, parents, and elected school officials to surrender control of the American public school system to public school students. I dissent.

Justice Harlan's dissent was based on the premise that the school officials had acted in good faith in their responsibility to maintain discipline and good order in their schools.

CASE 41

A TEACHER WEARS A BLACK ARMBAND TO CLASS

James v. Board of Education of Central School District No. 1
461 F.2d 566 (1972)

We have seen how the Supreme Court handled the issue of students who defied school regulations and wore black armbands to class to express opposition to the war in Vietnam. What do you think would happen to teachers if they did the same thing? Would the courts treat them the same way?

The *Tinker* case was decided in February, 1969 and in November of the same year an episode took place in Addison, New York, which was to test the issue of the teacher's right to wear armbands to class as an expression of opposition to the war in Vietnam.

Charles James was an English teacher in the eleventh grade of the high school in that town. The Quakers in that area had decided to participate in the Vietnam Moratorium—a form of continuing protest against the war. James, who had joined the Quakers, decided to participate in the Moratorium by wearing a black armband on November 14, 1969. When he was asked by the principal why he was wearing it, James replied that he was opposed to killing. When asked to remove the band, James refused and he was suspended.

Throughout the controversy which followed, James maintained that his act was based on religious conviction and moral conscience. The Board of Education claimed that it was a political act and, therefore, unethical conduct. The Board permitted James to return to his job on the condition that he would not engage in political activities in school. James did return, and, the following month, he wore the black armband again during the December Moratorium. He was suspended and later fired.

The case was appealed to the New York State Commissioner of Education and James lost. The Commissioner reasoned that, in approaching controversial issues, the teacher must present fairly all viewpoints. When the teacher wears a black armband, he presents favorably only one side of the issue. The American Civil Liberties Union decided to make a federal case out of the issue.

In 1971 the case was filed in the United States District Court with the request that James be reinstated in his job and awarded $25,000 in damages. The complaint argued that James's right to freedom of speech and religion had been violated and that the Board had violated due process of law by failing to give him a hearing before dismissal. The complaint further indicated that at the Addison High School teachers had worn crucifixes and Masonic pins and that one classroom had on the bulletin board a sign which read: "Peace With Honor." The school board replied that it had done nothing illegal, that James had acted in a political manner, and that he had disobeyed the letter which reinstated him on condition that he engage in no political activities. James had been discharged because he had been insubordinate. Probably, in the back of the minds of all participants was the question whether the court would or would not apply the *Tinker* case rule to the *James* case.

In 1971 the United States District Judge ruled that James had ignored State Education Department rulings in relation to neutrality and objectivity in presenting such controversial subjects as the Vietnam Moratorium. The school board had won in the lower court.

In preparing the appeal, James' lawyer decided to build his case around the free speech issue of the *Tinker* case rather than the freedom of religion position which James had maintained. On May 21, 1972 a unanimous United States Court of Appeals decided in favor of James. The judges based their opinion on the *Tinker* case. James had exercised his right to freedom of speech—symbolic speech—in a school atmosphere where there had been no disruption of discipline. Judge Kaufman's opinion pointed out that, as in the *Tinker* case, school authorities had permitted other signs or symbols. A sign in an Addison High School classroom, "Peace With Honor," indicated that the school board's "regulation against political activity in the classroom may be no more than the fulcrum to censor only that expression with which it disagrees." The Supreme Court refused to review this decision.

The case was sent back to the lower court and the school board was ordered to reinstate James, which it did. The board, however, refused to give him back pay. On June 30, 1973 they terminated James' contract and the case was back in the courts again. An important constitutional principle had been vindicated, but a person's life and career were still enmeshed in legal uncertainty.

NOTE

THE TINKER CASE

IMPLICATIONS FOR THE SCHOOL ENVIRONMENT

Inevitably, student-principal issues were bound to follow the *Tinker* precedent into the courts and the following cases helped to clarify the nature of that decision.

ISSUES TO BE ANALYZED (CASES 42-46)

CASE 42

A student named Guzick appeared in his high school in Cleveland, Ohio, carrying pamphlets and wearing a button which read:

April 5 Chicago
G.I.—Civilian
Anti-War
Demonstration
Student Mobilization Committee

He also carried pamphlets calling for students to participate in the anti-Vietnam war demonstration in Chicago. The principal ordered him to remove the button: He refused and was suspended.

The school had a rule against insignia not related to school activities. It had arisen out of problems relating to sororities and fraternities and had been enforced for forty years, although it was not in writing.

Prior to this case, students had come to the school wearing such buttons as "White is Right," "Black Power," and "Happy Easter, Dr. King" and fights had resulted. Since the racial composition of the school had changed from all-White to 70% Black, racial tensions tended to polarize students and the buttons added to the potential for disorder.

In view of these facts, how would you decide this case?

Do you see any differences between this case and the *Tinker* case?

CASE 43

In a North Carolina school, three types of armbands relating to the Vietnam War were worn. There had been incidents among the factions, marching in the hallways, chanting threats of violence and disrespect towards teachers and the flag. More than one-third of the students were children of military personnel from a nearby base. School authorities forbade the wearing of armbands.

Would you differentiate this case from Tinker? Compare this case with the Guzick case. Would you decide them the same way?

CASE 44

Students of Mexican descent wore black berets to school as "a symbol of their Mexican culture," to "show unity among Mexicans," and as a "symbol of their dissatisfaction with society's treatment of their race." For a while the school authorities permitted it. When, however, according to the school officials, the students became arrogant, disrespectful, blocked hallways, and threatened teachers, the students were suspended.

Does the *Tinker* case apply?

CASE 45

In a Texas school, Mexican-American students wore brown armbands to express their grievances over certain educational policies. The school board there issued a regulation against wearing "apparel decoration that is disruptive, distracting, or provocative." Notice that the regulation does not refer to brown armbands.

Compare Cases 44 and 45. Does the *Tinker* rule apply?

CASE 46

Anticipating that the Vietnam Moratorium of October 15, 1969 would create disruptions in the schools, Dallas school authorities prohibited the wearing of black armbands to school on that day. Those who wore them to school were suspended from most schools. In some schools black armbands were worn for several hours and in one school they were worn all day. Those who wore white armbands were not excluded. Peace symbols had been worn previously without punishment.

How does this case fit into the *Tinker* pattern?

DECISIONS IN CASES 42–46

CASE 42

Guzick v. Debrus

431 F.2d 594 (1970)

The United States Court of Appeals in the Sixth Circuit upheld the school authorities. There are several differences between this case and *Tinker*. In this case there was a long-standing rule against all non school-related buttons, while in the *Tinker* case there was no such uniform rule against insignia. In addition, the racial composition of the high school contained the potential for racial collisions. In the words of the court:

> In our view, school authorities should not be faulted for adhering to a relatively non-oppressive rule that will indeed serve our ultimate goal of meaningful integration of our public schools.

As for the issue of freedom of speech, the court replied:

> We must be aware that in these contentious times that America's classrooms and their environs will lose their usefulness as places in which to educate our young people if pupils come to school wearing the badges of their respective disagreements, and provoke confrontations with their fellows and their teachers.

The Supreme Court refused to review this case.

CASE 43

Hill v. Lewis

323 F.Supp. 55 (E.D.N.C.1971)

The Court supported the school authorities because there was reasonable cause to fear disruption and violence. Which, in your opinion, were the material facts which the court used to justify its opinion?

CASE 44

Hernandez v. School District No. 1, Denver, Colorado

315 F.Supp. 289 (D.Colorado 1970)

The court upheld the suspensions because the evidence supported the reasonable conclusion that the berets were used as symbols of power to disrupt discipline in the school, as well as to dominate the student body.

CASE 45

Aguirre v. Tahoka Independent School District

311 F.Supp. 664 (N.D.Texas, 1970)

This time the federal district court upheld the students because "the facts as here found put this case on all fours with that decided by the United States Supreme Court" in *Tinker*. In the first place, the court concluded that the new dress rule was really directed at one group—those who wore the armbands. In the second place, the court found that some of the disruptions claimed by the school authorities were not supported by the evidence.

CASE 46

Butts v. Dallas Independent School District

436 F.2d 728 (5th Circuit 1971)

The trial court decided in favor of the school authorities, but the United States Court of Appeals reversed. The judges concluded that the regulation "was improvised . . . for the occasion." Although disruption on October 15th was a contingency, this did not justify suspending "the exercise of what we are taught by *Tinker* is a constitutional right." The judges then went on to say:

> Our difference with the trial court therefore is that we do not agree that the precedential value of the *Tinker* decision is nullified whenever a school system is confronted with disruptive activities or the possibility of them. Rather we believe that the Supreme Court has declared a constitutional right which school authorities must nurture and protect, not extinguish, unless they find the circumstances allow them no practical alternative. As to the existence of such circumstances, they are the judges, and if within the range where reasonable minds may differ, their decisions will govern. But there must be some inquiry, and establishment of substantial fact, to buttress the determination.

FREEDOM OF EXPRESSION: LIFE STYLES AND DRESS CODES

Each generation seems to develop a life style unique to its times and it is often expressed in hair length, beards, dress, speech, attitudes, and manners. Such life styles often trigger problems because of what is generally referred to as the generation gap. School officials are vested with the responsibility of maintaining discipline, decorum, and a learning atmosphere. Young people in the schools feel the pressure of their peers to conform to contemporary modes of conduct and appearance. When the two come into conflict, "the sparks fly upward" and sometimes reach the court.

Up to the present the Supreme Court has refused to hear hair style and dress code cases. Justice Black did have an opportunity to express his views on hair style when he was asked to sit as a Circuit Court Justice in the Fifth Circuit. Each Supreme Court Justice is assigned a circuit as part of his duties. Since there are nine Justices and eleven circuits Chief Justice Burger and Justice Brennan are each assigned two circuits.

CASE 47

In the case of *Karr v. Schmidt, Principal of Coronado High School,* 401 U.S. 1201, 91 S.Ct. 592, 27 L.Ed.2d 797 (1971), Justice Black was asked to act on an "Emergency Motion to Vacate a Stay of Injunction Pending Appeal." The El Paso school authorities issued rules providing that haircuts of boys must not "hang over the ears or the top of the collar of a standard dress shirt and must not obstruct vision." Failure to comply meant suspension. Karr refused and was suspended. The District Court held that the hair length rule violated the Due Process and Equal Protection Clauses of the United States Constitution. It issued an injunction against the school board. The United States Court of Appeals stayed and suspended the injunction. Justice Black was then asked to vacate the stay of the Court of Appeals and reinstate the injunction against the school board.

Justice Black refused to do so in sweeping terms reminiscent of his dissent in the *Tinker* case.

> The motion in this case is presented to me in a record of more than 50 pages, not counting a number of exhibits. The words used throughout the record such as "Emergency Motion" and "harassment" and "irreparable damages" are calculated to leave the impression that this case over the length of hair has created or is about to create a great national "crisis." I confess my inability to understand how anyone would thus classify this hair length case. The only thing about it that borders on the serious to me is the idea that anyone should think the Federal Constitution imposes on the United States courts the burden of supervising the length of hair that public school students should wear. The records of the federal courts, including ours, show a heavy burden of litigation in connection with cases of great importance—the kind of litigation our courts must be able to handle if they are to perform their responsibility to our society. Moreover, our Constitution has sought to distribute the powers of government in this Nation between the United States and the States. Surely the federal judiciary can perform no greater service to the Nation than to leave the States unhampered in the performance of their purely local affairs. Surely few policies can be thought of that States are more capable of deciding than the length of the hair of schoolboys. There can, of course, be honest differences of opinion as to whether any government, state or federal, should as a matter of public policy regulate the length of haircuts, but it would be difficult to prove by reason, logic, or common sense that the federal judiciary is more competent to deal with hair length than are the local school authorities and state legislatures of our 50 States. Perhaps if the courts will leave the States free to perform their own constitutional duties they will at least be able successfully to regulate the length of hair their public school students can wear.
>
> Motion denied.

A motion to overrule Justice Black's opinion was denied by the Supreme Court on March 1, 1971. Subsequently, all fifteen judges in the Fifth Circuit decided in favor of the school board. (See page 130.)

The hairstyle cases have confronted the courts with a unique issue. Unlike clothing which can be worn, discarded, or changed to conform to dress codes, hairstyles become a part of the person and cannot be readily changed, except perhaps by the wearing of wigs. That, of course, creates another type of problem.

CASE 48

The case of *Ferrell v. Dallas Independent School District* (392 F.2d 697—1968) dealt with three Dallas high school students who were members of a musical group. They had Beatle-type haircuts which they regarded as necessary for their performance as rock and roll musicians.

The school had a regulation requiring students to cut or trim their hair as a prerequisite to enrollment. Ferrell and his friends refused and were not permitted to enroll. At the trial the principal testified that boys who wore long hair to school created disciplinary problems. They were harassed by other boys; obscene language was used; threats were made; and challenges to fight were issued. This was substantiated by some students.

In their turn, Ferrell and his fellow musicians replied that the school regulations violated their right to liberty—freedom of expression—and their right to property—protected under the Due Process Clause of the Fourteenth Amendment.

The United States Court of Appeals was unimpressed with this line of reasoning and agreed with the principal. The state, said the majority opinion, has compelling reasons to maintain an effective and efficient school system and it has the power to eliminate conditions which hinder or interfere with the state's efforts to provide the best possible education for its students. To accomplish this a state has the constitutional power to restrict the constitutional right of freedom of expression, provided its actions are neither arbitrary, capricious, unreasonable, or discriminatory. In this case the principal acted properly.

As for interference with a musician's career, the court responded:

> It is common knowledge that many young performers are required to use special attire and makeup, including wigs or hairpieces, for their public appearances.

The dissenting opinion by Judge Tuttle refers to this case as something of a "tempest in a teapot." Three teenage schoolboys are barred because the length of their hair did not suit school authorities. That, for him, is not a defensible explanation. If school authorities feared disruptions, the proper course of action is not to deprive students of their constitutional rights. It is the disrupters who should have been warned of the consequences of their acts. Expression of individuality by students whose appearance may not please others is deserving of constitutional protection.

CASE 49

New Rider v. Board of Education of School District No. 1, Pawnee County, Okl.

28d F.2d (1973)

What do you think happened when a group of male Pawnee Indians at Pawnee High School, a public school in Oklahoma, decided to wear their hair parted in the middle with a long braid on each side? Would school authorities permit it, if there is a regulation forbidding hair to reach the shirt collar or ears?

The young Indian explained that they were following "the old traditional ways" and that their hairstyle was "one way of telling people that I am proud to be an Indian." Others testified that the young men were doing this because of a "new-found heritage" and that they were trying to "regain their tradition, to learn their culture."

The school defended its regulation on the basis that it sought to achieve the objective of "instilling pride and initiative among students leading to scholarship attainment and high school spirit and morale." One school superintendent testified that permitting the Indians to wear their hair one way while restricting the hair length of white students would be "disruptive" because an "integrated school system cannot countenance different groups and remain one organization."

It was admitted that the new hairstyle did not cause any disruption in the school. Nevertheless, the young men were suspended from school indefinitely.

In *New Rider v. Board of Education of Independent School District No. 1, Pawnee County, Okl.*, 480 F.2d 693, the United States Court of Appeals supported the school board. The students, through their lawyers, petitioned the Supreme Court for a writ of certiorari to hear the case and the Justices refused in December, 1973. Justice Douglas dissented and Justice Marshall agreed.

Both Justices felt that the entire Court should have heard the case because it involved an important constitutional issue. An excerpt from their dissent will disclose how they relate this case to *Tinker* and how they introduce the historic factor.

> Petitioners . . . were in fact attempting to broadcast a clear and specific message to their fellow students and others—their pride in being Indian. This, I believe, should clearly bring this case within the ambit of Tinker v. Des Moines School District, 393 U.S. 503, where we struck down a school policy which refused to allow students to wear black armbands in protest of the Vietnam War. We recognized that such armbands were closely akin to pure speech and were entitled to First Amendment protection, . . . at least where, as here,

there was no finding that the operation of the school was substantially endangered by the symbolic speech. . . . But as we noted in *Tinker*, this Court long ago recognized that our constitutional system repudiates the idea that a State may conduct its schools "to foster a homogeneous people." . . .

The effort to impose uniformity on petitioners is especially repugnant in view of the history of white treatment of the education of the American Indian. In the late 1800's, at about the same time that the Dawes Severalty Act of 1887 fragmented Indian tribal land holdings and allotted land to individual Indians with the effect of breaking up tribal structures, the Bureau of Indian Affairs (BIA) began operating a system of boarding schools with the express policy of stripping the Indian child of his cultural heritage and identity. . . .

The results of such a policy, mirrored in the policy of the school in this case to force all students into one homogeneous mold even when it impinges on their racial and cultural values, has been disastrous for the young Indian child who is taught in school that the culture in which he has been reared is not important or valid. The Subcommittee recognized that such a coercive assimilation policy, denigrating and seeking to abolish cultural differences, frustrates Indian children and leads "the community and the child [to] retaliate by treating the school as an alien institution." . . .

In the Fifth Circuit (Alabama, Florida, Georgia, Louisiana, Mississippi, Texas, and Canal Zone), so many cases relating to hair style and grooming reached the federal courts that in an unusual move, fifteen judges of the Court of Appeals, sitting en banc, finally decided the case of *Karr v. Schmidt*, 460 F.2d 609 (5 Cir., 1972) in an 8 to 7 (referred to on p. 126) vote with this declaration:

> Where a complaint merely alleges the constitutional invalidity of a high school hair and grooming regulation, the district courts are directed to grant an immediate motion to dismiss for failure to state a claim for which relief can be granted.

An examination of the lower court rulings on dress codes and hairstyles discloses two lines of reasoning that judges have followed:

In Favor of the School

1. The regulation must be specific and understandable.

2. There must be a compelling interest to accomplish an educational objective.

3. The regulation must be reasonable.

4. The regulation must not be applied in a capricious, arbitrary, unreasonable, and discriminatory manner.

5. Schools can forbid dress that constitutes a health hazard, is "obscene," or is so distracting as to interfere with learning.

In Favor of the Student

1. The regulation violates freedom of expression protected by the First and Fourteenth Amendments. (The *Liberty* Argument)

2. The regulation violates the right to privacy protected by the First, Fourth, Fifth and Ninth Amendments.

3. The regulation deprives the student of Due Process of Law protected by the Fourteenth Amendment.

4. The regulation deprives the student of Equal Protection of the Laws Clause of the Fourteenth Amendment.

CASE 50

A TEACHER REFUSES TO WEAR A NECKTIE TO CLASS

East Hartford Education Association v. Board of Education of the Town of East Hartford

562 F. 2nd 838 (1977)

Brimley, a teacher of English and filmmaking at a Connecticut high school, refused to wear a tie to class, despite the tie-and-jacket regulation of the school authorities. His reason was that a tieless teacher can establish greater rapport with students and teach more effectively. He also took the position that a turtle neck sweater or an open collar with jacket was evidence to students that the teacher was not tied to establishment conformity.

The Board gave him permission to wear informal attire to his filmmaking class, but insisted that he wear jacket and tie to his English class. He refused, was reprimanded, and he appealed the reprimand to the federal courts. The local teachers' organization joined in his appeal.

Brimley challenged the constitutionality of the dress code for public school teachers on two main grounds. He argued that his refusal to wear a tie was protected under the First Amendment's right to freedom of expression, as incorporated into the Fourteenth Amendment's due process of law clause. The idea of liberty under these amendments permits "symbolic speech". The informal attire was a form of "symbolic speech," since it communicated a statement by Brimley on current affairs, as well as a comprehensive view of society. This freedom of expression assisted him in his rapport with his students and made him a more effective teacher.

Brimley also based his appeal on the Fourteenth Amendment's declaration that no state can deprive a person of liberty without due process of law. This "liberty" claim, he argued, creates a right to privacy in the way a person chooses to dress.

The Board of Education responded that it was acting under authority delegated to it by the state. The dress code was designed "to promote respect for authority and traditional values as well as discipline in the classroom," "a professional image for teachers," and "good grooming among students".

The federal district judge dismissed Brimley's complaint. Brimley appealed to the United States Court of Appeals for the Second District and the three judge court decided in Brimley's favor by a 2 to 1 decision. Then one of the judges in the Second Circuit petitioned for an *en banc* hearing of the case. This means that *all* the judges in the Second Circuit were being asked to rule on the merits of the case. A majority of the judges agreed to the petition for this kind of hearing.

Ten judges re-examined the issues and decided in favor of the school board. The two judges who had voted in favor of Brimley in the three-judge hearing now dissented from the *en banc* ruling.

The majority found no "basic constitutional values" involved. In balancing the freedom of expression arguments against the Board of Education's power to make routine decisions concerning teacher's dress, the Board must prevail. The dress code was reasonably related to the Board's power to promote respect for authority and traditional values, as well as discipline in the classroom. On the other hand, Brimley had other means available to communicate his views on society to his students. He could have told his students his views "in a temperate way" without interfering with his teaching duties. The majority concludes that the "First Amendment claim made here is so insubstantial as to border on the frivolous." A teacher's sartorial choice does not come within the protective shield of the First Amendment.

As for Brimley's argument that he has a "liberty" claim arising out of the due process clause of the Fourteenth Amendment, the court found that *Kelley v. Johnson* (the policeman's grooming case discussed on page 134) was applicable. There is a distinction between a privacy claim made by a government employee and that of a member of the general public. Although the functions of policemen and teachers differ widely, a dress code is presumed to be constitutional unless it can be shown that the demands of the code are "so irrational that it may be branded arbitrary." Since Brimley failed to do this, the code is a constitutional exercise of the Board's power.

The two dissenting judges had sided with Brimley in the prior ruling. Here once again they argue that an important constitutional right is involved. What connection, they ask, is there these days between discipline, decorum, and respect in the classroom and a dress code for teachers? They suggest that the "majority confuses traditional values with mindless orthodoxy." When a court is confronted with a First Amendment issue, it is the obligation of the judges to scrutinize the issues with care. This is no trivial matter to the individual and to society.

The dissent concludes with the observation that the majority gives away the real reason for its ruling by indicating that judges do not have a "roving commission" to right the wrongs of society. Article III of the Constitution requires judges to interpret the Constitution. Failure to do so is an abdication of judicial responsibility.

CASE 51

A POLICE OFFICER CHALLENGES HAIR LENGTH REGULATIONS

Kelley, Commissioner of the Suffolk Police Department v. Johnson

425 U.S. 238, 96 S.Ct. 1440, 47 L.Ed.2d 708 (1976)

The Police Department of Suffolk County in New York State issued rules and regulations concerning hair length, side burns, mustaches, beards, goatees, and wigs. The hair length requirement provided:

> Hair shall be neat, clean, trimmed, and present a groomed appearance. Hair will not touch the ear or the collar except the closely cut hair on the back of the neck. Hair in front will be groomed so that it does not fall below the band of properly worn headgear. In no case will the bulk or length of the hair interfere with any proper wear of any authorized headgear . . .

Johnson, a police officer and President of the Patrolmen's Benevolent Association, attacked the hair length regulation as an unconstitutional violation of his right to freedom of expression under the First and Fourteenth Amendments, as well as his guarantee of due process and equal protection of the law under the Fourteenth Amendment. The Police Department responded that the regulation was needed for some standard of uniformity of appearance, for the *esprit de corps* of the department, and for the safety of the police officer in apprehending a suspect in close contact.

With whom would you side in this controversy? On what principle would you base your decision?

The Supreme Court handed down a 6 to 2 decision, with Justice Stevens abstaining. Justice Rehnquist's opinion for the majority supported the Police Department. We are not dealing here, he said, with the rights of citizens at large, but with a public employee who must abide by restrictions which are rationally connected with his job. One who joins the Police Department in Suffolk County agrees to wear a uniform, salute the flag, refrain from smoking in public, and abide by grooming regulations which are relevant for the job.

The issue here is not whether the state can prove a genuine public need, but whether there is a rational connection between hair length and the organization and high morale of a police force. The majority concluded that there was such a connection and decided that there was no violation of the police officer's liberty.

Justice Powell's concurring opinion stressed that this ruling dealt only with uniformed police forces, and could not be construed to apply "in a different context." He obviously was concerned that this decision might be used as a precedent in hair regulation cases.

Justice Marshall dissented and Justice Brennan concurred. "Liberty," said the dissenters, "extends to the full range of conduct which the individual is free to pursue." This surely must mean that the individual is free to dress "according to his own taste." Justice Marshall elaborates this position:

An individual's personal appearance may reflect, sustain, and nourish his personality and may well be used as a means of expressing his attitude and lifestyle. In taking control over a citizen's personal appearance, the Government forces him to sacrifice substantial elements of his integrity and identity as well. To say that the liberty guarantee of the Fourteenth Amendment does not encompass matters of personal appearance would be fundamentally inconsistent with the value of privacy, self-identity, autonomy, and personal integrity that I have always assumed the Constitution was designed to protect.

THURGOOD MARSHALL
1908–

Associate Justice
1967–

This rule also applies to police officers, Marshall said. When the majority takes the position that hair uniformity will make identification of police easier, it misses the point. Police are not identified by the length of their hair. As for *esprit de corps*, Johnson, who is President of the Patrolmen's Benevolent Association, is challenging this regulation in his official capacity. This means that *esprit de corps* may be low because of this regulation.

CHAPTER 13

ACADEMIC FREEDOM

Although the idea of academic freedom is not mentioned in the Constitution, it is today regarded as one of the freedoms included in the First Amendment. The origins of academic freedom are generally traceable to the German universities. The rationale for this idea of freedom in the school and university is that learning and teaching must be directed to the search for truth and its dissemination throughout society. In recent years, the term "academic freedom" has been expanded to include other school-related activities.

Academic freedom cases involve students and teachers. Examples of these have been discussed: The *Tinker* case, the *James* case, the *Epperson* case, and the *Russo* case. In each of these cases, we noted a confrontation between school authorities and students or teachers involving First Amendment rights. Professor Ladd has designated this situation as a clash between the Puritan and the Madison Models of school governance. The former is based on the proposition that the school authorities generally know best what is good for students. Their training and experience qualify them for their roles as decision-makers. The Madison Model regards the rights of students as central to the education process because the schools are training grounds for democracy.

The Madison Model recognizes that there are times when restrictions are necessary because of compelling reasons (violence, destruction, learning environment), but these limitations must be weighed against the rights granted to all people under the First Amendment.

In the cases of students, academic freedom cases include hair style and dress codes, student newspapers, student clubs, and the right to petition. In the case of teachers, academic freedom issues include dress style, selection of materials for student use, use of language or teaching methods, and the right to join associations.

When it comes to the use of teaching materials, teachers are generally safe except when a student or a parent objects on grounds of morality or obscenity. Issues of this nature are generally resolved on the following guidelines: Are the teaching materials and teaching strategies relevant to the subject matter? Are the materials appropriate to the age and maturity levels of the students? Will they disrupt the discipline of the school? Do the materials and the methods conform to acceptable professional standards? Is the judge sympathetic to academic freedom? In the following pages we shall juxtapose viewpoints of judges on this issue.

LOYALTY OATHS AND LOYALTY LEGISLATION

The loyalty oath is one of the techniques used by governments to insure the loyalty of their citizens and their employees. How effective a loyalty oath really is in practice is difficult to tell. Sometimes a loyal citizen will refuse to take the oath on grounds of conscience, while one who is disloyal will not hesitate to do so because he or she feels that there will be little likelihood of discovering the truth about them.

In the late 1940's and 1950's state legislatures enacted loyalty legislation to counteract the dangers of Communism and subversion. The Feinberg Law, passed in 1949, required boards of education in New York State to prepare lists of subversive organizations and to discharge any educator who belonged to any of these organizations. In 1952 in *Adler v. Board of Education*, 342 U.S. 485, 72 S.Ct. 380, 96 L.Ed. 517, the Supreme Court upheld this law by a 6 to 3 ruling. Justice Minton's opinion for the Court contained the rationale for the Court's decision.

> A teacher works in a sensitive area in a schoolroom. There he shapes the attitude of young minds towards the society in which they live. In this, the state has a vital concern. It must preserve the integrity of the schools. That the school authorities have the right and the duty to screen the officials, teachers, and employees as to their fitness to maintain the integrity of the schools as a part of ordered society, cannot be doubted. One's associates, past and present, as well as one's conduct, may properly be considered in determining fitness and loyalty. From time immemorial, one's reputation has been determined in part by the company he keeps. In the employment of officials and teachers of the school system, the state may properly inquire into the company they keep, and we know of no rule, constitutional or otherwise, that prevents the state, when determining the fitness and loyalty of such persons, from considering the organizations and persons with whom they associate.

The same year in another case, *Wieman v. Updegraff*, 344 U.S. 183, 73 S.Ct. 215, 97 L.Ed. 216, the Supreme Court unanimously voided an Oklahoma law requiring a lengthy loyalty oath attesting to the fact that the state employee did not belong to any subversive organization and that they would take up arms in defense of the United States. A group of college instructors challenged this law. Justice Frankfurter's concurring opinion has been oft-quoted in a defense of academic freedom.

> To regard teachers—in our entire educational system, from the primary grades to the university—as the priests of our democracy is therefore not to indulge in hyperbole. It is the special task of teachers to foster those habits of openmindedness and critical inquiry which alone make for responsible citizens, who, in turn, make possible an enlightened and effective public opinion. Teachers must fulfill their function

by precept and practice, by the very atmosphere they generate; they must be exemplars of open-mindedness and free inquiry. They cannot carry out their noble task if the conditions for the practice of a responsible and critical mind are denied to them. They must have the freedom of responsible inquiry, by thought and action, into the meaning of social and economic ideas, into the checkered history of social and economic dogma. They must be free to sift evanescent doctrine, qualified by time and circumstance, from that restless, enduring process of extending the bounds of understanding and wisdom, to assure which the freedom of thought, of speech, of inquiry, of worship are guaranteed by the Constitution of the United States against infraction by National or State Government.

Here we have the classic confrontation: The defense of the teacher's right to academic freedom and the support for the State's right to screen its teachers for fitness and loyalty.

In 1964 in *Baggett v. Bullitt,* 377 U.S. 360, 84 S.Ct. 1316, 12 L.Ed. 2d 377, the Washington Loyalty Oath was declared an unconstitutional violation of the Due Process Clause of the Fourteenth Amendment. The 7 to 2 ruling found this law to be so vague, uncertain, and broad that a public servant might have difficulty in differentiating "what is and is not disloyal."

Two years later, in *Elfbrandt v. Russell,* 384 U.S. 11, 86 S.Ct. 1238, 16 L.Ed.2d 321, a 5 to 4 Court voided the Arizona loyalty oath law on the ground that it presumed a person to be guilty if he belonged to certain organizations until he proved himself innocent. In 1967 the Court returned to the Feinberg Law, which it had declared to be constitutional, but this time in a 5 to 4 decision, in *Keyishian v. Board of Regents of New York,* 385 U.S. 589, 87 S.Ct. 675, 17 L.Ed.2d 629, the majority found the language of the law to be imprecise. Membership in the Communist Party, they said, is not enough to disqualify a teacher from public service. It must be shown that the teacher knew of and had specific intent to further the aims of the proscribed organization.

Once again the clash of opposing view points is heard.

Justice Brennan's opinion for the majority discusses the subject of academic freedom in these words:

Our Nation is deeply committed to safeguarding academic freedom, which is of transcendent value to all of us and not merely to the teachers concerned. That freedom is therefore a special concern of the First Amendment, which does not tolerate laws that cast a pall of orthodoxy over the classroom. "The vigilant protection of constitutional freedoms is nowhere more vital than in the community of American schools." . . . "The classroom is peculiarly the marketplace of ideas." The Nation's future depends upon leaders trained through wide exposure to that robust exchange of ideas which discovers truth "out of a multitude of tongues, [rather] than through any kind of authoritative selection." . . .

Justice Clark's dissent responded with equal eloquence.

The majority says that the Feinberg Law is bad because it has an "overbroad sweep." I regret to say—and I do so with deference—that the majority has by its broadside swept away one of our most precious rights, namely, the right of self-preservation. Our public educational system is the genius of our democracy. The minds of our youth are developed there and the character of that development will determine the future of our land. Indeed, our very existence depends on it. The issue here is a very narrow one. It is not freedom of speech, freedom of thought, freedom of press, freedom of assembly, or of association, even in the Communist Party. It is simply this: May the State provide that one who, after a hearing with full judicial review, is found to have wilfully and deliberately advocated, advised, or taught that our Government should be overthrown by force or violence or otherwise unlawful means; or to have wilfully and deliberately printed, published, etc., any book or paper that so advocated and to have *personally* advocated such doctrine himself; or to have wilfully and deliberately become a member of an organization that advocates such doctrine, is prima facie disqualified from teaching in its university? My answer, in keeping with all of our cases up until today, is "Yes"!

There is another aspect of academic freedom which is unique because it pits the administrators and teachers, who are now on the same side, against a group of parents or community leaders. The issue generally takes the form of textbook selection, or books or magazines used in school, or courses, like sex education and family life, or curricular materials. In legal terms, the equation takes the form of a right and a power on a collision course. The parents have the right to guide the upbringing of their children, while the state has the power to develop requirements for citizenship education. In exercising its power, the state must not engage in capricious, arbitrary, and unreasonable conduct. On the other hand, the position of the parents in opposing the school authorities must not only be reasonable, but they must also bear the burden of proof in the case. It all comes down to whether the issue is a legal one or an educational one. If it is an educational problem, courts will tend to let the educators decide it. If the issue passes over to the due process area of the Constitution, the tendency will be for the courts to step in.

As we shall see in the following chapters, the issue of academic freedom extends into freedom of the press and the right to assemble peaceably through associations. In this chapter we have set up the clash of values which will continue to resound as long as there are teachers, students, administrators, boards of education, parents, and college trustees pressing on the rights and responsibility equations in the world of education.

SECTION IV

FREEDOM OF THE PRESS

AMENDMENT I

Congress shall make no law . . . abridging the freedom of . . . the press . . .

AMENDMENT XIV

. . . nor shall any state deprive any person of . . . liberty . . . without due process of law.

Were it left to me to decide whether we should have a government without newspapers, or newspapers without a government, I would prefer the latter.

Thomas Jefferson

If there be any among us who would wish to dissolve this union or change its republican form, let them stand undisturbed as monuments of the safety with which error of opinion may be tolerated where reason is left free to combat it.

Thomas Jefferson
First Inaugural Address

Some degree of abuse is inseparable from the proper use of everything; and in no instance is this more true than in that of the press.

James Madison
Report on the Virginia
Resolutions of 1798

The liberty of the press is the right to publish with impunity, truth with good motives, for justifiable ends, though reflecting on government, magistracy, or individuals.

Alexander Hamilton
quoted in *People v. Croswell,* 1 N.Y. Common Law
Reports 717 (1804)

INTRODUCTION

Those who invented movable type and the printing press could not foresee the ultimate results of their work. They laid the foundation for a revolution in knowledge and a revolution in communications which we are still experiencing. Books, newspapers, leaflets, pamphlets, and magazines began to spread a variety and multiplicity of ideas. Later, radio and television and the movies joined the parade of media influencing the thoughts and feelings of men and women.

It was inevitable that freedom of the press would bring with it the freedom to criticize, as well as the freedom to support government policies and public officials. It was just as inevitable that government officials would try to suppress viewpoints that conflicted with official policy. Out of this confrontation came government censorship—a practice that exists to this very day in many countries.

Censorship takes one of two forms and, in legal language, they are referred to as *prior restraint* and *post restraint*. The former prohibits the publication of any book, article, magazine, or newspaper before it is read and approved by the official censor or licensor. In England, where prior censorship was the rule for many years, it was the custom to give two copies of the material to be published to the censor. This practice was designed to make sure that, if approved, the material would be published exactly as submitted. Changes were forbidden.

Post restraint is the policy of imposing punishment after the distribution of a publication. Under this practice the censoring body judges the materials and if it concludes that the law has been violated, punishment is imposed. Obviously, there is greater uncertainty under post restraint than under prior restraint, since interpretations containing laws relating to the contents of publications may differ widely. But there is also greater freedom.

There is, of course, a school of thought that opposes all forms of censorship. The arguments of Socrates and Milton, which we referred to in the preceding section, justify the policy that the market place of ideas should be open to anyone who believes he or she has something to say. John Stuart Mill's famous essay *On Liberty* is studded with memorable quotations in defense of this position. Perhaps the most quoted passage is the following.

> If all mankind minus one were of one opinion, and only one person were of the contrary opinion, mankind would be no more justified in silencing that one person, than he, if he had the power, would be justified in silencing mankind. Were an opinion a personal possession of no value except to the owner; if to be obstructed in the enjoyment of it were simply a private injury, it would make some difference whether the

injury was inflicted only on a few persons or on many. But the peculiar evil of silencing the expression of an opinion is, that it is robbing the human race; posterity as well as the existing generation; those who dissent from the opinion, still more than those who hold it. If the opinion is right, they are deprived of the opportunity of exchanging error for truth: if wrong, they lose, what is almost as great a benefit, the clearer perception and livelier impression of truth, produced by its collision with error.

With this defense of liberty, as applied to freedom of the press, we face the question: Is it absolute or limited? If it is limited, what are the guidelines to be followed?

In trying to answer this question, we are faced with an avalanche of subjects, cases, and precedents. From this wealth of materials we have selected a few which help to illuminate the major problems and the alternative solutions that are available under our constitutional system.

JUSTUS IN THE MINNEAPOLIS STAR

"It's better this way—people won't have to think"

CHAPTER 14

CRITICISM OF PUBLIC OFFICIALS

When men and women attain public office today they become fair game for journalists, editorial writers, cartoonists, TV commentators, and the average citizen. It was not always so.

In England the crime of seditious libel—criticism of public officials—was a serious offense and tried in the feared Court of Star Chamber. "To speak ill of the government" or to cast blame on public officials was enough to send one before this court in which the inquisitional procedures included torture.

The crime of seditious libel was part of the criminal law of colonial America and the most famous trial in this country involving freedom of the press dealt with a printer who was charged with the seditious libel of a governor.

CASES

CASE 52

THE CASE OF JOHN PETER ZENGER (1735)

The Zenger case is one of the staple products of American history. Students in elementary, junior, and senior high school, as well as in colleges and universities, have been confronted with this great case. By the time a student graduates from high school, the name of Peter Zenger should ring a familiar bell.

A brief summary of the highlights of this trial are in order here because this episode marks a change in the law. Described as "the morning star of that liberty which subsequently revolutionized America," the decision in the Zenger case eventually influenced the wording of the First Amendment.

Zenger was a printer, not a writer. The writers who hated Governor Cosby of New York asked Zenger to print their articles. He did so knowing that the printer, not the writer, would suffer the consequences of the Governor's displeasure and hostility. It was James Alexander, who was the editor of the paper, *New York Weekly Journal,* and he and the newspaper became the opposition press in New York.

The articles attacked Cosby as an "idiot", a "Nero", a "rogue" and a lawbreaker. Stories cited instances in which the Governor had openly violated the law.

Since Zenger was the printer, he was arrested, charged with seditious libel, and tried in August, 1735. The problem confronting Zenger was that the truth was no defense to libel at that time. If Zenger argued that he was printing the truth, the court could rule out his line of reasoning as being irrelevant. As a matter of fact, the principle seemed to be: "The greater the truth, the greater the libel."

Zenger had the good fortune to have as his lawyer in this crucial case, the famous old Andrew Hamilton, who, in addition to his legal skills, was the architect of Independence Hall in Philadelphia. He combined these skills in building a defense for Zenger which, like Independence Hall, has served as a memorial to the idea of liberty. In arguing on behalf of his client that truth was a defense when one was charged with seditious libel, Andrew Hamilton pleaded his cause with great eloquence.

> I am truly very unequal to such an undertaking on many accounts. And you see I labor under the weight of many years, and am borne down with great infirmities of body; yet old and weak as I am, I should think it my duty, if required, to go to the utmost part of the land where my service could be of any use in assisting to quench the flame of prosecutions upon informations set on foot by the government to deprive a people of the right of remonstrating (and complaining too) of the arbitrary attempts of men in power. Men who injure and oppress the people under their administration provoke them to cry out and complain; and then make that very complaint the foundation for new oppressions and prosecutions. I wish I could say there were no instances of this kind. But to conclude; the question before the Court and you gentlemen of the jury is not of small nor private concern, it is not the cause of a poor printer, nor of New York alone, which you are now trying: No! It may in its consequence affect every freeman that lives under a British government on the main of America. It is the best cause. It is the cause of liberty; and I make no doubt but your upright conduct this day will not only entitle you to the love and esteem of your fellow citizens; but every man who prefers freedom to a life of slavery will bless and honor you as men who have baffled the attempt of tyranny; and by an impartial and uncorrupt verdict, have laid a noble foundation for securing to ourselves, our posterity, and our neighbors that to which nature and the laws of our country have given us a right—the liberty—both of exposing and opposing arbitrary power (in these parts of the world, at least) by speaking and writing truth. . . .

Impressed with the reasoning of the venerable Hamilton, the jury found Zenger "not guilty" and opened the door to public criticism of government officials provided the charges were true. It would be comforting to be able to say that the *Zenger* precedent was followed immediately everywhere. That is not true. It took time for this rule of law to become the law of the land. After all, not every jury was as courageous as the Zenger jury in defying the Court in its insistence that truth could not be used as a defense in libel actions.

Let us suppose, now, that a newspaper publishes critical comments about public officials which are not factually true. Does that in and of itself make the newspaper liable for damages? This question came before the Supreme Court more than two hundred years after the *Zenger Case.*

CASE 53

New York Times v. Sullivan

376 U.S. 254, 84 S.Ct. 710, 11 L.Ed.2d 686 (1964)

On March 29, 1960 the *New York Times* carried a full page advertisement entitled, "Heed Their Rising Voices", referring to the widespread non-violent demonstrations by thousands of Southern Blacks to affirm their "right to live in human dignity as guaranteed by the U. S. Constitution and the Bill of Rights." The ad went on to say that the Blacks had been met by a "wave of terror." The third and sixth paragraphs read as follows:

Third paragraph:

"In Montgomery, Alabama, after students sang 'My Country, 'Tis of Thee' on the State Capitol steps, their leaders were expelled from school, and truckloads of police armed with shotguns and tear-gas ringed the Alabama State College Campus. When the entire student body protested to state authorities by refusing to re-register, their dining hall was padlocked in an attempt to starve them into submission.

Sixth paragraph:

"Again and again the Southern violators have answered Dr. King's peaceful protests with intimidation and violence. They have bombed his home almost killing his wife and child. They have assaulted his person. They have arrested him seven times—for 'speeding,' 'loitering' and similar 'offenses.' And now they have charged him with 'perjury'—a *felony* under which they would imprison him for *ten years.* . . ."

The ad appeared over the names of 64 well-known persons. Below these appeared the names of four Black Alabama clergymen, as well as the officers of the Committee to Defend Martin Luther King and the Struggle for Freedom in the South.

L. B. Sullivan was one of three elected Commissioners of the City of Montgomery, Alabama, and his job was to supervise the Fire and Police Departments. He brought this civil libel action against the *Times* and four Black Alabama clergymen, claiming that he had been defamed by the ad.   The jury awarded him $500,000 in damages and an appeal was made to the Supreme Court.

The *Times* argued that the ad was presented to it by a respectable person and that it could be assumed that the 64 prominent persons whose names appeared there would justify the content of the ad. The *Times* saw no need to check the accuracy of the charges, in view of the roster of persons involved.   Furthermore, argued the *Times*, there was nothing in the ad to connect Sullivan personally with the charges made.   In addition, the paper took the position that freedom of the press guaranteed by the First and Fourteenth Amendments justified its action.

Sullivan's lawyers argued that the ad had many inaccuracies which could have been easily verified.   The Supreme Court agreed, saying:

> It is uncontroverted that some of the statements contained in the two paragraphs were not accurate descriptions of events which occurred in Montgomery.   Although Negro students staged a demonstration on the State Capitol steps, they sang the National Anthem and not "My Country, 'Tis of Thee."   Although nine students were expelled by the State Board of Education, this was not for leading the demonstration at the Capitol, but for demanding service at a lunch counter in the Montgomery County Courthouse on another day.   Not the entire student body, but most of it, had protested the expulsion, not by refusing to register, but by boycotting classes on a single day; virtually all the students did register for the ensuing semester.   The campus dining hall was not padlocked on any occasion, and the only students who may have been barred from eating there were the few who had neither signed a preregistration application nor requested temporary meal tickets.   Although the police were deployed near the campus in large numbers on three occasions, they did not at any time "ring" the campus, and they were not called to the campus in connection with the demonstration on the State Capitol steps, as the third paragraph implied.   Dr. King had not been arrested seven times, but only four; and although he claimed to have been assaulted some years earlier in connection with his arrest for loitering outside a courtroom, one of the officers who made the arrest denied that there was such an assault.

> On the premise that the charges in the sixth paragraph could be read as referring to him, respondent [Sullivan] was allowed to prove that he had not participated in the events described.   Although Dr. King's home had in fact been bombed twice when his wife and child were there, both of these occasions antedated respondent's tenure as Commissioner, and the police were not only not implicated in the bombings, but had made every effort to apprehend those who were.   Three of Dr. King's four arrests took place before respondent became Commissioner. Although Dr. King had in fact been indicted (he was subsequently acquitted) on two counts of perjury, each of which carried a possible five-year sentence, respondent had nothing to do with procuring the indictment.

Were these errors sufficient to justify damages for libel?

The decision of the Court was unanimous and Justice Brennan delivered the opinion of the Court. The problem with the lower court rulings, said Justice Brennan, is that they did not consider the motives of those who made or printed the statements. It is possible for the press to print a story or an ad containing factual errors. To hold that such errors affecting the reputation of a public official is libelous without permitting a showing of honest mistakes would discourage the press from printing many important articles.

We are required for the first time in this case to determine the extent to which the constitutional protections for speech and press limit a state's power to award damages in a libel action brought by a public official against critics of his official conduct . . . A rule compelling the critic of official conduct to guarantee the truth of all his factual assertions—and to do so on pain of libel judgments virtually unlimited in amount—leads to a comparable "self-censorship." . . . Under such a rule, would-be critics of official conduct may be deterred from voicing their criticism, even though it is believed to be true and even though it is in fact true, because of doubt whether it can be proved in court or fear of the expense of having to do so. They tend to make only statements which "steer far wider of the unlawful zone." . . . The rule thus dampens the vigor and limits the variety of public debate. It is inconsistent with the First and Fourteenth Amendments.

The constitutional guarantees require, we think, a federal rule that prohibits a public official from recovering damages for a defamatory falsehood relating to his official conduct *unless he proves that the statement was made with "actual malice"—that is, with knowledge that it was false or with reckless disregard of whether it was false or not.* . . . (Italics added)

Justice Black wrote a separate opinion, in which Justice Douglas concurred. The Court, declared Justice Black, did not go far enough. The rule, in his view, should be:

An unconditional right to say what one pleases about public affairs is what I consider to be the minimum guarantee of the First Amendment.

Justice Goldberg also wrote a separate opinion in which Justice Douglas concurred. His view, like that of Justice Black is that the Court stopped short of what the law should be. To ask a jury to search the mind of one accused of libel for malice is to ask the average man and woman to probe a complex phenomenon. Such an approach creates too many problems.

The rule of Law in the *Sullivan* case has been applied to public figures. A man or woman who has achieved success in his field and is so recognized by the media cannot collect for defamation of character unless there is proof of actual malice. There must be proof of lies knowingly printed.

CASE 54

An interesting application of the rule of law in the *The New York Times* Case is presented in *Pickering v. Board of Education*, 391 U.S. 563, 88 S.Ct. 1731, 20 L.Ed.2d 811 (1968). Pickering, a teacher, wrote a letter to the local newspaper, criticizing the Board of Education for its handling of a bond issue and for its allocation of funds. The theme of the letter was that the Board was trying to push tax-supported athletics down the throats of the taxpayers to the detriment of other aspects of education. It is admitted that Pickering made several errors of fact in his letter concerning the budget and the Board. Charged with making false statements and casting aspersions on the members of the Board, Pickering was given a hearing and then was fired.

The Supreme Court, with one Justice dissenting in part, held that the *New York Times* rule applied in this case. Justice Marshall concluded his opinion for the Court:

> In sum, we hold that, in a case such as this, absent proof of false statements knowingly and recklessly made by him, a teacher's exercise of his right to speak on issues of public importance may not furnish the basis for his dismissal from public employment.

The Court did note that where the relationship between a superior and a subordinate in public employment is of such a personal and intimate nature that criticism would undermine the working relationship, the ruling might be different.

CHAPTER 15

THE PENTAGON PAPERS CASE: PRIOR RESTRAINTS ON NEWSPAPERS

CASE 55

New York Times v. United States

United States v. Washington Post Company

403 U.S. 713, 91 S.Ct. 2140, 29 L.Ed.2d 822, June 30, 1971

It had the elements of a mystery. The Pentagon had contracted with the Rand Corporation, a think tank, to do a thorough history of United States policy relating to Vietnam. Eventually, the research resulted in a 47-volume study entitled *History of U. S. Decision-Making Process on Vietnam Policy*. The materials were classified as top secret.

Daniel Ellsberg was one of the men assigned to this job. A hawk with reference to the Vietnam war, he apparently was so influenced by the documents that came to his attention that his views on the war changed radically and he became a dove. Determined to bring to the attention of the American people and to Congress what he believed to be half-truths, misrepresentations and lies by presidents and government officials, Ellsberg took eighteen of these volumes out of the files of the Rand Corporation, had them photocopied, and then returned them. These were all marked *Top Secret*, but Ellsberg argued that this set belonged to three government officials, one of whom gave him permission to read them.

Later, when Ellsberg and Russo, the man who helped him, were tried for this act, the government maintained that they had stolen the documents. Since that case later resulted in a mistrial, neither Russo nor Ellsberg was ever tried again and the issue of their guilt under the law remains undetermined.

In order to publicize what they regarded as crimes against the American people by government officials, Ellsberg and Russo turned the photocopied materials over to the *New York Times*. After studying the materials for three months, the *Times* decided to publish them and on June 13, 1971 the first of the articles appeared. The government tried to get an injunction against the *Times* to stop any further publication on the ground that exposing the top secret documents would injure the war effort, as well as strain relations among the United States and its allies. The *New York Times* replied that the First Amendment prohibits censorship of the press, especially prior to publication.

The United States District Court ruled for the *Times*, but the U. S. Court of Appeals reversed. At the same time, the *Washington Post* began the publication of installments of the *Pentagon Papers* and when the government tried to get an injunction, both the U. S. District Court and the U. S. Court of Appeals sided with the newspaper.

The case was then appealed to the Supreme Court. Since prior restraint was the issue—censorship before publication, speed was of the essence. The longer the courts delayed, the longer the publication would be delayed. With unprecedented speed, the Supreme Court decided the case in four days. Arguments were heard on June 26, 1971; the ruling was handed down on June 30, 1971.

As can be expected, this was a tough case for the nine Justices. On the one hand, there was the claim by the newspapers that freedom of the press is protected by the First Amendment. On the other hand, there was the position of the government that the President is Commander-in-Chief of the Army and Navy and the chief architect of American foreign policy. He and his assistants have the power to decide which documents should be classified as Top Secret. When this is done, no one can see or read these documents without permission. The newspapers had no right to see or publish these documents, declared the Government, especially since Ellsberg did not have any right to their possession. By passing them on to the newspapers, he was committing a crime, so the argument went, and the newspapers had to share that guilt because they were not entitled to possession. Furthermore, argued the Government, publication of the documents would result in grave and irreparable injury to the public interest.

The War At Home

—from *Herblock's State of the Union* (Simon & Schuster, 1972)

The response of the *Times* and *Washington Post* was that freedom of the press means exactly what it says. The events in the Pentagon Papers were really events of the past, known to foreign governments, and should also be known to the American people, since lives and billions of dollars had been expended in this longest war in our history.

> How would you decide this conflict in values? Can you think a way out of this dilemma?

If it is any consolation to you, the Court had so much trouble with this case that the result was a 6 to 3 ruling. The decision of the majority was presented in a *per curiam* opinion—an unsigned opinion giving the decision. Having done this, each of the nine Justices then went on to write his own opinion, giving his own reasons. It is quite an intellectual adventure to assess what each one had to say.

Let us begin with the *per curiam* (unsigned) opinion of the majority. It is brief and to the point.

> . . . Any system of prior restraints of expression comes to this Court bearing a heavy presumption against its constitutional validity. . . . The Government "thus carries a heavy burden of showing justification for the imposition of such a restraint." . . . The District Court for the Southern District of New York in the *New York Times* case, . . . and the District Court for the District of Columbia and the Court of Appeals for the District of Columbia Circuit, . . . in the *Washington Post* case held that the Government had not met that burden. We agree. . . .
>
> The stays entered June 25, 1971, by the Court are vacated. The judgments shall issue forthwith.
>
> So ordered.

The nine opinions which follow are arranged on a continuum ranging from the liberal to the conservative. The first opinion is that of Justice Black, in which Justice Douglas concurred, and it is in the most liberal tradition of both Justices. For these two Justices the issue raised by this case had only one possible answer.

> I adhere to the view that the Government's case against the Washington Post should have been dismissed and that the injunction against the New York Times should have been vacated without oral argument when the cases were first presented to this Court. I believe that every moment's continuance of the injunctions against these newspapers amounts to a flagrant, indefensible, and continuing violation of the First Amendment. . . . In my view it is unfortunate that some of my Brethren are apparently willing to hold that the publication of news may sometimes be enjoined. Such a holding would make a shambles of the First Amendment.

Our Government was launched in 1789 with the adoption of the Constitution. The Bill of Rights, including the First Amendment, followed in 1791. Now, for the first itme in the 182 years since the founding of the Republic, the federal courts are asked to hold that the First Amendment does not mean what it says, but rather means that the Government can halt the publication of current news of vital importance to the people of this country.

In seeking injunctions against these newspapers and in its presentation to the Court, the Executive Branch seems to have forgotten the essential purpose and history of the First Amendment. . . . Both the history and language of the First Amendment support the view that the press must be left free to publish news, whatever the source, without censorship, injunctions, or prior restraints.

In the First Amendment the Founding Fathers gave the free press the protection it must have to fulfill its essential role in our democracy. The press was to serve the governed, not the governors. The Government's power to censor the press was abolished so that the press would remain forever free to censure the Government. The press was protected so that it could bare the secrets of government and inform the people. Only a free and unrestrained press can effectively expose deception in government. And paramount among the responsibilities of a free press is the duty to prevent any part of the government from deceiving the people and sending them off to distant lands to die of foreign fevers and foreign shot and shell. In my view, far from deserving condemnation for their courageous reporting, the New York Times, the Washington Post, and other newspapers should be commended for serving the purpose that the Founding Fathers saw so clearly. In revealing the workings of government that led to the Vietnam war, the newspapers nobly did precisely that which the Founders hoped and trusted they would do. . . .

Justice Douglas's opinion, concurred in by Justice Black, begins with a reaffirmation of the theme that the First Amendment means exactly what it says. Neither Congress nor the President can place any restraints on freedom of the press. Furthermore, says the Justice, there is no law on the books which prohibits the newspapers from publishing the Vietnam documents. As a matter of fact, there has been wide distribution of sets of the Pentagon Papers and the President had sent a set to Congress. Anyone who reads this material is reading history, the story of the past, not future events.

As for those who justify the need for governmental secrecy in cases of this type, Justice Douglas responds:

The dominant purpose of the First Amendment was to prohibit the widespread practice of governmental suppression of embarrassing information. It is common knowledge that the First Amendment was adopted against the widespread use of the common law of seditious libel to punish the dissemination of material that is embarrassing to the powers-that-be. . . . The present cases will, I think, go down in history as the most dramatic illustration of that principle. A debate of large proportions goes on in the Nation over our posture in Vietnam.

That debate antedated the disclosure of the contents of the present documents. The latter are highly relevant to the debate in progress.

Secrecy in government is fundamentally anti-democratic, perpetuating bureaucratic errors. Open debate and discussion of public issues are vital to our national health. On public questions there should be "uninhibited, robust, and wide-open" debate. . . .

The stays in these cases that have been in effect for more than a week constitute a flouting of the principles of the First Amendment. . . .

WILLIAM O. DOUGLAS
1898–

Associate Justice
1935–1975

Justice Brennan's opinion stresses that the general rule must continue to be no restraints on freedom of the press—not even temporary injunctions. "So far as I can determine," says the Justice, "never before has the United States sought to enjoin a newspaper from publishing information in its possession." Certainly there are times when an injunction may be necessary. In wartime, for example, a government could prohibit interference with recruitment or the publication of sailing dates of transports or the number or location of troops. These are emergency situations. The government made no such claims here. What the government contended was that the publication of the Pentagon Papers "could" or "might" or "may" prejudice the national interest: This is not sufficient to warrant an injunction because:

> . . . The First Amendment tolerates absolutely no prior judicial restraints of the press predicated upon surmise or conjecture that untoward consequences may result.

Justice Stewart begins his opinion, in which Justice White concurred by posing the dilemma confronting the Court. Since the advent of the nuclear missile age, the President possesses enormous power in the areas of national defense and international relations. This power is virtually unchecked. Perhaps the only practical check on this power is "an informed and critical public opinion which alone can here protect the values of democratic government." He goes on to say:

> For this reason, it is perhaps here that a press that is alert, aware, and free most vitally serves the basic purpose of the First Amendment. For without an informed and free press there cannot be an enlightened people.

POTTER STEWART
1915–
Associate Justice
1958–

The problem here is that secrecy is often necessary in matters of national security and international relations. Secrecy for its own sake, however, must be avoided.

For when everything is classified, then nothing is classified, and the system becomes one to be disregarded by the cynical or the careless, and to be manipulated by those intent on self-protection or self-promotion. I should suppose, in short, that the hallmark of a truly effective internal security system would be the maximum possible disclosure, recognizing that secrecy can best be preserved only when credibility is truly maintained.

Perhaps the way out of the dilemma posed by the right of the people to know versus the responsibility of the President to conduct foreign policy is through "specific and appropriate criminal laws to protect government property and preserve government secrets." In this case, however, the Court has not been asked to interpret any laws or regulations. It is being asked to grant an injunction against the press. This request, concludes Justice Stewart cannot be granted because there is no evidence that disclosure of the Pentagon Papers "will result in direct, immediate, and irreparable damage to our nation or its people."

Justice White's opinion, in which Justice Stewart concurred, approaches the issue from another position. He believes that the publication of the documents "will do substantial damage to public interests." The remedy for this type of conduct, however, is a criminal action against the newspapers, not a request for an injunction. Prior restraint—censorship before publication—must be based on overwhelming evidence of "substantial dangers to the national interests." Since Congress has not enacted any guidelines to assist the Court in evaluating documents on the measuring rod of grave or irreparable damage or danger to the national interest, it is difficult to curb the press before publication. At a criminal proceeding after publication of the documents, proof of criminal conduct on the part of the newspapers can be weighed and judged under the laws enacted by Congress and under the procedures of due process. An action for an injunction was not the proper remedy in this case.

With Justice Marshall's concurring opinion, the Court's decision was supported by six Justices. Justice Marshall, like the others, felt it necessary to differentiate his position. He pointed out that ours is a government of separation of powers. Congress makes the law; the Executive enforces the law; and the Judiciary interprets the law. On two occasions in 1917 and in 1953 the Congress was asked to enact a law prohibiting the publication of classified information relating to national defense that might be useful to the enemy. On each occasion Congress refused. Now the President comes to the courts and requests that they censor newspapers. What Congress refused to do, the combination of the President and the Supreme Court cannot do. It would be a dangerous precedent to use an injunction to accomplish what Congress refused to enact. This would be government by injunction—a course of action to be rejected within the framework of a trial.

The three dissenters agreed on one point. Here, they said, we have one of the most important cases in American history and it is being rushed through the courts. Eighteen volumes of documents have to be studied and certain of these documents may be crucial to our national security. Yet, within a period of less than three weeks the case has moved from the U. S. District Courts to the Supreme Court and, now, the case is being decided in four days. Why the feverish haste?

Chief Justice Burger begins his dissent with this theme.
These cases are not simple . . . We do not know the facts of the cases. No District Judge knew all the facts. No Court of Appeals Judge knew all the facts. No member of this Court knows all the facts. Why are we in this posture, in which only those judges to whom the First Amendment is absolute and permits of no restraint in any circumstances or for any reason, are really in a position to act?
I suggest we are in this posture because these cases have been conducted in unseemly haste. . . .

The *New York Times*, points out the Chief Justice, had "unauthorized possession" of the "purloined documents" for three to four months before it published them. It had the time to analyze 7,000 pages of complex materials. Shouldn't the judiciary have the same opportunity?

Chief Justice Burger then proceeds to read the *Times* a lesson in citizenship.

> To me it is hardly believable that a newspaper long regarded as a great institution in American life would fail to perform one of the basic and simple duties of every citizen with respect to the discovery or possession of stolen property or secret government documents. That duty, I had thought—perhaps naively—was to report forthwith, to responsible public officers. This duty rests on taxi drivers, Justices, and the *New York Times*. The course followed by the *Times*, whether so calculated or not, removed any possibility of orderly litigation of the issues. If the action of the judges up to now has been correct, that result is sheer happenstance.

The result of this "melancholy series of events," remarks the Chief Justice, "is that we literally do not know what we are acting on." He points out that at times the lawyers on both sides were not able to answer factual points raised by the judges. Although they had literally worked "around the clock," even the lawyers could not digest the mass of materials. He concludes with the observation:

> We all crave speedier judicial processes but when judges are pressured as in these cases the result is a parody of the judicial function.

In his judgment the case should be sent back to the District Court for a trial in accordance with traditional judicial procedures.

> The opinion of Justice Harlan, in which Justice Blackmun and Chief Justice Burger concurred, also speaks of the "frenzied train of events" and "irresponsibly feverish" actions. What makes this opinion unique among the dissenters is that it lists questions of fact, of law, and of judgment, that must be answered before a conclusion can be reached on the merits of the case.

Like Justice Marshall, Justice Harlan builds his decision around separation of powers. Unlike Justice Marshall, Justice Harlan concludes that the judiciary must show great restraint in interfering with the President's power over foreign affairs. The judiciary can inquire into two issues only. Does the subject matter of the dispute fall within the President's foreign relations power? Would disclosure impair the national security, according to the views of the Secretary of State or Secretary of Defense? The answers to these two questions should form the basis for the Court's rulings. Since this was not done in these cases, he would send them back to the lower court for reconsideration.

Justice Blackmun begins his opinion with the same quote which marks the opening of Justice Harlan's opinion.

> Great cases, like hard cases, make bad law. For great cases are called great, not by reason of their real importance in shaping the law of the future, but because of some accident of immediate overwhelming interest which appeals to the feelings and distorts the judgment. These immediate interests exercise a kind of hydraulic pressure . . . .

This statement by the famous Justice Oliver Wendall Holmes, has been invoked by judges whenever they are confronted with sensational cases. It is often used to warn that the pressure of events may lead to hasty judgments. What is needed is a trial free of "pressure, panic and sensationalism."

Justice Blackmun points out that the issues before the Court deal only with a few documents designated as critical. Therefore, he concludes, permit the newspapers to publish those which are not in issue and focus the cases on those which are in dispute.

Like Chief Justice Burger, Justice Blackmun found it necessary to give both newspapers a lecturette in civic education.

> I strongly urge, and sincerely hope, that these two newspapers will be fully aware of their ultimate responsibilities to the United States of America. . . . I hope that damage has not already been done. If, however, damage has been done, and if, with the Court's action today, these newspapers proceed to publish the critical documents and there results therefrom "the death of soldiers, the destruction of alliances, the greatly increased difficulty of negotiation with our enemies, the inability of our diplomats to negotiate," to which list I might add the factors of prolongation of the war and of further delay in the freeing of United States prisoners, then the Nation's people will know where the responsibility for these sad consequences rests.

CHAPTER 16

FREEDOM OF THE PRESS IN THE SCHOOLS

Do secondary school student newspaper editors have the same rights under our Constitution as do the editors and publishers of the public press? Do secondary school students have the right to put out their own newspaper—sometimes referred to as "underground" newspapers? Does the *Tinker* case apply to the student press?

As in the case of hair styles and dress codes, there are two schools of thought. The case of *Eisner v. Stamford (Connecticut) Board of Education*, 440 F.2d 803 (2d Cir. 1971) dealt with students in a Connecticut public high school who produced and distributed a mimeographed newspaper entitled the *Stamford Free Press*. The first three issues were distributed off school grounds. When they requested permission to distribute the issue on school grounds, the Board of Education issued a regulation which prohibited the distribution of written or printed material on school grounds or in school buildings without prior approval of the school administration. The directive contained the following guidelines:

> No material shall be distributed which, either by its content or by the manner of distribution itself, shall interfere with the proper and orderly operation and discipline of the school, will cause violence or disorder, or will constitute an invasion of the rights of others.

The students were prohibited from distributing their paper and they sought an injunction and a declaratory judgment. The federal district court declared the Board's policy an unconstitutional prior restraint on freedom of the press, because the Board's regulations were vague and did not provide "procedural safeguards."

The United States Court of Appeals agreed with the ruling that the Board's policy was unconstitutional but for reasons different from those of the lower court. It was the judgment of the Court of Appeals that prior restraints are permissible under the *Tinker* rule if school authorities can reasonably predict "substantial disruption of or material interference with school." In weighing the scales of students' rights and school discipline, it is necessary for the school authorities to set up specific procedural safeguards for the review of the materials to be distributed. These safeguards must prescribe:

(1) a definite brief period within which review of submitted material will be completed,

(2) to whom and how material may be submitted for clearance.

In a subsequent ruling, a third directive was added:

(3) prompt review procedures where permission is denied.

Although the *Eisner* case of the Second Circuit is the leading authority on its approval of prior restraint provided there are the aforementioned procedural safeguards, the Seventh Circuit has presented an opposing principle. In *Fujishima v. Board of Education (Chicago)*, 460 F.2d 1355 (7th Cir. 1972), three students were suspended. Two had circulated several hundred copies of an underground newspaper before and between classes and during lunch breaks. During a fire drill in school, the third student had handed out leaflets dealing with the Vietnam War and an unsigned copy of a petition calling for a teach-in on the war. The applicable school regulation forbade the distribution on school premises of "any books, tracts, or other publications . . . unless . . . approved by the General Superintendent of Schools."

The Court of Appeals ruled prior restraints in school unconstitutional and declared that the *Eisner* case was "unsound constitutional law."

When it comes to obscenity and libel, the courts will tend to be far more severe in their rulings than when the issue is vulgarity or profanity. The language of the street and the contemporary mode of communication among youth tend to be treated more sympathetically than the outright erotic or the libel of a school official. Instructions to student editors and student publishers in Codes of Responsibility advocate the rule of prudence encompassed within responsible journalism.

CHAPTER 17

FREE PRESS—FAIR TRIAL

Up to this point, we have focused our attention on the nature of a free press. We have examined issues relating to the freedom of the press to criticize public officials. We have also analyzed a Supreme Court ruling prohibiting prior restraint or government censorship of newspapers. The opinions of the Court have shown great respect for the power of the press to satisfy the public need and right to know what is going on in the city, the state, the nation, and the world.

In recent years an interesting problem has developed. The First Amendment's freedom of the press has been on a collision course with the Sixth Amendment's right to a "speedy and public trial, by an impartial jury." It is obvious that newspaper and television coverage of a sensational crime can prejudice the community against an accused to the point where it becomes difficult to select an impartial jury. If or when this happens, what can or should be done? How do we resolve the dilemma of two great valued rights in collision? Which one deserves priority? How can we decide what to do? Let us see how the Supreme Court has grappled with this value conflict.

In answering these questions, it must be remembered that the right to a free press and the right to a fair trial apply both in federal and state cases. Amendments I and VI apply to federal cases. The Supreme Court has ruled that these two important rights also apply to the states under the Fourteenth Amendment's provision that "no state shall deprive any person of life, liberty, and property without due process of law."

CASES

CASE 56

SAM SHEPPARD, THE UNIDENTIFIED INTRUDER, AND THE CLEVELAND PRESS

Sheppard v. Maxwell, Warden

384 U.S. 333, 86 S.Ct. 1507, 16 L.Ed.2d 600 (1966)

It has remained a mystery to this very day. On July 4, 1954 Marilyn Sheppard was bludgeoned to death in the upstairs bedroom of her home. Her husband, Sam Sheppard, told police that he had been sleeping in the downstairs living room, when he had been awakened by a noise. He went upstairs to investigate and was knocked unconscious. When he regained consciousness, he saw that his wife was probably dead. He then checked his son's room and found that he had not been touched. Hearing a noise he hurried downstairs, saw a "form", chased it, fought with it, and was knocked unconscious again. When he recovered, he phoned his friends and they came at once and phoned the police.

The Sheppards were a prominent family in Bay Village, Ohio, a suburb of Cleveland, and the story hit the headlines at once. The headlines and stories which were featured on the front pages of the Cleveland newspapers were:

"Doctor Balks At Lie Test"

"Why No Inquest? Do It Now, Dr. Gerber"

"Why Don't Police Quiz Top Suspect?"

"Why Isn't Sam Sheppard in Jail?"

"Quit Stalling—Bring Him In."

Among the front page editorials that appeared between the day of the murder and the day of the inquest was one which declared that "someone is getting away with murder" because of "friendships, relationships, hired lawyers, a husband who ought to have been subjected instantly to the same third-degree to which any other person under similar circumstances is subjected." The implications seemed to be that the authorities were treating the socially prominent Sheppard with kid gloves.

When the inquest took place, it was held in a school gymnasium with reporters, television cameras, radio technicians, and hundreds of spectators. At one point, Sheppard's counsel was ejected by the Coroner, who received cheers, hugs, and kisses from some of the women in the audience.

Sheppard was arrested and his trial began two weeks before the November general election. Both the trial judge and the chief prosecutor were candidates for re-election. The names and addresses of the jurors were published in the newspapers. During the trial the jurors were not sequestered, but were permitted to go home. The courtroom was so crowded with reporters, cameramen, television and radio personnel that there was much confusion and it was difficult for witnesses and counsel to be heard.

Sheppard was found guilty and his appeals to the state courts of appeal, as well as to the Supreme Court in 1956, were denied. In 1965 Sheppard retained the services of a young lawyer, F. Lee Bailey, who decided to institute a writ of habeas corpus proceeding in the

United States District Court. This "great writ" requires that a person who claims that he is being illegally detained be brought before a judge to determine the legality of his confinement. This writ is generally sought by those who claim that their conviction violated due process of law requirements. He won in the District Court, lost in the United States Court of Appeals, and appealed to the United States Supreme Court.

> If you had to decide this case, what would you have done? How would you have reasoned? Do you think Sheppard deserved another trial?

With only Justice Black dissenting without opinion, the Court decided that Sheppard had been denied due process of law. Justice Clark's opinion turns first to the role of the press.

> A responsible press has always been regarded as a handmaiden of effective judicial administration, especially in the criminal field. Its function in this regard is documented by an impressive record of service over several centuries. The press does not simply publish information about trials that guards against the miscarriage of justice by subjecting the police, prosecutors, and judicial processes to extensive public scrutiny and criticism. This Court has, therefore, been unwilling to place any direct limitations on the freedom traditionally exercised by the news media . . . we have consistently required that the press have a free hand, even though we sometimes deplored its sensationalism.

There comes a time, however, when the press and other media can interfere with "the essential requirement of the fair and orderly administration of justice." When "prejudice, passion, and excitement" invade the temple of justice, it is difficult for the jury's verdict to be based solely on the evidence presented in court.

Sheppard had not been granted a change of venue, nor had the jury been sequestered. Jurors had been subjected to so much newspaper, radio and television coverage that they became celebrities. They did not receive adequate instructions from the trial judge not to read or listen to anything concerning the case.

In the words of Justice Clark:

> For months the virulent publicity about Sheppard and the murder had made the case notorious . . . Furthermore, the trial began two weeks before a hotly contested election at which both Chief Prosecutor Mahon and Judge Blythin were candidates for judgeships . . . The fact is that bedlam reigned at the courthouse during the trial and newsmen took over practically the entire courtroom, hounding most of the participants in the trial, especially Sheppard . . .

> The carnival atmosphere at trial could easily have been avoided since the courtroom and the courthouse premises are subject to the control of the court . . . Bearing in mind the massive pretrial publicity, the judge should have adopted stricter rules governing the use of the courtroom by newsmen . . . the court should have insulated the witnesses . . . the court should have made some effort to control the release of leads, information, and gossip to the press by police officers, witnesses, and the counsel for both sides.

In other words, according to Justice Clark, both the press and the trial judge were to blame for a denial of due process. Therefore, concluded the Justice,

> Since the state trial judge did not fulfill his duty to protect Sheppard from the inherently prejudicial publicity which saturated the community and to control disruptive influences in the courtroom, we reverse the denial of the habeas petition. The case is remanded to the District Court with instructions to issue the writ and order that Sheppard be released from custody unless the State puts him to his charges again within a reasonable time.

Sheppard was given a second trial and was found not guilty.

The case had a significant ripple effect. The American Bar Association, as well as local bar associations, published reports suggesting standards of conduct for judges, prosecutors, lawyers and other criminal justice personnel in criminal proceedings. The American Newspaper Publishers Association responded with a report of its own on suggested procedures for reporting criminal trials.

The issue of free press—fair trial continues with the problem of massive publicity surrounding sensational cases. A recent attempt by a trial judge to resolve the problem with a "gag" order reached the Supreme Court in 1976.

CASE 57

A TRIAL JUDGE ISSUES A "GAG ORDER" AGAINST THE MEDIA

Nebraska Press Association v. Stuart, Judge, District Court of Lincoln County, Nebraska

427 U.S. 539, 96 S.Ct. 2791, 49 L.Ed.2d 683 (1976)

As in the Sheppard case, the events that took place on October 18, 1975 involved a sensational crime that hit the front pages of newspapers and television screens. Six members of the Henry Kellie family were found brutally murdered in their home in Sutherland, Nebraska, a small community of 850.

Ervin Charles Simants was regarded as the prime suspect. His description was released to reporters and he was apprehended, arrested, and arraigned the following day. Within the next three days, the media coverage was becoming so extensive that both the prosecutor and Simants' lawyer feared that it would be impossible to impanel an impartial jury and conduct a fair trial. By this time everyone had learned the lesson of the *Sheppard* case. Both attorneys asked the County Court judge to issue an order prohibiting the publication of prejudicial news. On October 22nd, the judge issued an order prohibiting everyone in attendance from releasing "in any form or manner whatsoever any testimony or evidence adduced." The order also required the press to observe the Nebraska Bar-Press Guidelines, setting forth voluntary standards for reporting crimes and criminal trials.

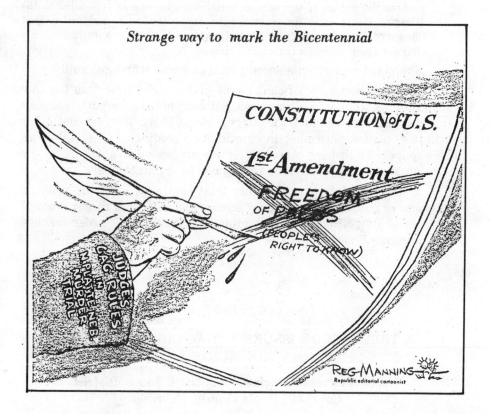

Several press and broadcast associations, as well as publishers, protested the restrictive order imposed by the County Court. The District Court modified the County Court order and, when this was appealed to the Nebraska Supreme Court, the highest court in the state modified the order once again. This time the media were prohibited from reporting on only three matters:

(a) the existence and nature of any confessions or admissions made by the defendant to law enforcement officers,

(b) any confessions or admissions made to any third parties, except members of the press, and

(c) other facts "strongly implicative" of the accused.

This order, which expired when the jury was impaneled, was appealed to the Supreme Court. In the meantime, Simants had been convicted of murder and sentenced to death. While his appeal was pending in the Nebraska Supreme Court, the United States Supreme Court decided the constitutionality of the so-called "gag order."

The Supreme Court agreed unanimously on the decision, but four opinions were written in view of the significance of the free press-fair trial confrontation. Chief Justice Burger delivered the opinion of the Court, in which two other Justices concurred. He began with an interesting history of the issue:

> The problems presented by this case are almost as old as the Republic. Neither in the Constitution nor in contemporaneous writings do we find that the conflict between these two important rights was anticipated, yet it is inconceivable that the authors of the Constitution were unaware of the potential conflicts between the right to an unbiased jury and the guarantee of freedom of the press. The unusually able lawyers who helped write the Constitution and later drafted the Bill of Rights were familiar with the historic episode in which John Adams defended British soldiers charged with homicide for firing into a crowd of Boston demonstrators; they were intimately familiar with the clash of the adversary system and the part that passions of the populace sometimes play in influencing potential jurors. They did not address themselves directly to the situation presented by this case; their chief concern was the need for freedom of expression in the political arena and the dialogue in ideas. But they recognized that there were risks to private rights from an unfettered press.
> . . .
> The trial of Aaron Burr in 1807 presented Chief Justice Marshall, presiding as a trial judge, with acute problems in selecting an unbiased jury. Few people in the area of Virginia from which jurors were drawn had not formed some opinions concerning Mr. Burr or the case, from newspaper accounts and heightened discussion both private and public. . . .

The trial of Bruno Hauptmann in a small New Jersey community, for the abduction and murder of the Charles Lindbergh's infant child, probably was the most widely covered trial up to that time, and the nature of the coverage produced widespread public reaction. Criticism was directed at the "carnival" atmosphere that pervaded the community and the courtroom itself. Responsible leaders of press and the legal profession—including other judges—pointed out that much of this sorry performance could have been controlled by a vigilant trial judge and by other public officers subject to the control of the court. . . .

The excesses of press and radio and lack of responsibility of those in authority in the Hauptmann case and others of that era led to efforts to develop voluntary guidelines for courts, lawyers, press and broadcasters. . . . The effort was renewed in 1965 when the American Bar Association embarked on a project to develop standards for all aspects of criminal justice, including guidelines to accommodate the right to a fair trial and the rights of a free press. . . . The resulting standards, approved by the Association in 1968, received support from most of the legal profession. . . . In the wake of these efforts, the cooperation between bar associations and members of the press led to the adoption of voluntary guidelines like Nebraska's.

. . .

Guidelines, says the Chief Justice, are not enough because they may not be binding on everyone.

In practice, of course, even the most ideal guidelines are subjected to powerful strains when a case such as Simants' arises, with reporters from many parts of the country on the scene. Reporters from distant places are unlikely to consider themselves bound by local standards. They report to editors outside the area covered by the guidelines, and their editors are likely to be guided only by their own standards. To contemplate how a state court can control acts of a newspaper or broadcaster outside its jurisdiction, even though the newspapers and broadcasts reach the very community from which jurors are to be selected, suggests something of the practical difficulties of managing such guidelines.

Chief Justice Burger then goes on to say that cases like that of Sam Sheppard had alerted the courts to the dangers of massive prejudicial pretrial publicity on the thinking of potential jurors. The question in this case is whether a "gag order" is a constitutionally permissible method of preventing the press from influencing jurors and denying an accused the right to a fair trial.

The Chief Justice concedes that this issue is not an easy one to resolve because the "authors of the Bill of Rights did not undertake to assign priorities as between the First Amendment and Sixth Amendment rights, ranking one as superior to the other." Nevertheless, he goes on to say, we have developed a tradition that opposes censorship or prior restraints on the press. Granted that the trial judge was right in concluding that the intense and pervasive pretrial publicity, would impair the defendant's right to a fair trial, was the "gag order" the only means available to protect the accused? The *Sheppard* case had enumerated other ways of trying to assure an accused a fair trial:

(a) change of trial venue to a place less exposed to the intense publicity that seemed imminent in Lincoln County;

(b) postponement of the trial to allow public attention to subside;

(c) the use of searching questioning of prospective jurors to screen out those with fixed opinions as to guilt or innocence;

(d) the use of emphatic and clear instructions on the sworn duty of each juror to decide the issues only on evidence presented in open court.

These four measures were available and could have been used to protect Simants' rights. Prior restraint must be a last resort until all else has failed.

Could the "gag order" really have protected Simants in a small community of 850, where rumor and gossip travel quickly and cannot be stopped? The Chief Justice did not think that it could.

A third reason why the "gag order" was constitutionally unacceptable was its vagueness. It implied that confessions at public hearings could not be reported. This is contrary to the law which permits the press to report events that take place in the courtroom. The order also prohibited the publication of "implicative" information, a term "too vague" and "too broad" under the First Amendment.

In view of these reasons, the "gag order" is an unconstitutional infringement on freedom of the press.

Justice White agrees with the Chief Justice's opinion but goes much further. He doubts whether "gag orders" of the press would ever be justified.

Justice Powell also agrees with the Court's judgment but feels it necessary to clarify his position. To justify a prior restraint order, it must be shown that there is "a high likelihood of preventing, directly and irreparably, the impaneling" of an impartial jury.

Justice Brennan writes a long concurring opinion, in which Justices Marshall and Stewart joined. Prior restraints on the press are "the essence of censorship" and are to be condemned, in cases of this type, since judges have available to them "a broad spectrum of devices for ensuring that fundamental fairness is accorded the accused." Past decisions have indicated that at certain times and under certain circumstances prior censorship might be constitutional. In time of war it might be imposed if the evidence disclosed that publication would result in "direct, immediate, and irreparable damage to our Nation and its people" or "must *inevitably*, *directly*, and *immediately* cause the occurrence of an event kindred to imperiling the safety of a transport already at sea." To permit "gag orders" or prior censorship in this type of case would create a new and dangerous precedent.

It should be observed, declares Justice Brennan, that most of the restrained information was already in the public domain. This could have been prevented, since court personnel and attorneys are officers of the court and the judge could have instructed them concerning the release of information.

To counter the impact of prejudicial publicity, the trial judge could use the *voir dire* ("to tell the truth") examination of prospective jurors to detect prejudice, and the continuance of the trial or a change of venue to counter prejudicial publicity. Judges are not so helpless that they need "gag orders" as a weapon to assure a fair trial. In the last analysis, there is available the road to appeal.

Justice Brennan, in denying the power to issue "gag orders" concludes:

> However, the press may be arrogant, tyrannical, abusive, and sensationalist, just as it may be incisive, probing, and informative. But at least in the context of prior restraints on publication, the decision of what, when, and how to publish is for editors, not judges. . . . Every restrictive order imposed on the press in this case was accordingly an unconstitutional prior restraint on the freedom of the press . . .

Justice Stevens, in a brief concurring opinion, agrees with Justice Brennan's sweeping condemnation of "gag orders."

A reading of the opinions discloses that five Justices (Brennan, Marshall, Stevens, Stewart, and White) have taken the position that they would oppose "gag" orders by judges as a means of combatting prejudicial pretrial publicity.

SOME CONCLUDING THOUGHTS

Two great constitutional principles—free press and fair trial—continue to be on a collision course and the courts will continue to be confronted by newspaper and television coverage which will raise issues of priority of values. In trying to grapple with these issues, a number of approaches are available:

(1) The press should be free to publish the news with a minimum of restraints for two reasons: a threat of criminal or civil penalties after publication *chills* freedom of expression, while prior restraint *freezes* it. Only the gravest natural emergency justifies censorship.

(2) When a person's life or liberty may be at stake in a trial, the press must exercise self-restraint in reporting the events surrounding the episode. By inflaming the minds of prospective jurors and arousing prejudice and hatred, an accused is doomed to conviction.

(3) Chief Justice Burger has commented that:

The authors of the Bill of Rights did not undertake to assign priorities as between First Amendment and Sixth Amendment rights, ranking one as superior to the other.

According to this position, a balancing of these two principles will determine which deserves priority in any given situation.

At this time, it is evident that judges who issue "gag orders" will not be supported by our High Court unless it can be clearly shown that change of venue, postponement of the trial, *voir dire* examination of prospective jurors, and the instructions of judges will not succeed in creating the atmosphere for an impartial trial. Then—and only then—may some of the Justices be willing to concede that the media may have gone too far in its prejudicial pretrial publicity.

CHAPTER 18

OBSCENITY AND PORNOGRAPHY

One of the most troublesome subjects in American society and in American law is that which deals with obscenity and pornography. On the one hand, there are charges of filth, lewd, smut, and dirt. On the other hand, there are replies of literary, artistic, serious, and creative. Behind this battle of words, of charges and counter-charges, is an awesome problem. Where does one draw the line between the individual's freedom to express thoughts, views, feelings, and fantasies and society's responsibility to protect the morals and welfare of the community?

This confrontation has taken a variety of forms. Attempts have been made to remove books from classrooms and libraries; legislation has been enacted requiring licensing or previewing of films; shows and "topless" bars have been banned; and the use of the mails has been prohibited for certain types of material. Inevitably, these conflicts of values have found their way into the courts.

So many cases have been decided and so many principles have been proclaimed that it would require a massive volume to do them justice. Instead of delving into the thicket of these rulings, we shall try to summarize the state of the law in the summer of 1977.

Chief Justice Burger, in referring to the cases in this area remarked:

> We have seen a variety of views among the members of the Court unmatched in any other course of constitutional adjudication.

The reason for this multitude of tongues is that the Court is dealing with censorship, a practice which runs headlong into the wall of the First Amendment. How strong that wall really is depends on the views of the Justices. Let us look at some examples:

> . . . implicit in the history of the First Amendment is the rejection of obscenity as utterly without redeeming importance. This rejection for that reason is mirrored in the universal judgment that obscenity should be restrained, reflected in the international agreement of over 50 nations, in the obscenity laws of all the 48 states, and in the 20 obscenity laws enacted by the Congress from 1842 to 1956 . . . . We hold that obscenity is not within the area of constitutionally protected speech or press. . . .

However, sex and obscenity are not synonymous. Obscene material is material which deals with sex in a manner appealing to prurient interest.

> Justice Brennan for the majority in
> *Roth v. United States*
> *Alberts v. California*
> 354 U.S. 476, 77 S.Ct. 1304, 1 L.Ed.
> 2d 1498 (1957)

It is with regret that I write this dissenting opinion. However, the public should know of the continuous flow of pornographic material reaching this Court and the increasing problem States have in controlling it. *Memoirs of a Woman of Pleasure*, the book involved here, is typical. I have "stomached" past cases for almost ten years without much outcry. Though I am not known to be a purist—or a shrinking violet—the book is too much even for me. It is important that the Court has refused to declare it obscene and thus gives it further circulation. In order to give my remarks the proper setting I have been obliged to portray the book's contents, which gives me embarrassment.

> Justice Clark dissenting in
> *A Book Named "John Cleland's*
> *Memoirs of A Woman of Pleasure"*
> *v. Attorney General of Massachu-*
> *setts*, 383 U.S. 413, 86 S.Ct. 975, 16
> L.Ed.2d 1 (1966)

I would give the broad sweep of the First Amendment full support. I have the same confidence in the ability of our people to reject noxious literature as I have in their capacity to sort out the true from the false in theology, economics, politics, or any other field.

> Justice Douglas in the *Roth* case cited
> above

Censorship reflects a society's lack of confidence in itself. It is a hallmark of an authoritarian regime. Long ago those who wrote our First Amendment chartered a different course. They believed that a society can be truly strong only when it is truly free. . . . the Constitution protects coarse expression as well as refined, and vulgarity no less than elegance. A book worthless to me may convey something of value to my neighbor. In the free society to which our Constitution has committed us, it is for each to choose for himself.

> Justice Stewart dissenting in
> *Ginzburg v. United States*
> 383 U.S. 463, 86 S.Ct. 942, 16 L.Ed.
> 2d 31 (1966)

By the mid-1950's the Court finally arrived at what seemed like a working rule, consisting of three criteria:

1. The dominant theme of the material taken as a whole, not on the basis of selected passages, appeals to a prurient in-

terest in sex. Prurient is defined as having a tendency to excite lustful thoughts.

2. The material is patently offensive because it affronts contemporary community standards—the conscience of the community—relating to the description or representation of sexual matters. The test of the publication should be its impact on the average person in the community, not on the young and immature. This was interpreted to mean the national community rather than the local one.

3. The material is utterly without redeeming social value.

By the mid-1960's a fourth criteria was added in the case of *Ginzburg v. United States*, 383 U.S. 463, 86 S.Ct. 942, 16 L.Ed.2d 31 (1966). Ginzburg had used the US mails to advertise three publications. The charge against him was not that the publications were obscene, but rather that the advertising of these materials through the mails was aimed specifically at "the sordid business of pandering—appealing to the erotic interest of the customers." In other words, the advertising promised to deliver materials which could satisfy the prurient interests of the buyer.

Ginzburg invoked the First Amendment, but he could not convince more than four Justices (Black, Harlan, Douglas, and Stewart). Justice Brennan, writing the opinion of the Court, concluded that materials can be obscene in one context and not in another. In this case, the material was advertised in such a manner that it resulted in "an exploitation of interest in titillation by pornography." By accentuating sexual matters, the advertising gave the publications the cast of obscenity.

The four dissenters wrote ringing defenses of First Amendment Freedoms and denounced censorship, especially that which converts non-obscene materials to pornographic simply because of the advertising.

In 1973 the Court returned once again to "the intractable obscenity problem," in the words of Justice Harlan, and once again, there was sharp disagreement. In *Miller v. California*, 413 U.S. 15, 93 S.Ct. 2607, 37 L.Ed.2d 419 the Court was confronted with a violation of the California obscenity law. The defendant was accused of mailing brochures of four "adult-type" books and a film, depicting men and women engaged in sexual acts. The problem revolved, in part, on the issue as to whether the material should be judged according to national standards, as seemed to be the practice up to this time, or whether the test should be the standards in the state of California.

Five of the Justices agreed on what now seem to be the present (1977) criteria for judging obscenity. In the words of Chief Justice Burger, writing for the majority:

> The basic guidelines for the trier of fact must be: (a) whether "the average person, applying contemporary community standards" would find that the work, taken as a whole, appeals to the prurient interest. . . . (b) whether the work depicts or describes, in a patently offensive way, sexual conduct specifically defined by the applicable state law, and (c) whether the work, taken as a whole, lacks serious literary, artistic, political, or scientific value. We do not adopt as a constitutional standard the *"utterly* without redeeming social value" test of *Memoirs v. Massachusetts* . . . ;

He goes on to say:

> Sex and nudity may not be exploited without limit by films or pictures exhibited or sold in places of public accommodation any more than live sex and nudity can be exhibited or sold without limit in such public places. At a minimum, prurient, patently offensive depiction or description of sexual conduct must have serious literary, artistic, political, or scientific value to merit First Amendment protection. . . .

The Chief Justice could not let the arguments of the four dissenters go unanswered.

> The dissenting Justices sound the alarm of repression. But, in our view, to equate the free and robust exchange of ideas and political debate with commercial exploitation of obscene material demeans the grand conception of the First Amendment and its high purposes in the historic struggle for freedom. It is a "misuse of the great guarantees of free speech and free press . . .." . . . The First Amendment protects works which, taken as a whole, have serious literary, artistic, political or scientific value, regardless of whether the government or a majority of the people approve of the ideas these works represent. "The protection given speech and press was fashioned to assure unfettered interchange of *ideas* for the bringing about of political and social changes desired by the people," *Roth v. United States* . . .. But the public portrayal of hard core sexual conduct for its own sake, and for the ensuing commercial gain, is a different matter.

The significance of this ruling is that it replaces the national standard of what is patently offensive by a local community standard for judging obscene material. A national standard, stresses the Chief Justice, is an abstract formulation, while contemporary community standards would be more familiar to lay jurors.

With this decision, the Court, perhaps unthinkingly, opened a Pandora's box of standards. What is a local community? Is it the city, the town, or the state? Isn't it possible for a rural community and an urban community in the same region to have different community standards of pornography?

It should also be noted that this ruling replaced the "utterly without redeeming social value" criterion with a more demanding guideline: the work, taken as a whole, must lack serious literary, artistic, political, or scientific value. The latter rule makes it easier to condemn material as obscene.

The four dissenting Justices wrote two opinions. Justice Douglas restated his well-known views:

> . . . "obscenity" is not mentioned in the Constitution or Bill of Rights. And the First Amendment makes no such exception from "the press" which it undertakes to protect nor, as I have said on other occasions, is an exception necessarily implied, for there was no recognized exception to the free press at the time the Bill of Rights was adopted which treated "obscene" publications differently from other types of papers, magazines, and books. So there are no constitutional guidelines for deciding what is and what is not "obscene." The Court is at large because we deal with tastes and standards of literature.

The dissent of Justice Brennan, concurred in by Justices Stewart and Marshall, found the California obscenity law so "overbroad" as to be unconstitutional.

CASE 59

Does it make any difference if an obscenity law is enacted to protect minors? Will the Court draw a distinction between the reading materials designed for adults and acceptable under the law and, at the same time, condemn the sale of the same materials to minors?

New York State had enacted a criminal obscenity statute which prohibited the sale to minors under 17 years of age material defined to be obscene on the basis of its appeal to minors, regardless of whether it would be regarded as obscene for adults. Among the provisions of the law was one which declared it a crime knowingly to sell to a minor under 17 "any picture which depicts nudity . . . and which is harmful to minors." The accused, the owner of a stationery store and luncheonette, sold several "girlie" magazines to a 16-year old boy. He was convicted under the law and appealed through the courts.

In a 6 to 3 decision, the Supreme Court upheld the conviction. Justice Brennan, speaking for the majority, agreed that the magazines in question were not obscene for adults. The legislature could, however, single out minors for state protection for the following reasons:

> The well-being of its children is of course a subject within the State's constitutional power to regulate, and, in our view, two interests justify the limitations . . . upon the availability of sex material to minors under 17, at least if it was rational for the legislature to find that the minors' exposure to such material might be harmful. . . .

The legislature could properly conclude that parents and others, teachers for example, who have this primary responsibility for children's well-being are entitled to the support of laws designed to aid discharge of that responsibility. . . .

The State also has an independent interest in the well-being of its youth . . . an interest "to protect the welfare of children" and to see that they are "safeguarded from abuses" which might prevent their "growth into free and independent well-developed men and citizens." The only question remaining, therefore, is whether the New York Legislature might rationally conclude, as it has, that exposure to the materials proscribed . . . constitutes such an "abuse."

Justice Brennan goes on to say that, since the majority cannot say that there is no rational relationship of the law to the objective of safeguarding minors from harm, the New York law is constitutional.

Justice Stewart concurred with this thought:

I think a State may permissibly determine that, at least in some precisely delineated areas, a child—like someone in a captive audience— is not possessed of that full capacity for individual choice which is the presupposition of First Amendment guarantees. . . .

Justice Douglas dissented on familiar grounds, with Justice Black concurring:

. . . As I read the First Amendment, it was designed to keep the State and the hands of all state officials off the printing presses of America and off the distribution systems for all printed literature. . . .

Justice Fortas dissented on the ground that no attempt had been made by the Court to determine whether the material was obscene and whether there had been pushing or pandering.

The obscenity-pornography controversy will continue in the years to come in many communities. Films, plays, books, and songs will be condemned and defended. Boards of Education will continue to be confronted with requests to remove textbooks and library books from the schools.

Out of this confrontation of public morality and public law will continue to emerge principles defining the nature and scope of the idea of liberty. In time it will reflect the temper of the times and the philosophies of the Justices.

CHAPTER 19

FREEDOM OF EXPRESSION IN WARTIME
AND IN TIMES OF CRISIS

The Constitution and the Bill of Rights read exactly the same, whether in peace time or war time. The words may be the same, but the interpretations differ. War brings with it clouds of suspicion and waves of hate, and the climate of opinion favors self-preservation at all costs. Among the casualties of war are the rights of dissenters, non-conformists, and groups whose allegiance to the war effort is questioned by the majority, as well as by law-makers and other public officials. This hostility occurs during both hot and cold wars.

In the undeclared war with France in 1798, The Federalist Party enacted the Alien and Sedition Acts. The Sedition Act, one of the first national laws in American history to interfere with freedom of expression, declared that anyone who uttered or published any "false, scandalous, or malicious" statements concerning the Government of the United States, the Congress, or the President "with intent to defame . . . or to bring . . . into contempt or disrepute" shall be punished by a fine not exceeding $2000 or by imprisonment not exceeding two years. The object of the law was to discredit and to weaken Thomas Jefferson's Republican Party. Under this law twenty-five persons were arrested and ten were convicted and punished. When Jefferson became President in 1801, he pardoned all who had been convicted and the Sedition Act was permitted to expire. It was not revived until World War I.

Why wasn't the constitutionality of the Sedition Law tested before the Supreme Court? It was not until 1803 that John Marshall announced his famous ruling in *Marbury v. Madison* that the Supreme Court had the power under the Constitution to declare a law of Congress unconstitutional. This principle of judicial review had not, as yet, been invoked.

Perhaps one of the most interesting sidelights on the 1798 Sedition Law is the comment made by Justice Brennan in the *New York Times v. Sullivan* case (1964). He used that occasion to observe that the judgment of history had declared this law unconstitutional.

When the United States entered World War I, in 1917, Congress enacted the Espionage Act, which declared unlawful espionage activities, as well as any attempts to cause insubordination in the armed forces. In 1918, this law was amended by the Sedition Act, penalizing any "disloyal, profane, scurrilous, or abusive language" regarding our form of government, the Constitution, the flag, and the uniform of the armed forces.

This time the two laws were carried to the Supreme Court and they were upheld in *Schenck v. United States*, 249 U.S. 47, 39 S.Ct. 247, 63 L.Ed. 470 (1919) and *Abrams v. United States*, 250 U.S. 616, 40 S.Ct. 17, 63 L.Ed. 1173 (1919). It was in the *Schenck* case that Justice Holmes, speaking for a unanimous Court, announced his much discussed and debated "clear and present danger" rule.

OLIVER WENDELL HOLMES
1841–1935

Associate Justice
1902–1932

We admit that in many places and in ordinary times the defendants in saying all that was said in the circular would have been within their constitutional rights. But the character of every act depends upon the circumstances in which it is done. . . . The most stringent protection of free speech would not protect a man in falsely shouting fire in a theatre and causing a panic. . . . The question in every case is whether the words used are used in such circumstances and are of such a nature as to create a clear and present danger that they will bring about the substantive evils that Congress has a right to prevent. It is a question of proximity and degree. When a nation is at war many things that might be said in time of peace are such a hindrance to its effort that their utterance will not be endured so long as men fight and that no court could regard them as protected by any constitutional right.

The Clear and Present Danger Rule has been used as one of the guidelines in deciding freedom of expression cases both in peacetime and in wartime. For example, in the *Feiner* case (pages 103–104 and 107–109 above), in which an unpopular speaker was confronted by a hostile audience, the Court invoked the rule against the speaker on the ground that the episode had created a clear and present danger to those involved.

Although the Sedition Act was repealed in 1921, the post-World War I period saw the prosecution of men and women under state syndicalism and sedition laws. The pervasive fear of those with "radical leanings" led to arrests, convictions and the expulsion of five elected members of the Socialist Party from the New York State legislature.

In 1940, the year after World War II started, Congress passed the first peacetime sedition act in American history, the Alien Registration Act, commonly called the Smith Act. The law made it a crime to teach or to advocate, or to conspire to teach and advocate the overthrow of the United States Government by force or violence. After World War II, the Smith Act was invoked against the leaders and members of the Communist Party. This law was upheld in *Dennis v. U. S.* (Case 62). The Cold War between the Soviet Union and the United States led to the passage of additional legislation. The Internal Security Act of 1950, known as the McCarran Act, imposed registration requirements and travel and federal employment disqualifications on members of Communist-action organizations. In 1954 Congress enacted the Communist Control Act which was designed to outlaw the party.

In the 1960's a series of Supreme Court rulings declared parts of the McCarran Act unconstitutional. The Court was equally unsympathetic to state loyalty legislation and loyalty oaths.

All of this is a part of the history of the idea of liberty and it holds forth important lessons for all who are interested in ebb and flow of interpretations concerning the rights of individuals and organizations in time of peace and in time of war.

SECTION V

THE RIGHT PEACEABLY TO ASSEMBLE

In no country in the world has the principle of association been more successfully used or applied to a greater multitude of objects than in America. Besides the permanent associations which are established by law under the names of townships, cities, and counties, a vast number of others are formed and maintained by the agency of private individuals. . . . In the United States associations are established to promote the public safety, commerce, industry, morality, and religion.

Alexis de Tocqueville. *Democracy in America* (1835)

Freedom of Assembly is an essential element of the American democratic system. . . . The right of assembly lies at the foundation of our system of government. The cornerstone of that system is that government—all government, whether federal, state or local—shall be based on the consent of the governed. But "the consent of the governed" implies not only that the consent shall be uncoerced but also that it shall be grounded on adequate information and discussion. Otherwise the consent would be illusory and a sham.

Bill of Rights Committee of the American Bar Association (Brief Amicus Curiae submitted in the case of *Hague v. CIO* (1939))

INTRODUCTION

The last two rights in the First Amendment are the right of the people peaceably to assemble and the right to petition the government for a redress of grievances. Historically these two rights were so related that the two provisions were read as one: The right of the people peaceably to assemble *in order to* petition the government for a redress of grievances. In this section we shall examine the right to assemble as a separate right because over the years it has been joined with other rights and with due process of law clauses to emerge into the right of association.

Americans are great joiners. The list is almost endless: Boy Scouts and Girl Scouts, fraternities and sororities, social clubs and political clubs, unions and manufacturers' associations, sports clubs and musical societies and lots more. This is one aspect of the right to assemble peaceably and, as we shall see, it is more complex in application than it appears in print.

Another aspect of the right to assemble peaceably is the street meeting or the assembly in a hired hall. It can be described as a limited one-shot affair, a meeting held for a specific purpose at a specified time. It does not have the continuity of the Association. Such street affairs or assemblages as the marches on Washington, vigils for or against some public policy, or gathering in parks represent this second type of assembly. A third aspect of this right arises out of loyalty legislation designed to discourage membership in unpopular or subversive organizations.

Where does one draw the line between a lawful assembly and an unlawful one? Where does one draw the line between a lawful street meeting and an unlawful one? Does it matter in the eyes of the law if the organization is the Ku Klux Klan, the Socialist Party, the Communist Party, the National Association for the Advancement of Colored People, the American Civil Liberties Union, or the John Birch Society? Does it matter in the eyes of the law if one of these groups holds a street meeting where the audience may be hostile?

The chapter on *The Right to Assemble Peaceably in Associations* begins with fraternities and sororities and ends with the right of teachers and students to join associations. In between these two educational issues, we deal with the Communist Party, the Ku Klux Klan, and the National Association for the Advancement of Colored People. Each in turn found itself involved in constitutional issues and each brought to our High Court value confrontations of significance. How the nine Justices grappled with each of these cases is an illuminating study of the quest for principles to resolve problems.

The chapter which follows examines the issues in *Street Meetings* relating to the issuance of permits—an important right and an important power on a collision course.

RELIGIOUS NEWS SERVICE PHOTO

CHAPTER 20

THE RIGHT TO ASSEMBLE PEACEABLY
IN ASSOCIATIONS

The right to form or join associations is not found in the First Amendment. In any event, it is not stated in specific words. The right of association, nevertheless, has been taken for granted for many years. More than a century ago, Alexis de Tocqueville, the famous French observer of the American scene, wrote in his *Democracy in America:*

> In no country in the world has the principle of association been more successfully used or applied to a greater multitude of objects than in America.

Where are the constitutional roots of this important right? They include the right to assemble peaceably and the right to petition. To these must be added the Due Process Clauses of the Fifth and Fourteenth Amendments providing that neither Congress nor the states may deprive any person of life, liberty, or property without due process of the law. Add to these the Ninth Amendment which declares that the enumerated rights "shall not be construed to deny or disparage others retained by the people." Against this backdrop, the right of association is connected with the First, Fifth, Ninth, and Fourteenth Amendments.

Now, let us try to analyze some of the important cases related to this important right.

ISSUES TO BE ANALYZED

CASES 60–68

Decide each of these cases by weighing the interests of the association with the interests of the Community. Use principles of law which have been developed in preceding cases. The decisions are presented on pp. 189–197.

CASE 60

A STATE BARS STUDENTS FROM JOINING FRATERNITIES

The State of Mississippi passed a law abolishing fraternities, sororities and other similar organizations at the University of Mississippi. Anyone who belonged to the prohibited societies was disqualified from graduation, honors, or prizes. Students who applied for admission were required to sign pledges that they did not belong to the proscribed organizations and would not join while a student.

J. P. Waugh applied for admission to the University, but refused to sign the pledge because, in his opinion, the statute violated the Fourteenth Amendment. He charged, specifically, that the Mississippi statute deprived him, without reason, "of his property and property right, liberty and his harmless pursuit of happiness, and the equal protection of the laws."

How would you expect the state to answer these arguments? What does this case have to do with peaceable assembly?

As a judge, how would you decide this type of case? On what principles would you base your judgment?

CASE 61

DEJONGE SPEAKS AT A COMMUNIST PARTY MEETING

Dick DeJonge, a member of the Communist Party, attended a meeting of the Communist Party in Portland, Oregon. The meeting was called to protest illegal raids on workers' halls and homes and against the shooting of striking longshoremen by Portland police. DeJonge spoke before 150–300 persons and he protested conditions in the county jail, the action of city police in the maritime strike, the raids on Communist headquarters and workers' halls, and the part of steamship companies and stevedoring companies in breaking the maritime longshoreman's and seamen's strike.

DeJonge was arrested and charged with conducting and presiding over a meeting of the Communist Party, an organization which "did then and there unlawfully and feloniously teach and advocate the doctrine of criminal syndicalism and sabotage." The Oregon law defined criminal syndicalism as "the doctrine which advocates crime, physical violence, sabotage, or any unlawful acts or methods as a means of accomplishing or effecting industrial or political change or revolution."

DeJonge was found guilty and sentenced to seven years. He appealed his conviction.

On what grounds would you sustain it or overrule it? Do you think the year in which the speech was delivered is relevant? If so, the meeting was held on July 27, 1934.

CASE 62

ELEVEN LEADERS OF THE COMMUNIST PARTY ARE CHARGED WITH VIOLATING THE SMITH ACT

The period following World War II was filled with international tensions. The wartime alliance between the United States and the Soviet Union was ended and an era of hostility, referred to as the Cold War, emerged. Suspicions and fear of Communist activity led to investigations and prosecutions. The most sensational trial in 1949 was the prosecution of leaders of the Communist Party.

They were indicted for violating the Smith Act of 1940. The Act made it a crime to knowingly advocate or teach the overthrow of the United States government by force or violence; to organize, become a member of any group or assembly of persons who teach, advocate, or encourage the overthrow of the United States government by force or violence; or to conspire to commit such acts.

The trial before Judge Medina lasted nine months and was marked by numerous disruptions. All eleven defendants were found guilty. The United States Court of Appeals affirmed and the defendants appealed to the Supreme Court on two grounds:

1. The Smith Act as applied in this case violates the First Amendment rights of speech, press, and assembly;

2. The Smith Act is so vague as to violate the First and Fifth Amendments.

Do you think that the two arguments advanced by the defendants carry any weight? They were charged with teaching and advocating. Does this mean that they were using speech but were not engaged in any acts? Are these terms clear: "teach," "advocate," "force," "violence"?

How do you think the Justices of the Supreme Court answered these questions at that time? How would they have answered them today?

CASE 63

A KU KLUX KLAN LEADER ADVOCATES THE
USE OF FORCE

Brandenburg, a leader of the Ku Klux Klan in Ohio, invited an announcer-reporter to attend a Klan meeting. With the cooperation of the organizers of the meeting, the reporter and a cameraman attended and filmed the meeting. Portions of the film were later shown on local and national television.

The film showed hooded figures around a large wooden cross, which was burned. Some of the people were armed.

Brandenburg, dressed as a Klansman, addressed the meeting with these words:

> This is an organizers' meeting. We have had quite a few members here today which are—we have hundreds, hundreds of members throughout the State of Ohio. I can quote from a newspaper clipping from the Columbus Ohio Dispatch, five weeks ago Sunday morning. The Klan has more members in the State of Ohio than does any other organization. We're not a revengent organization, but if our President, our Congress, our Supreme Court, continues to suppress the white, Caucasian race, it's possible that there might have to be some revengence taken.

> We are marching on Congress July the Fourth, four hundred thousand strong. From there we are dividing into two groups, one group to march on St. Augustine, Florida, the other group to march into Mississippi. Thank you.

In addition to these remarks, he made derogatory references about Blacks and Jews.

Subsequently, he was arrested and convicted for violating the Ohio Criminal Syndicalism Statute which prohibits "advocat[ing] . . . the duty, necessity, or propriety of crime, sabotage, violence, or unlawful methods of terrorism as a means of accomplishing industrial or political reform" and of "voluntarily assembl[ing] with any society, group or assemblage of persons formed to teach or advocate the doctrines of 'criminal syndicalism'." Brandenburg was fined $1,000 and sentenced to one to ten years imprisonment.

The appeal was based on the First and Fourteenth Amendments. Assume that you were hired by Brandenburg to conduct his appeal, how would you have developed your argument? Assume that Brandenburg is so unpopular that he could not obtain counsel. The American Civil Liberties Union is asked to defend him and they, in turn, ask you, a Jew or a Black, to represent him. Would you do so? If you agreed, how would you proceed?

CASES 64–66

THE NATIONAL ASSOCIATION FOR THE ADVANCEMENT OF COLORED PEOPLE IS ASKED TO DISCLOSE ITS MEMBERSHIP LISTS

Can an organization be asked to make public its membership lists? What is the purpose behind such legislation?

After the unanimous Supreme Court ruling in *Brown v. Board of Education* in 1954 declaring that segregated education in public schools violated the Equal Protection Clause of the Fourteenth Amendment, several Southern states took measures to either outlaw the NAACP or to drive it out of the state. It was the NAACP that had initiated the *Brown* case, as well as many others relating to racial discrimination.

CASE 64

Alabama had a foreign corporations law requiring out-of-state corporations to file corporate charters with the Secretary of State and to designate a local place of business and a local agent. The NAACP, a New York non-profit corporation, believed it was exempt from the law. Alabama sued to oust the NAACP from the state and the court granted the motion for the production of records, papers, the names of agents and a list of all its members. The NAACP complied with the order except that it refused to disclose its membership list on the ground that this violated the First and Fourteenth Amendments, which safeguarded the right to assemble peaceably.

Do you agree with the NAACP? Why?

CASE 65

Little Rock, Arkansas, imposed an annual license tax on businesses, corporations, and professions. The law was amended in 1957 to require any organization in the city to give the City Clerk on request, a list of its members who paid dues. This information was to be made public.

The NAACP refused on the ground that disclosure of a list of its members would lead to harassment, economic reprisals, threats, and violence. Little Rock officials defended their position on the ground that the power to tax is a basic function of local government.

> With whom do you side in this case?

CASE 66

Louisiana passed two anti-subversion laws which were applied to the NAACP. Each chapter of that organization was required to file a list of names and addresses of its members, together with affidavits declaring that none of the officers was subversive.

> What distinctions do you see between the Alabama and Louisiana laws? Do these distinctions make a difference? How would you decide this case?

CASE 67

CAN EDUCATORS BE REQUIRED TO DISCLOSE TO THE STATE ALL THE ORGANIZATIONS TO WHICH THEY BELONG?

In 1958 the Arkansas legislature passed a law requiring all educators in the public schools and colleges, as a condition of employment, to file an affidavit annually disclosing the names and addresses of all associations to which they belonged, made contributions to, or paid dues within the past five years. The purpose, in the words of the law, was to assist the people in Arkansas in solving its desegregation problems. Obviously, the objective was to discover the names of educators who belong to the NAACP or other organizations favoring desegregation.

Shelton, a teacher employed in the Little Rock Public School System for twenty-five years, declined to file the affidavit and he was dismissed. He instituted an action in federal court and was joined by the Arkansas Teachers Association. At the trial, it was disclosed that he was a member of the NAACP, but not a member of any subversive organization.

At the same time, two teachers started a state court action against the law. Carr, an associate professor at the University of Arkansas, refused to file the affidavit, but he did submit a written statement listing his professional organizations and he denied belonging to any subversive group. Gephardt, a teacher at Little Rock's Central High School, filed an affidavit stating that he never belonged to a subversive organization, that he belonged to the Arkansas Education Association and to the American Legion, and that he was willing to answer any question which relates constitutionally to his professional qualifications. Both lost their jobs.

Their cases were appealed to the Supreme Court, which posed two issues:

1. Does a state have the power to inquired into the competence and fitness of those it hires to teach?

2. Can a state compel a teacher to disclose every organization to which he or she belongs?

How would you answer these questions? What constitutional provisions are involved?

CASE 68

MEMBER OF THE STUDENTS FOR A DEMOCRATIC SOCIETY TRY TO ESTABLISH A CHAPTER ON A COLLEGE CAMPUS

In September 1969, a group of students at Central Connecticut State College, a state-supported institution of higher learning, decided to organize a local chapter of Students for a Democratic Society, known as the SDS. In accordance with the procedures at the college, they filed their request for official recognition as a campus organization with the Student Affairs Committee, a committee of faculty and students. They specified in their application that the club would have three objectives: a forum for developing an analysis of American society; "an agency for integrating thought and action so as to bring about constructive changes"; and "a coordinating body for relating the problem of leftist students" with other groups on the campus.

By a 6 to 2 vote the committee approved the application on the premise that, since the Young Americans for Freedom, the Young Democrats, the Young Republicans, and the Liberal Party were represented on the campus, the "left-wing" students should also have their club.

The president of the college rejected the application for several reasons. His major objection was that this local branch of the SDS was not independent from the national SDS, which had been associated with episodes of violence and disruption on campuses. The local SDS students maintained that they were independent from the national group.

When the students found that they would not be granted recognition, they went to the federal courts claiming that their First Amendment rights of freedom of expression and association had been violated.

What do you think? Does the *Tinker* rule apply here? Can a college draw up a "Student Bill of Rights" relating to permissible speech and unacceptable conduct and require any group that wants a college charter to agree to abide by this declaration? If a college can do this, what do you think ought to be included and excluded from this declaration of student's rights and responsibilities?

DECISIONS IN CASES 60–68

CASE 60

J. P. Waugh v. Board of Trustees of University of Mississippi

237 U.S. 589, 35 S.Ct. 720, 59 L.Ed. 1131 (1915)

The Supreme Court was unanimous and, speaking through Justice McKenna, it ruled:

> It is said that the fraternity to which complainant belongs is a moral and of itself a disciplinary force. This need not be denied. But whether such membership makes against discipline was for the State of Mississippi to determine. It is to be remembered that the University was established by the state and is under the control of the state, and the enactment of the statute may have been induced by the opinion that *membership in the prohibited societies divided the attention of the students and distracted from that singleness of purpose which the State desired to exist in its public educational institutions.* It is not for us to entertain conjectures in opposition to the views of the state and annul its regulations upon disputable considerations of their wisdom or necessity. (Emphasis supplied.)

In other words, the right to peaceable assembly can be curtailed by the state through the exercise of its police power. The state can issue disciplinary regulations reasonably related to education.

The same approach has been taken by state courts in interpreting regulations of school boards abolishing fraternities, sororities, and other secret organizations in the schools. Among the reasons advanced by the courts to justify such statutes are: material interference with the purposes of public education, the fostering of "a clannish spirit of insubordination to school authority," interference with "the good order, harmony, discipline, and general welfare of the school," distraction from scholarship and studious habits, and harm to the reputation of the school and to the personal character of the members.

(See David Fellman. *The Constitutional Right of Association.* Chicago: University of Chicago Press, 1963.)

CASE 61

DeJonge v. Oregon

229 U.S. 353, 57 S.Ct. 255, 81 L.Ed. 278 (1937)

Chief Justice Hughes delivered the unanimous opinion of the Court. The conviction was reversed for the following reasons:

His sole offense as charged, and for which he was convicted and sentenced to imprisonment for seven years, was that he had assisted in the conduct of a public meeting, albeit otherwise lawful, which was held under the auspices of the Communist Party. . . .

A like fate might have attended any speaker, although not a member, who "assisted in the conduct" of the meeting. However innocuous the object of the meeting, however lawful the subjects and tenor of the addresses, however reasonable and timely the discussion, all those assisting in the conduct of the meeting would be subject to imprisonment as felons if the meeting were held by the Communist Party. . . .

In other words, if the Oregon law were interpreted strictly, anyone who "assisted in the conduct" of the meeting was subject to indictment, trial, and conviction. Such a law violates the fundamental right of peaceable assembly.

It follows from these considerations that, consistently with the Federal Constitution, peaceable assembly for lawful discussion cannot be made a crime. The holding of meetings for peaceable political action cannot be proscribed. Those who assist in the conduct of such meetings cannot be branded as criminals on that score. The question, if the rights of free speech and peaceable assembly are to be preserved, is not as to the auspices under which the meeting is held but as to its purpose; not as to the relations of the speakers, but whether their utterances transcend the bounds of the freedom of speech which the

Constitution protects. If the persons assembling have committed crimes elsewhere, if they have formed or are engaged in a conspiracy against the public peace and order, they may be prosecuted for their conspiracy or other violation of valid laws. But it is a different matter when the State, instead of prosecuting them for such offenses, seizes upon mere participation in a peaceable assembly and a lawful public discussion as the basis for a criminal charge.

For all the aforementioned reasons, the Oregon statute "is repugnant to the due process clause of the Fourteenth Amendment."

CASE 62

Dennis v. United States

341 U.S. 494, 71 S.Ct. 857, 95 L.Ed. 1137 (1951)

In a 6 to 2 ruling, the Supreme Court sustained the conviction. The issues raised here were so challenging that five opinions were written. Justice Clark did not take part in the case.

Chief Justice Vinson delivered the opinion of the Court, in which Justices Reed, Burton, and Minton concurred. The issue is posed as follows:

> The question in this case is whether the statute which the legislature has enacted may be constitutionally applied. In other words, the Court must examine judicially the application of the statute to the particular situation, to ascertain if the Constitution prohibits the conviction. We hold that the statute may be applied where there is a 'clear and present danger' of the substantive evil which the legislature had the right to prevent. Bearing, as it does, the marks of a "question of law," the issue is properly one for the judge to decide.

The Justices arrived at the conclusion that there was a "clear and present" danger on the basis of the following findings by the trial court and the Court of Appeals:

> . . . that the Communist Party is a highly disciplined organization, adept at infiltration into strategic positions, use of aliases, and double-meaning language; that the Party is rigidly controlled; that Communists, unlike other political parties, tolerate no dissension from the policy laid down by the guiding forces, but that the approved program is slavishly followed by the members of the Party; that the literature of the Party and the statements and activities of its leaders, petitioners here, advocate, and the general goal of the Party was, during the period in question, to achieve a successful overthrow of the existing order by force and violence. . . .

As for the argument that there is a right to rebel against dictatorial government, the Court replies:

> The obvious purpose of the statute is to protect existing Government, not from change by peaceable, lawful and constitutional means, but

from change by violence, revolution and terrorism. That it is within the *power* of the Congress to protect the Government of the United States from armed rebellion is a proposition which requires little discussion. Whatever theoretical merit there may be to the argument that there is a 'right' to rebellion against dictatorial governments is without force where the existing structure of the government provides for peaceful and orderly change.

Agreed that Congress has the power to protect the country from an armed overthrow, were the means employed by the Government in this case constitutional? The Court replies:

Overthrow of the Government by force and violence is certainly a substantial enough interest for the Government to limit speech. Indeed, this is the ultimate value of any society, for if a society cannot protect its very structure from armed internal attack, it must follow that no subordinate value can be protected. . . . If Government is aware that a group aiming at its overthrow is attempting to indoctrinate its members and to commit them to a course whereby they will strike when the leaders feel the circumstances permit, action by the Government is required. . . . For that is not the question. Certainly an attempt to overthrow the Government by force, even though doomed from the outset because of inadequate numbers or power of the revolutionists, is a sufficient evil for Congress to prevent.

The Court then concluded:

We hold that . . . [the provisions of the Smith Act] do not inherently, or as construed or applied in the instant case, violate the First Amendment and other provisions of the Bill of Rights, or the First and Fifth Amendments because of indefiniteness. Petitioners intended to overthrow the Government of the United States as speedily as the circumstances would permit. Their conspiracy to organize the Communist Party and to teach and advocate the overthrow of the Government of the United States by force and violence created a "clear and present danger" of an attempt to overthrow the Government by force and violence. They were properly and constitutionally convicted for violation of the Smith Act. The judgments of conviction are affirmed.

Justice Jackson's concurring opinion emphasized that Congress could enact legislation punishing conspirators without waiting for the occurrence of an overt act. Justice Frankfurter's concurring opinion was based on the balancing doctrine: weighing the individual's right to freedom of expression versus organized society's need for national security. Self-preservation dictated the passage of the Smith Act and the Supreme Court is obligated to respect this judgment of the Congress.

The dissents were written by Justices Black and Douglas. The former condemned the Smith Act as a "virulent form of prior censorship of speech and press" and by implication, peaceable assembly. He concluded with a prophetic observation:

> Public opinion being what it now is, few will protest the conviction of these Communist petitioners. There is hope, however, that in calmer times, when present pressures, passions and fears subside, this or some later Court will restore the First Amendment liberties to the high preferred place where they belong in a free society.

Justice Douglas found that this case involved speech alone, not "speech plus acts of sabotage or unlawful conduct." Treating speech alone as the equivalent of treason or sedition violates the American tradition of human rights.

NOTE ON
THE SUPREME COURT AND THE COMMUNIST PARTY

A number of cases relating to Communists and the Communist Party came before the Court in the years following the *Dennis* case and the Government had limited success.

In 1952 a number of so-called second-string Communists were convicted under the conspiracy provisions of the Smith Act. The High Court threw out the convictions on the ground that the three-year statute of limitations had run out. The Communist Party had been organized in 1945 and indictments under the Smith Act had to be issued prior to 1948. It had not been done in this case. The Court's 5 to 2 opinion in *Yates v. United States* (1958) stressed an important point. It differentiated between advocacy of abstract doctrines or ideas and advocacy of action. The former is permissible; the latter is unlawful.

In 1961 the membership provisions of the Smith Act came before the Court. In *Scales v. United States*, a divided Court, 5 to 4, held the membership provisions to mean "active" membership as distinguished from "passive" membership. In *Noto v. United States*, a unanimous Court concluded that the Government had failed to prove that the Communist Party was engaged in advocacy of action in contrast to advocacy of abstract ideas.

CASE 63

Brandenburg v. Ohio

395 U.S. 444, 89 S.Ct. 1827, 23 L.Ed.2d 430 (1969)

In a *per curiam* (unsigned) opinion by the Court, the Justices reversed the conviction on

> . . . the principle that the constitutional guarantees of free speech and free press do not permit a state to forbid or proscribe advocacy of the use of force or of law violation except where such advocacy is directed to inciting or producing imminent lawless action and is likely to incite or produce such action.

The opinion went on to say that "the mere abstract teaching of the moral propriety or even moral necessity for a resort to force and violence, is not the same as preparing a group for violent action and steeling it to such action." Measured by this test, the Ohio Syndicalism Act is unconstitutional under the First and Fourteenth Amendments because it punishes persons who assemble voluntarily with a group to teach or advocate the doctrines of criminal syndicalism. Mere advocacy must be distinguished from incitement to imminent lawless action.

Justices Black and Douglas concurred with the hope that this ruling had relegated to the limits of constitutional history the "clear and present danger" rule—a rule which they regarded as a clear and present danger to the First Amendment Freedoms.

CASE 64

National Association for the Advancement of Colored People v. Alabama

357 U.S. 449, 78 S.Ct. 1163, 2 L.Ed.2d 1488 (1958)

The Court's unanimous opinion upheld the NAACP refusal to turn over its membership list to state authorities. Justice Harlan's opinion for the Court declared that the Association is "but a medium through which its individual members seek to make more effective the expression of their own views." He goes on to say:

> Effective advocacy of both public and private points of view, particularly controversial ones, is undeniably enhanced by group association . . . It is beyond debate that freedom to engage in association for the advancement of beliefs and ideas is an inseparable aspect of the "liberty" assured by the Due Process Clause of the Fourteenth Amendment . . .

Justice Harlan underscored the obvious purpose of this type of state action. It can lead to "economic reprisals, loss of employment, threat of physical coercion, and other manifestations of public hostility" toward the members of the association. Such legislation is often aimed at reducing membership through fear and, thereby, diminishing the financial resources and the power of the association.

CASE 65

Bates v. City of Little Rock

361 U.S. 516, 80 S.Ct. 412, 4 L.Ed. 2d 480 (1960)

Once again, the Court decided in favor of the NAACP in a unanimous decision. Once again, the Justices, speaking through Justice Stewart, concluded that the disclosure of the membership list would lead to harassment, bodily harm, economic reprisals, and community hostility towards the individual members. At the same time, the NAACP would lose membership, as well as its influence as an organization.

Justice Stewart's opinion emphasized that the right of peaceable assembly, like freedom of expression, are "at the foundation of a government based upon the consent of an informed citizenry." He goes on to say that "it is now beyond dispute that freedom of association for the purpose of advancing ideas and airing grievances is protected by the Due Process Clause of the Fourteenth Amendment from invasion by the States."

As for Little Rock's argument that it was using its taxing power in a legal manner, the Court found no relationship between an occupation license tax and compulsory disclosure of membership lists.

Justices Black and Douglas wrote a concurring opinion emphasizing that the right of peaceable assembly includes the freedom of association and that both principles are "applicable to all people under our Constitution irrespective of their race, color, politics, or religion."

CASE 66

Louisiana ex rel. Gremillion v. National Association for the Advancement of Colored People

366 U.S. 293, 81 S.Ct. 1333, 6 L.Ed.2d 301 (1961)

In delivering the brief opinion of the Court, Justice Douglas said:

> We deal with a constitutional right, since freedom of association is included in the bundle of First Amendment rights made applicable to the States by the Due ·Process Clause of the Fourteenth Amendment . . . And where it is shown . . . that disclosure of membership lists results in reprisals against and hostility to the members, disclosure is not required.

He concluded with the warning that "regulatory measures . . . no matter how sophisticated, cannot be employed in purpose or in effect to stifle, penalize, or curb the exercise of First Amendment rights."

CASE 67

Shelton v. Tucker

364 U.S. 479, 81 S.Ct. 247, 5 L.Ed.2d 231 (1960)

In a 5 to 4 ruling the Supreme Court condemned the Arkansas law on the grounds of its "unlimited and indiscriminate sweep" and its comprehensive interference with associational freedom. All nine Justices agreed that a state had the power to inquire into the fitness and competence of its teachers by requiring disclosure of associational activities relevant to those matters. Where the majority and minority of the Justices parted company was on the extent of the disclosure. What was to be gained, asked Justice Stewart for the majority, by having teachers disclose "every conceivable kind of associational tie—social, professional, political, avocational, or religious"? It is obvious that many of these "could have no possible bearing upon the teacher's occupational competence or fitness."

Justice Stewart was understandably concerned by the effect of this law on teachers who "serve at the absolute will of those to whom disclosure must be made." The pressure on teachers to avoid associational ties is great. How much greater will be the impact of this law on the right to assemble peaceably and the freedom to associate freely. This law, so sweeping in nature and so dangerous to the atmosphere of freedom in which teachers do their best work is an unconstitutional infringement of "the fundamental personal liberties" protected by the First and Fourteenth Amendments.

The four dissenters—Justices Harlan, Frankfurter, Clark, and Whittaker—concluded that the Arkansas law represented a constitutional use of a state's power to determine the competency and fitness of teachers. If this law should be abused by the local authorities in any way—the firing of teachers, for example—the Court stood ready to remedy any injustices. As for the argument that the Arkansas law is too sweeping in that it requires disclosure of *all* organizations to which a person belonged or contributed during the preceding five years, such disclosure may be useful to a local board of education. It may disclose that a teacher belongs to so many organizations that they "consume his time and energy and interest at the expense of his work or even of his professional dedication."

CASE 68

Healy v. James

408 U.S. 169, 92 S.Ct. 2338, 33 L.Ed.2d 266 (1972)

The federal district court agreed with the college. The United States Court of Appeals affirmed. The Supreme Court reversed and remanded the case to the lower court to clarify certain questions.

Justice Powell, in delivering the opinion of court, begins with an examination of the right of students to form associations.

> Among the rights protected by the First Amendment is the right of individuals to associate to further their own beliefs. While the freedom of association is not explicitly set out in the amendment, it has long been held to be implicit in the freedoms of speech, assembly, and petition. . . . There can be no doubt that denial of official recognition, without justification, to college organizations burdens or abridges that associational right. The primary impediment to free association flowing from non-recognition is the denial of use of campus facilities for meetings and other appropriate purposes. . . .

As is to be expected, Justice Powell then asks whether a college can ever justify an action which infringes on these important rights. The answer can be found in the *Tinker* case, among others. What the college authorities did here was a form of prior restraint, and therefore the college bears the "heavy burden" of demonstrating that it was justified in its actions. It can do so only by presenting proof that, in the words of *Tinker*, the proposed club would substantially and materially interfere with the discipline and work of the college.

The fear that the local chapter of the SDS would follow robot-like in the footsteps of the National Organization presents a guilt-by-association argument that is unacceptable. The students said they were and would be independent.

The fact that the president found the views and philosophy of the students repugnant was no reason for the denial of the charter. The college, acting as an agency of the state is bound by the First and Fourteenth Amendments. Differences of opinion or disagreement over philosophy do not justify infringement of First Amendment Freedoms.

There is a line between mere advocacy and advocacy "directed to inciting or producing imminent lawless action." In this case there was no substantial evidence produced that the local chapter would probably have been a disruptive force on campus. Quoting *Tinker* again, Justice Powell notes that "undifferentiated fear or apprehension of disturbance . . . is not enough to overcome the right to freedom of expression."

Having said all this in favor of the students, Justice Powell then points out that one important ground still existed for the denial of the charter. The college had a "Student Bill of Rights" which delineated the line between permissible speech and impermissible conduct (depriving others of the opportunity to speak or be heard, damaging property, invading privacy of others, disrupting operation of the college, and interfering with the rights of others). Justice Powell felt that the case should be sent back to the lower court to clarify the stand of the college and the SDS students on this "Student Bill of Rights." It is necessary to determine whether the college requires campus organizations to comply with this code of conduct. If there is such a requirement, it is necessary to find out whether the SDS students intend to comply with this requirement. A college, says Justice Powell, can deny a charter to "any group that reserves the right to violate any valid campus rules with which it disagrees."

CHAPTER 21

STREET MEETINGS

By this time it is obvious that the right to assemble peaceably is intimately connected with the right of free speech. As we have seen, Irving Feiner called a street meeting to inform the audience of issues important to him and his group. The result was the confrontation between a speaker unpopular with several people in the audience and the inevitable dilemma for the police. Terminiello hired a hall for his followers and the result was bedlam.

Episodes of this type—the confrontation between the unpopular speaker and the hostile audience—have given rise to local ordinances limiting access to public places for purposes of street meetings. Designed to protect the lives, welfare, and safety of the people, these ordinances have inevitably come into conflict with the right to assemble peaceably, as well as the right to free speech. The following cases illustrate the dilemma and the proposed solutions.

ISSUES TO BE ANALYZED

CASES 69–71—The Decisions follow these three cases

CASE 69

"I AM THE LAW" HAGUE TRIES TO CENSOR THE C.I.O.

Frank "I am the Law" Hague was Mayor and political boss of Jersey City, New Jersey. He was anti-union and, when the Committee for Industrial Organization asked for a permit to hold a street meeting, it was refused by the Chief of Police. A city ordinance required a permit for a public meeting and it provided that such permits could be refused "for the purpose of preventing riots, disturbances, or disorderly assemblages." The permit was refused because it was alleged that the CIO was a Communist Organization, an allegation that was denied. The CIO gave as its reason for the holding of the meeting the need to explain to workingmen the purposes of the National Labor Relations Act.

The case is appealed to the courts. What are the issues? Is the historical period important? It was the era of the New Deal and the year was 1938.

CASE 70

A BAPTIST MINISTER HOLDS A RELIGIOUS MEETING IN THE STREET WITHOUT A PERMIT

New York City had an ordinance which made it unlawful to hold public meetings on the street without first obtaining a permit from the city police commissioner. The ordinance made it unlawful "to ridicule or denounce any form of religious belief."

Carl Jacob Kunz, a Baptist Minister, applied for and received a permit in 1946, but it was later revoked because at his meetings he had attacked Catholics and Jews. In 1947 he was denied a permit and the same action was taken in 1948. He held a street meeting without a permit, was arrested, and fined $10.00.

Kunz argues that his right to free speech and to hold street meetings have been denied. What do you think?

CASE 71

A JEHOVAH'S WITNESS HOLDS A RELIGIOUS MEETING IN A PUBLIC PARK WITHOUT A PERMIT

Poulos, a Jehovah's Witness applied for a permit to conduct religious services in a public park in Portsmouth, New Hampshire. The city's local ordinance read as follows:

> Section 22. License Required. No theatrical or dramatic presentation shall be performed or exhibited and no parade or procession upon any public street or way, and no open air public meeting upon any ground abutting thereon shall be permitted unless a license thereof shall first be obtained from the City Council.

The license fee was $300 a day and any person who violated the law could be fined $20.

Poulos offered to pay the fee and to comply with all requirements. The City Council refused to give him the license. Despite the refusal, Poulos held his meetings and was convicted and fined $20. His appeal was based on the following grounds:

1. No license can be required for conducting religious ceremonies in a public park because such a requirement violates the free speech and religion clauses of the First and Fourteenth Amendments.

2. Even if a license requirement were constitutional, the arbitrary refusal of the City Council amounts to a violation of the free speech and religion clauses of the First and Fourteenth Amendments.

Poulos does not raise the right to peaceable assembly argument.

> Would you have done so if you had been his attorney?
> How would you decide this case?

DECISIONS IN CASES 69–71

CASE 69

Hague v. C.I.O.

307 U.S. 496, 59 S.Ct. 954, 83 L.Ed. 1423 (1939)

In a 7 to 2 ruling the Supreme Court declared the ordinance void because it enabled the Director of Safety "to refuse a permit on his mere opinion" that it will prevent "riots, disturbances or disorderly assemblage." Under these circumstances an ordinance becomes "the instrument of arbitrary suppression of free expression of views on national affairs for the prohibition of all speaking."

Justice Robert's opinion is quoted often to clarify the dimensions of freedom of assembly.

> Wherever the title of streets and parks may rest, they have immemorially been held in trust for the use of the public and, time out of mind, have been used for purposes of assembly, communicating thoughts between citizens, and discussing public questions. Such use of the streets and public places has, from ancient times, been a part of the privileges, immunities, rights, and liberties of citizens. The privilege of a citizen of the United States to use the streets and parks for the communication of views on national questions may be regulated in the interest of all; it is not absolute, but relative, and must be exercised in subordination to the general comfort and convenience, and in consonance with peace and good order; but it must not, in the guise of regulation, be abridged or denied.

CASE 70

Kunz v. New York

340 U.S. 290, 71 S.Ct. 312, 95 L.Ed. 280 (1951)

Chief Justice Vinson's opinion for the majority declared the New York City ordinance unconstitutional on the ground that it gave "an administrative official discretionary power to control in advance the right of citizens to speak on religious matters on the streets of New York." It is a prior restraint on the exercise of First Amendment rights.

Where there are no guidelines in an ordinance to assist a local official in deciding whether a permit for a street meeting should be granted, we have an open invitation to censorship and suppression. If a permit is granted and the speaker and the audience engage in disorderly antics, communities have the means to punish this conduct.

Justice Jackson's dissent is a bitter condemnation of the majority's position. How can one expect standards or guidelines from a community, he asks, when the Supreme Court has offered no standards of its own. To permit "hateful and hate-stirring attacks on races and faiths" under the guise of First Amendment Freedoms is to belittle the great principles of liberty. A community should not be required to place its streets at the service of those who plan to hurl insults at the passerby.

CASE 71

Poulos v. New Hampshire

345 U.S. 395, 73 S.Ct. 760, 97 L.Ed. 1105 (1953)

Justice Reed's opinion for the Court, with Justices Black and Douglas dissenting, accepts the ruling of the New Hampshire Supreme Court that the ordinance is valid and that there is nothing in that ordinance which prevents the holding of religious services in Godwin Park at reasonable hours and times. The City Council, however, had no authority under that ordinance as written to deny the requested license. By doing so, it acted in an arbitrary manner. In other words, the ordinance does not interfere with free speech, or religious freedom; the actions of the City Council do.

Did the City Council's arbitrary decision justify defiance of the law? The answer is "No," because Poulos had available to him judicial remedies to question the arbitrariness of the City Council's decision. To take the law into one's hands is an unacceptable and even dangerous course of action. In the excerpts which follow from

Justice Reed's opinion, it is important to note the references to the right to assembly.

Justice Reed emphasizes the constitutionality of reasonable regulations on freedom of assembly:

> The principles of the First Amendment are not to be treated as a promise that everyone with opinions or beliefs to express may gather around him at any public place and at any time a group for discussion or instruction. . . . This Court . . . has indicated approval of reasonable nondiscriminatory regulation by governmental authority that preserves peace, order and tranquility without deprivation of the First Amendment guarantees of free speech, press and the exercise of religion. When considering specifically the regulation of the use of public parks, the Court has taken the same position.

Since, however, the public officials acted in an arbitrary and unlawful manner, why should the one who suffered because of this act have to go to the expense of a lawsuit? Justice Reed answers as follows:

> Delay is unfortunate but the expense and annoyance of litigation is a price citizens must pay for life in an orderly society where the rights of the First Amendment have a real and abiding meaning. Nor can we say that a state's requirement that redress must be sought through appropriate judicial procedure violates due process.

Justices Douglas and Black dissented. Both argued that the First Amendment rights are "preferred freedoms." To require a citizen to go to the time and expense of a lawsuit to correct an arbitrary and unreasonable ruling of a public official is another "subtle use of a creeping censorship loose in the land."

SECTION VI

THE RIGHT TO PETITION THE GOVERNMENT FOR REDRESS OF GRIEVANCES

In every stage of these Oppressions We have Petitioned for Redress in the most humble terms; Our repeated Petitions have been answered only by repeated injury.

Declaration of Independence
(1776)

The right to petition for the redress of grievances has an ancient history and is not limited to writing a letter or sending a telegram to a congressman; it is not confined to appearing before the local city council, or writing letters to the President or Governor or Mayor. . . . Conventional methods of petitioning may be, and often have been, shut off to large groups of our citizens. Legislators may turn deaf ears; formal complaints may be routed endlessly through a bureaucratic maze; courts may let the wheels of justice grind very slowly. Those who do not control television and radio, those who cannot afford to advertise in newspapers or circulate elaborate pamphlets may have only a more limited type of access to public officials. Their methods should not be condemned as tactics of obstruction and harassment as long as the assembly and petition are peaceable, as these were.

Justice Douglas—Dissenting opinion in *Adderly v. Florida* (1967)

INTRODUCTION

Petitions are a common method of protesting conditions and requesting government cooperation. People have petitioned local, state, and national government on such matters as traffic lights, parks, busing of students, taxes, environmental problems, consumer affairs, nuclear plants, foreign policy, and a variety and multiplicity of other issues. Petitions have taken the form of written statements, delegations of citizens, and protest marches.

The right to petition for redress of grievances, like the other First Amendment Rights, was not handed down to us on a silver platter. There were times in history when such petitions were regarded as seditious and criminal. In some countries today citizens would not think of petitioning for redress of grievances because to do so would invite the heavy hand of governmental retaliation.

Even for Americans, this right is not always welcomed or used. For example, Irving Brant, in his book on *The Bill of Rights* relates that on July 4, 1951, the *Capital Times*, a newspaper in Madison, Wisconsin, the home of the University of Wisconsin, decided to try an experiment to test the attitude of citizens toward a great American document. A petition was prepared declaring that those who signed it believed in the Declaration of Independence. Reporters then asked people on the street chosen at random to sign the petition. Only one person agreed to sign out of 112 interviewed. What reasons did they give? Many feared that they would lose their jobs, or be called Communists, or that it was a subversive document.

When the *New York Post* tried it, only 19 out of 161 were willing to sign. Among the reasons given were "suspicion, distrust, and hostility."

It is unfortunate that so few Americans know the history of this great right. Stated in the *Magna Carta* of 1215, one of the foundation stones of the liberties of Englishmen, this right to petition was used against King Charles I in the famous document, *The Petition of Right*. In 1689 the right to petition was incorporated into the English Bill of Rights with these resounding words:

> That it is the right of subjects to petition the King, and all commitments and prosecutions for such petitioning are illegal.

The American colonists, appealing to the rights of Englishmen, used the right to petition to protest their grievances against George III and Parliament. When the Declaration of Independence was written, one of the grievances against the British Government was stated as follows:

Our repeated Petitions have been answered only by repeated injury.

Incorporated into the First Amendment of the Bill of Rights, this right has been used throughout American history by those who have understood the uses of this form of protest. As we have seen above, some—perhaps too many—people regard the placing of their name on a document of this type as an act fraught with dire consequences. In some communities this may be so. As we shall see, however, more and more people seem to be resorting to the mass protest and the march as a more effective and less threatening means than signing a petition.

Two sensational historic examples of the right to petition were Coxey's Army and the Bonus March. Coxey's Army was a "living petition" of several hundred unemployed who marched to Washington, D. C., in 1894 to persuade the government to supply jobs for the unemployed. The Bonus Army of unemployed veterans marched to Washington, D. C. in 1932 to petition Congress for immediate payment of their promised bonuses. Both marches were unsuccessful.

Two points should be noted. Originally the right peaceably to assemble was joined to the right to petition for the redress of grievances. As we have seen, in time the right to assemble peaceably became recognized as a distinctive right with justification for the recently recognized constitutional right of association. The right to assemble peaceably is also intimately connected with freedom of expression. Inevitably, all the rights in the First Amendment are interconnected since they represent the touchstone of sincerity relating to respect for the dignity and integrity of the individual.

Today, the right to petition often takes the form of lobbying—trying to persuade government officials to pass laws favorable to the lobby or to kill bills harmful to the lobby. Lobbying is a lawful activity and in some jurisdictions lobbyists have been required to identify the interests they represent.

CHAPTER 22

MASS DEMONSTRATIONS, SIT-INS AND MARCHES

In this chapter the cases deal with a variety of forms of petitions by Blacks against racial discrimination. With written petitions proving of little avail, Black activists resorted to mass demonstrations, sit-ins in a public library, a demonstration at a county jail, and a march to a mayor's home. In each of these episodes, we shall see the Justices of the Supreme Court grappling with two desirable principles on a collision course.

CASES

CASE 72

A MASS DEMONSTRATION PROTESTS DISCRIMINATION AGAINST BLACKS

On March 2, 1961, 187 Black high school and college students held a mass demonstration to protest discrimination against Blacks in Columbia, the capital of South Carolina. In groups of fifteen they walked from a nearby church to the statehouse grounds bearing signs: "Down With Segregation" and "I am proud to be a Negro." The purpose of the demonstration was to publicize their dissatisfaction with discriminatory actions against Blacks and to seek the repeal of laws limiting the rights of Blacks..

A crowd of between 200 and 300 watched the demonstration. There was no obstruction of traffic and no evidence of trouble.

The demonstrators continued their march for 45 minutes. The police then ordered them to disperse within 15 minutes or be subject to arrest. They refused and remained on the grounds singing "The Star Spangled Banner" and other patriotic and religious songs. One of their leaders delivered a "religious harangue," according to the City Manager, who also described the proceedings as "loud," "boisterous," and "flamboyant."

The demonstrators were arrested, charged with breach of peace—"a violation of public order, a disturbance of the public tranquillity." The fines ranged from $10 or 5 days in jail to $100 or 30 days in jail.

The demonstrators based their appeal on freedom of expression and the right of petition. The police defended their action on the police power—the power to protect the lives, health, morals, welfare and safety of the people.

How would you resolve this conflict of values?

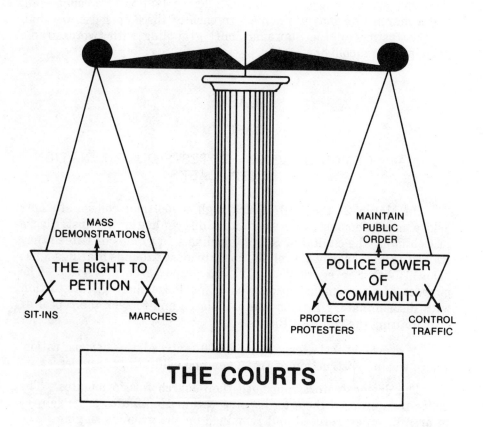

MASS
DEMONSTRATIONS

THE RIGHT TO
PETITION

SIT-INS   MARCHES

MAINTAIN
PUBLIC
ORDER

POLICE POWER
OF
COMMUNITY

PROTECT
PROTESTERS   CONTROL
TRAFFIC

THE COURTS

CASE 73

A SIT–IN IN A PUBLIC LIBRARY

The public library in Clinton, Louisiana was segregated. On March 4, 1964 Brown and four other Blacks decided to protest this discriminatory policy by "sitting in." They sat down in the library and refused to leave when the librarian asked them to do so. When the sheriff arrived, about 10 to 15 minutes after the sit-in had started, and asked them to leave, they again refused and were arrested and convicted of the breach of the peace law which read:

> Whoever with intent to provoke a breach of the peace, or under circum-
> stances such that a breach of the peace may be occasioned thereby:
> (1) crowds or congregates with others . . . in . . . a . . .
> public place or building . . . and who fails or refuses to disperse
> and move on, when ordered to do so by any law enforcement officer
> . . . or any other authorized person . . . shall be guilty of
> disturbing the peace.

The library is a place for reading, study, and contemplation. Should this type of protest be allowed? The State contended that Brown and his friends were loafing and making a nuisance of themselves. This can be very distracting. What do you think?

CASE 74

A DEMONSTRATION AT A COUNTY JAIL

Harriet Adderly and about 200 students at the Florida A & M University in Tallahassee went from their school to the county jail, about a mile away, to demonstrate their grievances against the government. Among the reasons for the protest were the persistence of racial segregation policies and practices, in general, and segregation of the jail, in particular. They were also protesting against arrests of demonstrators at an earlier protest meeting.

The county sheriff, the legal custodian of the jail and the jail grounds, tried to persuade them to leave. When they refused, he warned that he would arrest them for trespass. Some students left, while others remained and were arrested. They were charged with violation of a Florida statute which made it a crime for a person or persons to trespass upon the property of another with "a malicious and mischievous intent."

The students were convicted and they appealed on the grounds that their conviction infringed their right to assemble peaceably in order to petition for the redress of grievances.

What distinctions can you draw between Cases 72 and 74? In what ways are they similar? How do they differ? What principles can you formulate which will apply to them?

CASE 75

DICK GREGORY MARCHES TO MAYOR DALEY'S HOME

Dick Gregory and a group of about 85 followers had become dissatisfied with the Superintendent of Schools in Chicago because he had not moved speedily enough to desegregate the public schools. Believing that Mayor Daley had the power to remove the Superintendent, the group decided to march from City Hall to the Mayor's home, a distance of about five miles. A police lieutenant, four police sergeants, about forty policemen, an assistant city counsel, and the marchers' attorney accompanied the group.

When the demonstrators began marching around the Mayor's home, a crowd of more than 1,000 of the Mayor's sympathizers appeared. As was to be expected, the language became rough and threatening. Threats and obscenities, as well as rocks and eggs, were hurled at the marchers.

When, in the judgment of the Commanding Officer, the situation became dangerous, he asked Gregory and his marchers to leave the area. When they refused, they were arrested and charged with violating Chicago's disorderly conduct ordinance, which provided:

> All persons who shall make . . . or assist in making any improper noise, riot, disturbance, breach of the peace within the limits of the city; all persons who shall collect in bodies or crowds for unlawful purposes, or for any purpose, to the annoyance or disturbance of other persons . . . shall be deemed guilty of disorderly conduct and upon conviction thereof, shall be severely fined not less than one dollar nor more than two hundred dollars for each offense.

Gregory and his group were convicted.

Were the arrest and conviction justified?
Would it make any difference to you, if the charge were disobeying the order of a policeman? Explain.

DECISIONS IN CASES 72–75

CASE 72

Edwards v. South Carolina

372 U.S. 229, 83 S.Ct. 680, 9 L.Ed.2d 697 (1963)

The Court had little trouble with this case. With only Justice Clark dissenting, Justice Stewart's opinion for the majority criticized the actions of the state.

> . . . it is clear to us that in arresting, convicting, and punishing the petitioners . . . South Carolina infringed the petitioners' constitutionally protected rights of free speech, free assembly, and freedom to petition for the redress of their grievances.

> It has long been established that these First Amendment freedoms are protected by the Fourteenth Amendment from invasion by the States . . . The circumstances in this case reflect an exercise of these basic constitutional rights in their most pristine and classic form.

Justice Stewart then refers to the obvious connection between the grievances of the Blacks and their protest.

> The petitioners felt aggrieved by laws of South Carolina which allegedly "prohibited Negro privileges in this state." They peaceably assembled . . . and there peaceably expressed their grievances "to the citizens of South Carolina, along with the Legislative Bodies of South Carolina."

Justice Stewart found the South Carolina breach-of-peace so vague that even the South Carolina courts found that it was "not susceptible of exact definition."

The majority ruling then concludes with a defense of the First Amendment Freedoms.

> The Fourteenth Amendment does not permit a State to make criminal the peaceful expression of unpopular views.

Justice Clark's dissent centers on the legitimate exercise of police powers. The law-enforcement officers were on the scene and in their experienced judgment a "dangerous disturbance was imminent." He saw no reason why the Justices should substitute their judgment for that of the police in this case.

CASE 73

Brown v. Louisiana

383 U.S. 131, 86 S.Ct. 719, 15 L.Ed.2d 637 (1966)

The Court was badly split. A bare majority of five reversed the convictions, while the four dissenters were livid with rage.

Justice Fortas announced the judgment of the Court in an opinion in which Chief Justice Warren and Justice Douglas joined. The five Black young men had been convicted for sitting in the library from 10 to 15 minutes. There was nothing in the breach of peace law which made this conduct unlawful. This, however, said Justice Fortas, is not the point of this case. What really is at issue here is a fundamental right.

> We are here dealing with an aspect of a basic constitutional right—the right under the First and Fourteenth Amendments guaranteeing freedom of speech and of assembly, and freedom to petition the Government for a redress of grievances. . . . As this Court has repeatedly stated, these rights are not confined to verbal expression. They embrace appropriate types of action which certainly include the right in a peaceable and orderly manner to protest by silent and reproachful presence, in a place where the protestant has every right to be, the unconstitutional segregation of public facilities. . . .

In this case, the Louisiana statute was used deliberately to frustrate this right.

> . . . The statute was deliberately and purposefully applied solely to terminate the reasonable, orderly, and limited exercise of the right to protest the unconstitutional segregation of a public facility. Interference with this right, so exercised, by state action is intolerable under our Constitution. . . .

It is unfortunate, says Justice Fortas, that the stage of this drama should have been a library. It is doubly unfortunate that the drama dealt with racism.

> It is an unhappy circumstance that the locus of these events was a public library—a place dedicated to quiet, to knowledge, and to beauty. It is a sad commentary that this hallowed place in the Parish of East Feliciana bore the ugly stamp of racism. It is sad, too, that it was a public library which, reasonably enough in the circumstances, was the stage for a confrontation between those discriminated against and the representatives of the offending parishes. Fortunately, the circumstances here were such that no claim can be made that use of the library by others was disturbed by the demonstration. Perhaps the time and method were carefully chosen with this in mind. Were

it otherwise, a factor not present in this case would have to be considered. Here, there was no disturbance of others, no disruption of library activities, and no violation of any library regulations.

Justice Brennan concurred on the ground that the Louisiana statute was too broad and therefore, unconstitutional.

Justice White's concurring opinion concluded that, if the students had been white, they probably would not have been arrested. Since they were Black, he concludes that the convictions deny them the Equal Protection of the Laws.

Justice Black's dissenting opinion was joined by Justices Clark, Harlan, and Stewart. The first point to observe, declares the opinion, is that a library is not a public street and not subject to the same regulations.

> A tiny parish branch library, staffed by two women, is not a department store . . . nor a bus terminal . . . nor a public thoroughfare as in *Edwards v. South Carolina,* . . . . Short of physical violence, petitioners could not have more completely upset the normal, quiet functioning of the Clinton branch of the Audubon Regional Library. The state courts below thought the disturbance created by petitioners constituted a violation of the statute. So far as the reversal here rests on a holding that the Louisiana statute was not violated, the Court simply substitutes its judgment for that of the Louisiana courts as to what conduct satisfies the requirements of that state statute. . . .

Justice Black finds the majority ruling a new departure in constitutional law and a dangerous precedent.

> In this case this new constitutional principle means that even though these petitioners did not want to use the Louisiana public library for library purposes, they had a constitutional right nevertheless to stay there over the protest of the librarians who had lawful authority to keep the library orderly for the use of people who wanted to use its books, its magazines, and its papers. But the principle espoused also has a far broader meaning. It means that the Constitution, the First and the Fourteenth Amendments, requires the custodians and supervisors of the public libraries in this country to stand helplessly by while protesting groups advocating one cause or another, stage "sit-ins" or "stand-ups" to dramatize their particular views on particular issues. . . . The States are thus paralyzed with reference to control of their libraries for library purposes, and I suppose that inevitably the next step will be to paralyze the schools. Efforts to this effect have already been made all over the country. . . .
>
> . . . I am deeply troubled with the fear that powerful private groups throughout the Nation will read the Court's action, as I do— that is, as granting them a license to invade the tranquillity and beauty of our libraries whenever they have quarrel with some state

policy which may or may not exist. It is an unhappy circumstance in my judgment that the group, which more than any other has needed a government of equal laws and equal justice, is now encouraged to believe that the best way for it to advance its cause, which is a worthy one, is by taking the law into its own hands from place to place and from time to time. Governments like ours were formed to substitute the rule of law for the rule of force. Illustrations may be given where crowds have gathered together peaceably by reason of extraordinarily good discipline reinforced by vigilant officers. "Demonstrations" have taken place without any manifestations of force at the time. But I say once more that the crowd moved by noble ideals today can become the mob ruled by hate and passion and greed and violence tomorrow. If we ever doubted that, we know it now. The peaceful songs of love can become as stirring and provocative as the Marseillaise did in the days when a noble revolution gave way to rule by successive mobs until chaos set in. The holding in this case today makes it more necessary than ever that we stop and look more closely at where we are going. . . .

CASE 74

Adderly v. Florida

385 U.S. 39, 87 S.Ct. 242, 17 L.Ed.2d 149 (1966)

Once again, the Court was divided 5 to 4 with Justice Black, now speaking for the majority, and Justice Douglas representing the dissenters.

Justice Black attacks at once the argument that the present case is similar to the *Edwards* case.

The *Edwards* case, like this one, did come up when a number of persons demonstrated on public property against their State's segregation policies. They also sang hymns and danced, as did the demonstrators in this case. But here the analogies to this case end. In *Edwards*, the demonstrators went to the South Carolina State Capitol grounds to protest. In this case they went to the jail. Traditionally, state capitol grounds are open to the public. Jails, built for security purposes, are not. The demonstrators at the South Carolina Capitol went in through a public driveway and as they entered they were told by state officials there that they had a right as citizens to go through the State House grounds as long as they were peaceful. Here the demonstrators entered the jail grounds through a driveway used only for jail purposes and without warning to or permission from the sheriff.

The Florida trespass law, unlike the South Carolina breach-of-peace-statute was more limited in scope and its meaning was clear and understandable.

As for the argument that the students had been deprived of their constitutional rights, Justice Black responded:

[The only question remaining is] whether conviction of the state offense . . . unconstitutionally deprives petitioners of their rights to freedom of speech, press, assembly or petition. We hold it does not. The sheriff, as jail custodian, had power, as the state courts have here held, to direct that this large crowd of people get off the grounds. . . . The record reveals that he objected only to their presence on that part of the jail grounds reserved for jail uses. There is no evidence at all that on any other occasion had similarly large groups of the public been permitted to gather on this portion of the jail grounds for any purpose. Nothing in the Constitution of the United States prevents Florida from even-handed enforcement of its general trespass statute against those refusing to obey the sheriff's order to remove themselves from what amounted to the curtilage of the jailhouse. The State, no less than a private owner of property, has power to preserve the property under its control for the use to which it is lawfully dedicated. . . .

Justice Douglas' dissenting opinion was concurred in by Chief Justice Warren and Justices Brennan and Fortas. The opinion begins with an examination of the nature and scope of the right to petition.

The jailhouse, like an executive mansion, a legislative chamber, a courthouse, or the statehouse itself (*Edwards v. South Carolina, supra*) is one of the seats of governments whether it be the Tower of London, the Bastille, or a small county jail. And when it houses political prisoners or those who many think are unjustly held, it is an obvious center for protest. The right to petition for the redress of grievances has an ancient history and is not limited to writing a letter or sending a telegram to a congressman; it is not confined to appearing before the local city council, or writing letters to the President or Governor or Mayor. . . . Conventional methods of petitioning may be, and often have been, shut off to large groups of our citizens. Legislators may turn deaf ears; formal complaints may be routed endlessly through a bureaucratic maze; courts may let the wheels of justice grind very slowly. Those who do not control television and radio, those who cannot afford to advertise in newspapers or circulate elaborate pamphlets may have only a more limited type of access to public officials. Their methods should not be condemned as tactics of obstruction and harassment as long as the assembly and petition are peaceable, as these were.

The protest was a legitimate one and the fact that it is public property makes no difference.

There is no question that petitioners had as their purpose a protest against the arrest of Florida A. & M. students for trying to integrate public theatres. . . . There was no violence; no threat of violence; no attempted jail break; no storming of a prison; no plan or plot to do anything but protest. The evidence is uncontradicted that the petitioners' conduct did not upset the jailhouse routine; things went on as they normally would. None of the group entered the jail.

Justice Douglas warns:

We do violence to the First Amendment when we permit "this petition for redress of grievances" to be turned into a trespass action.

He concedes that there are times and circumstances when the right to petition must be exercised judiciously.

There may be some public places which are so clearly committed to other purposes that their use for the airing of grievances is anomalous. There may be some instances in which assemblies and petitions for redress of grievances are not consistent with other necessary purposes of public property. A noisy meeting may be out of keeping with the serenity of the statehouse or the quiet of the courthouse. No one, for example, would suggest that the Senate gallery is the proper place for a vociferous protest rally. And in other cases it may be necessary to adjust the right to petition for redress of grievances to the other interests inhering in the uses to which the public property is normally put. . . . But this is quite different from saying that all public places are off limits to people with grievances.

But, he warns, our rights are fragile principles which must be nurtured and safeguarded, especially at times when legitimate protest is in order.

Today a trespass law is used to penalize people for exercising a constitutional right. Tomorrow a disorderly conduct statute, a breach-of-the-peace statute, a vagrancy statute will be put to the same end. . . . In modern times, . . . such arrests are usually sought to be justified by some legitimate function of government. Yet by allowing these orderly and civilized protests against injustice to be suppressed, we only increase the forces of frustration which the conditions of second-class citizenship are generating amongst us.

CASE 75

Dick Gregory v. City of Chicago

394 U.S. 111, 89 S.Ct. 946, 22 L.Ed.2d 134 (1969)

It was a unanimous decision. Chief Justice Warren delivered the opinion of the Court, declaring the convictions unlawful. He regarded the case as such a simple one that it warranted only a brief opinion. In a few well-chosen words, he declares:

Petitioners' march, if peaceful and orderly, falls within the sphere of conduct protected by the First Amendment. . . . There is no evidence in this record that petitioners' conduct was disorderly.

Therefore .   .   .   convictions so totally devoid of evidentiary support violate due process .   .   .   .

However reasonable the police request may have been and however
laudable the police motives, petitioners were charged and convicted for
holding a demonstration, not for a refusal to obey a police officer.

For Justices Black and Douglas, this issue warranted more detailed consideration because it involved a very important case. Justice Black's concurring opinion, in which Justice Douglas joined,
focuses on the promises of the Constitution.

[This case] in a way tests the ability of the United States to keep the
promises its Constitution makes to the people of the Nation. Among
those promises appearing in the Preamble of the Constitution are the
statements that the people of the United States ordained this basic
charter "in Order to .   .   .   secure the blessings of Liberty to ourselves and our Posterity .   .   ."

The First Amendment, continues Justice Black, fulfilled that
promise in writing by guaranteeing the rights of free speech, press,
peaceable assembly, and petition. Beginning with the 1954 *Brown
v. Board of Education* desegregation ruling, these rights were put to
the acid test when Blacks sought to speed up desegregation through
picketing and mass demonstrations. The anticipated reaction by
those who favored the status quo was emotional and determined. The
result was confrontation and the sparks flew upward to the Supreme
Court. Where should the Court draw the line between lawful and
unlawful assembly and petition?

Justice Black recognizes that cities have the power to pass ordinances regulating demonstrations, but such laws must be narrowly
drawn so as to protect First Amendment Freedoms. In his judgment, the Chicago ordinance "might better be described as a meat-ax
ordinance, gathering in one comprehensive definition of an offense
a number of words which have a multiplicity of meanings, some of
which would cover activity specifically protected by the First Amendment." What, he asks for example is the meaning of "improper," "unlawful purposes," "annoyance or disturbance."

The testimony showed that Gregory and his group "in the face
of jeers, insults, and assaults with rocks and eggs .   .   .   maintained
a decorum that speaks well for their determination simply to tell
their side of their grievances and complaints." Nevertheless, the
jury in the case was told to ignore acts of violence committed by the
crowd of onlookers and attempts made by police to arrest trouble-
makers. Since it may very well be that the jury convicted the accused by a literal reading of the ordinance, the conviction was an unconstitutional violation of First Amendment Freedoms.

A narrowly drawn statute specifying clearly the types of conduct which are forbidden is permissible. The Chicago law does not
fall within this permissible category.

CONCLUDING THOUGHTS

Liberty lies in the hearts of men and women; when it dies there, no constitution, no law, no court can save it; no constitution, no law, no court can even do much to save it. While it lies there it needs no constitution, no law, no court to save it. . . . .

The spirit of liberty is the spirit which is not too sure that it is right; the spirit of liberty is the spirit which seeks to understand the minds of other men and women; the spirit of liberty is the spirit which weighs their interests alongside its own without bias . . . .

> Judge Learned Hand in *The Spirit of Liberty* edited by Irving Dilliard

But when men have realized that time has upset many fighting faiths, they may come to believe even more than they believe the very foundations of their own conduct that the ultimate good desired is better reached by free trade in ideas—that the very best truth is the power of thought to get itself accepted in the competition of the market, and that truth is the only ground upon which their wishes safely can be carried out. That at any rate is the theory of our Constitution. It is an experiment, as all life is an experiment.

> Supreme Court Justice Oliver Wendell Holmes, Jr. Dissenting opinion in *Abrams v. United States* (1919)

OLIVER WENDELL HOLMES
1841–1935

Associate Justice
1902–1932

We began our conclusion with two important quotations which represent the foundation stones of the idea of liberty. Each of these great judges believed that liberty rests in a quest for understanding the ideas that swirl around us as we move through time and space. This quest for the meaning of truth, justice, equality, property, power, religion, beauty, and morality, among other great ideas, requires an environment that is open to the cross-winds of all manner and types of thoughts and opinions. It is an environment in which each of us must grapple with the thoughts of others and in which each of us must test our ideas and opinions against the power of the ideas and opinions of others.

To have an environment that encourages this "free trade in ideas," the spirit of liberty must rest "in the hearts of men and women." This feeling for liberty must be nourished in our schools and in our communities. To accomplish this, it is necessary to encourage students in our schools and colleges and citizens in communities to understand that aspect of the law which is humanistically centered—the great value confrontations which have led to landmark rulings of our High Court.

    *   *   *   *   *   *   *   *   *   *

Our journey in the quest for an understanding of the idea of liberty has taken us through six areas: separation of church and state, freedom of religion, freedom of speech, freedom of the press, the right peaceably to assemble, and the right to petition the government for redress of grievances. In this journey we were confronted by a never-ending series of obstacles. We have stopped and examined value confrontations resulting from society's need for security and the individual's need to express thoughts, ideas, and opinions. We have seen that these value conflicts exist in the community and in the school. We have also observed that the Supreme Court has become the Great Umpire or Referee in resolving the most pressing issues. What should be obvious at this point is that the decisions of the Supreme Court represent solutions which are rarely final. The Court has changed its mind on issues for a variety of reasons. Justices retire, new ones are appointed, the climate of public opinion changes, domestic or international crises occur, research brings to light new evidence, and history continues to move us into a future with unforeseen challenges.

In the midst of all these changes, the idea of liberty remains as a persistent challenge. How will we treat the dissenter, the unpopular group, the nonconformist, the ones who annoy us and claim that they are descendants of Socrates' "gadfly"? Will we answer this challenge with the absolute or the preferred position of the First Amendment Freedoms, or the Clear and Present Danger Rule, or the State can do no wrong, the descendant of the ancient principle: "the King can do no wrong"?

In 1987 we shall be celebrating the Bicentennial of the drafting of the Constitution of the United States, the oldest living constitution. Four years after that event, we shall be celebrating the Bicentennial of the ratification of the Bill of Rights. What will be the meaning of the idea of liberty at that time? Will we have "free trade in ideas" or will we have neglected or forgotten the "spirit of liberty"? Perhaps those who understand the issues involved in the cases which have been collected in this volume will become the guardians of the idea of liberty—today and into the future.

GLOSSARY

AMEND—	To change, improve, correct.
AMENDMENT—	1. A change in a bill as it passes through a legislature or in a law already passed.
	2. A provision of the U.S. Constitution enacted after the original Constitution became law.
APPEAL—	Verb. To ask a higher court to review actions of a lower court in order to correct mistakes or injustices.
	Noun. The process of appealing a case.
APPELLATE—	A higher court that can hear appeals from a lower court.
ARBITRARY—	Depending on choice; selected at random or without reason.
CERTIORARI—	(Latin: to make sure) A request to a higher court to examine the record of a case and determine whether the lower court properly had jurisdiction and whether its proceedings were according to law. Certiorari is used to determine whether a fuller review is appropriate. In an effort to streamline its procedures and keep its case load within manageable limits, the U.S. Supreme Court has placed most classes of cases under the category of review by certiorari. This gives the Court the option of refusing to review many cases.
COMMON LAW—	"Judge-made" rather than "legislature-made" law. The body of law which has developed from judicial decisions based on customs and precedents, as distinct from laws enacted by legislatures and written in statutes and codes.
CONSTRUE— CONSTRUCTION	To decide the meaning and legal effect of a document by looking not only at the words themselves, but at the circumstances in which they were written, the intention of the writers, and related laws and writings. (As distinct from *interpret*: to decide the meaning by studying the words themselves.)
CREED—	A brief formula stating basic beliefs.
DEFRAY—	Provide for or arrange the payment of.
DILEMMA—	A forced choice between alternatives which are about equally desirable or undesirable.

DISSENTER—   One who does not conform to an established church or to a generally accepted pattern of thought or action.

DOCTRINE—   Something taught—an official teaching or position.

DOGMA—   An established belief or an officially held opinion.

DUE PROCESS
   OF LAW—   A course of legal action carried out in accordance with established rules and principles.

EN BANC—   (French: in the bench) A session of all the judges of a court meeting together rather than in separate sections. A decision requires the agreement of a majority of the judges participating in the *en banc* hearing.

HERESY—   Teachings or beliefs contrary to the officially ac-
HERETICAL   cepted belief, especially to the official teaching of a particular religion.

IDEOLOGY—   A systematic group of ideas or theories, especially
IDEOLOGICAL   about human life and society.

INALIENABLE—   Not able to be transferred or taken away.

INCRIMINATE—   To involve in a crime, cause to appear guilty.

JURISDICTION—   1. The geographical area in which a court or official has the right to operate.
                      2. The persons about whom or subjects about which a court has the power to make legally binding decisions.

MANDATE—   An authoritative command.

NONCONFORMIST—   One who does not conform to an established church or to a generally accepted pattern of thought or action.

OPINION—   A judge's statement of the decision reached in a case.

   MAJORITY
   OPINION—   The opinion agreed in by more than half the judges or justices hearing a case, sometimes called the opinion of the court.

   CONCURRING
   OPINION—   Agrees with the majority opinion, but gives different or added reasons for arriving at that opinion.

   DISSENTING
   OPINION—   Disagrees with the majority opinion.

PER CURIAM— (Latin: by the court) An opinion given jointly by the judges of a particular court and not signed by any individual judge. The opinion usually states the court's decision very briefly, indicating that the issue is clear cut. However, the judges may have varying reasons for joining in the decision and may express these in individual opinions.

PETITION— An earnest request; a formal written document embodying such a request.

PLAINTIFF— The complaining party in a legal action, the person who brings a lawsuit against another.

PLURALISTIC— Including a number of different elements. In a pluralistic society diverse ethnic, racial, and religious groups maintain their own traditions and interest within a broader civilization which they share.

PRECEDENT— A court decision on a question of law that gives direction on law to be used in deciding a similar question in a later case. A previous decision which a court cites in reaching a decision.

PROHIBITION— An act of forbidding by authority; an order to restrain or stop.

PROMULGATE— To issue and make known a law or policy as a means of putting it into effect.

RATIFY— To approve and confirm an act done previously. For example, state legislatures must ratify an amendment to the U.S. Constitution; the Senate must ratify a treaty signed by the President.

RECORD— A formal written account of a case including the actions taken, papers filed, rulings made, opinions written.

REDRESS— To set right, remedy, make up for, remove the cause of a complaint or grievance.

REMAND— Send back. A higher court may remand a case to a lower court with instructions to take some action in the case.

SECT— A group following a particular doctrine or leader, often having broken away from another group; a religious denomination.

SECTARIAN— Characteristic of a sect.

SECULAR— Not specifically religious, ecclesiastical or clerical; relating to the worldly or temporal.

SEDITION— SEDITIOUS	Inciting resistance to established authority.
STATUTE—	A law passed by a legislature.
SUE—	To bring a civil lawsuit.
SUPREME COURT—	The highest court of most states; the highest court of the United States. The U.S. Supreme Court is made up of a chief justice and associate justices appointed by the President. The U.S. Supreme Court has both appellate and original jurisdiction. Most cases reach it through its appellate jurisdiction. Appeals can be made at every level from local courts through federal courts of appeal and state supreme courts until they reach the U.S. Supreme Court. The Supreme Court has original jurisdiction (the ability to hear cases from their beginning) only if a state or an ambassador or other United States minister is one of the parties.

After hearing all arguments in a case, the justices discuss the case in private. They then give their opinions, beginning with the chief justice and proceeding in order of seniority. After the last opinion is stated they vote in reverse order. If the chief justice votes with the majority he can write the majority opinion, or he can select another justice to write it. If the chief justice votes with the minority, the production of the majority opinion rests with the senior justice voting with the majority. Any justice who disagrees with the majority opinion may write a dissenting opinion; any justice who agrees with majority opinion, but disagrees with some of the reasoning expressed in it or having additional arguments in support of it may write a concurring opinion.

Supreme Court decisions must be followed by lower courts in similar cases. However the Supreme Court itself need not abide by its earlier decisions if it becomes convinced that circumstances demand a new approach. After a major decision legislatures often revise laws to bring them into accord with the Constitution as interpreted by the decision.

TENET—	Something held, especially a brief or principle held in common by members of a group.
THEOCRACY— THEOCRATIC	Government of a state by divine guidance; a state governed by officials regarded as divinely guided.

TRIAL COURT—   The court in which a case is originally tried, as distinct from higher courts to which the case might be appealed.

VOIR DIRE—   (French: to speak truth) An examination of prospective jurors or witnesses under oath to answer honestly questions about their qualifications, competence, interest in the case, or knowledge about the case.

*

A BRIEF BIBLIOGRAPHY

There are many valuable books in this field. The following recommendations are among my favorites:

Abraham, Henry J. *Freedom and the Court.* (2nd Edition). New York: Oxford University Press, 1972.

Berns, Walter. *The First Amendment and the Future of American Democracy.* New York: Basic Books, 1976.

Black, Hugo L. *A Constitutional Faith.* New York: Alfred A. Knopf, 1968.

Chafee, Zacharias, Jr. *Free Speech in the United States.* Cambridge, Mass.: Harvard University Press, 1954.

Fellman, David. *The Constitutional Right of Association.* Chicago: University of Chicago Press, 1963.

Howe, Mark DeWolfe. *The Garden and the Wilderness.* Chicago: University of Chicago Press, 1965.

Handlin, Oscar and Mary Handlin. *The Dimensions of Liberty.* Cambridge, Mass.: Harvard University Press, 1961.

Haiman, Franklyn S. *Freedom of Speech.* Skokie, Illinois: National Textbook Company, 1976.

Kurland, Philip B. *Religion and the Law.* Chicago: Aldine Publishing Company, 1962.

Larson, Martin A. and C. Stanley Lowell. *The Religious Experience: The Growth and Dangers of Tax-Exempt Property in the United States.* Silver Springs, Maryland: American United Research Foundation, 1977.

Levy, Leonard W. *Legacy of Suppression.* Cambridge, Mass.: Harvard University Press, 1960.

Naylor, David. *Dissent and Protest.* Rochelle Park, New Jersey: Hayden Book Company, 1974.

Pfeffer, Leo. *Church, State and Freedom.* (Revised Edition) Boston: Beacon Press, 1967.

Pfeffer, Leo. *Religious Freedom.* Skokie, Illinois: National Textbook Company, 1977.

Schissel, Lillian. *Conscience in America: A Documentary History of Conscience in America* (1757–1967). New York: Dutton and Company, 1968.

*

INDEX

A

B

C

†